Multiculturalism, Muslims and Citizenship
A European Approach

Tariq Modood, Anna Triandafyllidou
and Ricard Zapata-Barrero

 Routledge
Taylor & Francis Group

LONDON AND NEW YORK

First published 2006 by Routledge
2 Park Square, Milton Park, Abingdon, Oxon, OX14 4RN

Simultaneously published in the USA and Canada
by Routledge
270 Madison Ave, New York, NY 10016

Routledge is an imprint of the Taylor & Francis Group

© 2006 Tariq Modood, Anna Triandafyllidou, Ricard Zapata-Barrero

Typeset in Goudy by Taylor & Francis Books
Printed and bound in Great Britain by
MPG Books Ltd, Bodmin

British Library Cataloguing in Publication Data
A catalogue record for this book is available from the British Library

Library of Congress Cataloguing- in-Publication Data
A catalog record for this book has been requested

ISBN 10: 0–415–35514–1 (hbk)
ISBN 10: 0–415–35515–X (pbk)

ISBN 13: 978–0–415–35514–8 (hbk)
ISBN 13: 978–0–415–35515–5 (pbk)

T&F informa
Taylor & Francis Group is the Academic Division of T&F Informa plc.

From Tariq to Glynthia

From Ricard to Isabel

And from Mum to my little Iasonas

Contents

List of tables   ix
Notes on contributors   x
Acknowledgements   xiii

1 European challenges to multicultural citizenship:
  Muslims, secularism and beyond   1
  ANNA TRIANDAFYLLIDOU, TARIQ MODOOD AND
  RICARD ZAPATA-BARRERO

2 Multiculturalism, citizenship and Islam in problematic
  encounters in Belgium   23
  HASSAN BOUSETTA AND DIRK JACOBS

3 British Muslims and the politics of multiculturalism   37
  TARIQ MODOOD

4 French secularism and Islam: France's headscarf affair   57
  RIVA KASTORYANO

5 The particular universalism of a Nordic civic nation:
  common values, state religion and Islam in Danish political culture   70
  PER MOURITSEN

6 Enemies within the gates: the debate about the
  citizenship of Muslims in Germany   94
  WERNER SCHIFFAUER

7 Religious diversity and multiculturalism in Southern
  Europe: the Italian mosque debate   117
  ANNA TRIANDAFYLLIDOU

8 The Muslim community and Spanish tradition:
  Maurophobia as a fact, and impartiality as a desideratum   143
  RICARD ZAPATA-BARRERO

9 Secularism and the accommodation of Muslims in Europe   162
  TARIQ MODOOD AND RIVA KASTORYANO

10 Europe, liberalism and the 'Muslim question'   179
   BHIKHU PAREKH

   Index   204

List of tables

7.1   Distribution of the articles analysed per newspaper   125
7.2   Thematic dimensions   126
7.3   Voices and thematic dimensions   127
9.1   Religion *vis-à-vis* state and civil society in three countries   166
9.2   Some dimensions of religion re private/public   167

Contributors

Hassan Bousetta (hassan.bousetta@ulg.ac.be) has a Doctorate in Social Sciences from the Katholieke Universiteit Brussel (Belgium), an MA in Political Science and Public Administration and an MA in the Sociology of Developing Countries, both from the University of Liège (Belgium). He is currently an FNRS fellow at the University of Liège. Bousetta was previously at the Katholieke Universiteit Leuven and is a former Marie Curie Visiting Fellow at the Centre for the Study of Ethnicity and Citizenship in the Department of Sociology of the University of Bristol (UK). From January 1997 till September 2000, he was involved in the Institute for Political Sociology and Methodology of the Katholieke Universiteit Brussel. His work focuses on the political participation of immigrant minorities and on local multicultural policies. Bousetta has also collaborated on a number of consultancy projects both for cities (Paris, Antwerp, Bristol) and networks of cities (Eurocities).

Dirk Jacobs (dirk.jacobs@ulb.ac.be) is Associate Professor in Sociology at the Université Libre de Bruxelles and Associate Professor at the Katholieke Universiteit Brussel (Belgium). Jacobs studied sociology at Ghent University (Belgium), obtained his PhD in Social Sciences at Utrecht University (the Netherlands) and is a former postdoctoral fellow of the National Fund for Scientific Research Flanders at the Institute of Social and Political Opinion Research (ISPO), Katholieke Universiteit Leuven. He is now affiliated to the *Groupe d'études sur l'Ethnicité, le Racisme, les Migrations et l'Exclusion* (GERME) at the Institut de Sociologie of the Université Libre de Bruxelles. His research fields are minority studies and political sociology. He has published in journals such as *International Migration Review*, *Journal of Ethnic and Migration Studies*, *Social Compass*, *Journal of International Migration and Integration* and *Regional and Federal Studies*.

Riva Kastoryano (kastoryano@ceri-sciences-po.org) has a PhD in Sociology from the Ecole des Hautes Etudes en Sciences Sociales. She is a senior research fellow at the CNRS (National Centre for Scientific Research) and teaches at the Institute for Political Studies in Paris. Her work focuses on relationships between identity and states, and on minority and community formation in Western democratic societies. Her most recent publications include *La France, l'Allemagne et leurs Immigrés. Négocier l'identité* (Paris: Armand Colin, 1997), also translated into English *Negotiating Identities: States and Immigrants in France and Germany* (Princeton University Press, 2002); *Quelle identité pour l'Europe? Le multiculturalisme à l'épreuve* (editor, Paris: Sciences-Po, 1998); *Nationalismes en mutation en Méditerranée Orientale* (co-editor, Paris: CNRS, 2002); *Staat – Schule – Ethnizität. Politische Sozialisation von Immigratenkindern in vier europäischen Ländern* (co-editor, Münster: Waxman Verlag, 2002).

Tariq Modood (t.modood@bristol.ac.uk) is Professor of Sociology, Politics and Public Policy and the founding Director of the Centre for the Study of Ethnicity and Citizenship at the University of Bristol, UK. He is also the co-founding editor of the international journal *Ethnicities*. His latest publications include *Multicultural Politics: Racism, Ethnicity and Muslims in Britain* (Minnesota and Edinburgh University Presses, 2005); *Ethnicity, Nationalism and Minority Rights* (co-editor, Cambridge University Press, 2004); and *Ethnicity, Social Mobility and Public Policy in the US and UK* (co-editor, Cambridge University Press, 2005). He was awarded an MBE for services to social sciences and ethnic relations in 2001 and elected a member of the Academy of Social Sciences in 2004.

Per Mouritsen (pm@ps.au.dk) is a Senior Lecturer in Political Science at the University of Aarhus. He has a PhD from the European University Institute, Florence, and holds an MA from the University of Warwick. Previously, he was a visiting scholar at the University of Copenhagen, the EUI and the University of Sydney. His recent work includes 'What's the Civil in Civil Society? Robert Putnam, Italy, and the Republican Tradition', *Political Studies*, 51, 4, 2003; 'The Republican Conception of Patriotism', in H. Sicakkan and Y. Lithman (eds), *Envisioning Togetherness* (Edwin Mellen, 2005); 'The Liberty of the People. On the Pluralism of Republican Arguments', in I. Honohan and J. Jennings (eds), *Republican Theory, Republican Practice* (Routledge, 2005), *Constituting Communities: Political Solutions to Cultural Conflict* (co-editor, Palgrave, 2006) and *What's the Culture in Multiculturalism? The Crisis of Normative Theory* (co-editor, Palgrave, 2006).

Bhikhu Parekh is Professor of Philosophy at the University of Westminster and Emeritus Professor of Political Theory at the University of Hull. He is the author of several books in political philosophy, the latest being *Rethinking Multiculturalism* (Macmillan/Harvard University Press, 2000). He is a Fellow of the British Academy, President of the Academy of Learned Societies for the Social Sciences, and recipient of the Sir Isaiah Berlin Prize for Lifetime Contribution to Political Philosophy.

Werner Schiffauer (schiffauer@euv-frankfurt-o.de) is Professor of Comparative Social and Cultural Anthropology at Europa-Universität Viadrina, Frankfurt/ Oder. He has worked on the transformation of rural and urban Turkey, on labour migration, the organization of diversity in European Societies and recently on Islam in Europe. His recent publications include: *Migration und kulturelle Differenz. Studie für das Büro der Ausländerbeauftragten des Senats von Berlin* (Berlin, 2002); *Die Gottesmänner – Türkische Islamisten in Deutschland* (Suhrkamp, 2000); *Fremde in der Stadt – Zehn Essays zu Kultur und Differenz* (Suhrkamp, 1997); *Civil Enculturation. Nation-State, School and Ethnic Difference in four European Countries* (co-author, Berghahn, 2004).

Anna Triandafyllidou (anna@eliamep.gr) is Senior Research Fellow at the Hellenic Foundation for European and Foreign Policy (ELIAMEP) and Research Fellow at the Robert Schuman Centre of Advanced Studies, European University Institute, Florence. Since 2002, she has been a Professor at the College of Europe in Bruges (Belgium). Her recent publications include: *Immigrants and National Identity in Europe* (Routledge, 2001); *Negotiating Nationhood in a Changing Europe* (Edwin Mellen, 2002); *Europeanisation, National Identities and Migration* (co-editor, Routledge, 2003); *Transcultural Europe* (co-editor, Palgrave, 2005); *Poles in Europe* (editor, Edwin Mellen, 2006).

Ricard Zapata-Barrero (ricard.zapata@upf.edu) is Professor of Political Theory at the Universitat Pompeu Fabra, Barcelona (Spain). His main lines of research deal with contemporary problems of liberal democracy in multicultural contexts, especially the relationship between democracy, citizenship and immigration. He is director of a postgraduate course on management of cultural diversity at UPF/IDEC (Inmigración y ciudadanía: la gestión de la diversidad cultural) and, since 2001, academic collaborator of the immigration programme of the CIDOB Foundation (Centre of International Relations and International Cooperation). He is also academic adviser on immigration in Catalonia. His most recent publications include: *Inmigración y procesos de cambio* (co-editor, Barcelona: Icaria, 2003); *Multiculturalidad e inmigración* (Madrid: ed. Síntesi, 2004); *Inmigración, innovación política y cultura de acomodación en España* (Barcelona: ed. Cidob, 2004).

Acknowledgements

This book has the partial character of the relay: not all those who were there at the start of the project are there at the end, while others have been picked up at various stages.

Tariq Modood and Adrian Favell produced a book project proposal that brought together Dirk Jacobs, Riva Kastoryano, Judith Squires and Anna Triandafyllidou with themselves, with Rainer Baubock supporting by email. It was funded by the European Consortium of Political Research (ECPR) and the Social Science Research Council (SSRC), New York. This enabled three productive meetings during which the group was joined by Hassan Bousetta and Ricard Zapata-Barrero. While some of the basic thinking behind the book was sketched at those meetings, not all the discussion that took place there materialized into text, and some of our colleagues' other priorities took them away from this project, while others were recruited subsequently, namely Per Mouritsen and Werner Schiffauer, to extend the range of national case studies and, in the case of Bhikhu Parekh, to provide us with a theoretical conclusion. We are grateful to both the funders and all the contributors to this book, including those who departed before anything was written. The authors thank Blackwell Publishing for use of a modified version of chapter three published in one of their journals.

We would also like to thank Nelius Carey for his assistance with copy-editing.

1 European challenges to multicultural citizenship

Muslims, secularism and beyond

*Anna Triandafyllidou, Tariq Modood and
Ricard Zapata-Barrero*

Introduction

After the relative prominence of multicultural citizenship theoretical debates and multicultural policy developments in the 1990s, we witness today a change of direction. This crisis of multiculturalism comes at a time of heightened security awareness as a result of the events of New York (9/11, 2001), Madrid (14/3, 2004) and most recently in London (7/7 and 21/7, 2005). European citizenship is disorientated, increasingly linking a religion (Islam) with violence and anti-Western values. The upsurge of international terrorism has led to the increasing securitization of migration agendas. Even though suspected terrorists are apparently to be found among the educated, middle-class, legal immigrants – the 'good' kind of immigrants for whom Western societies and economies have been competing in the past decade – the argument of terrorism is now used in the policy debate to justify tougher controls of migration in general. In this context of high security awareness, existing models and policies of immigrant integration and the accommodation of (Muslim) minority claims are questioned. The governments of several 'old' immigration hosts like the Netherlands, Britain or France are tempted to adopt assimilationist approaches to counteract what they perceive as a (relative) failure of their former multicultural policies. New hosts like Greece, Spain or Italy and 'old' hosts that did not consider themselves as such (for example, Germany) find it even harder to adopt a multicultural approach even if political elites recognize the need to integrate immigrants.

This book has a twofold objective. At the empirical and policy level, we highlight some of the weaknesses, the ambivalence and the major challenges of multicultural citizenship policies in Europe today. At the theoretical level, we argue that the debate on multiculturalism and citizenship has to be context oriented and develop new theoretical insights related to the specific European context. In Europe, multiculturalism challenges relate above all mainly to the successful integration and participation of Muslim citizens and residents into European societies. We shall therefore concentrate our empirical and theoretical enquiries on the ways in which Muslim claims and issues are integrated and accommodated in the multiculturalism agendas of the countries under study.

The book adopts an interdisciplinary approach and methodology. Although one of our aims is to address some important limitations of contemporary multiculturalism theory in political science, the authors of individual chapters combine political scientific, sociological and discursive methods in the undertaking of their case studies. This work thus makes a contribution to the multicultural citizenship theoretical and conceptual debate from a bottom-up approach that brings social reality closer to philosophical and theoretical enquiry.

Starting from a set of seven country studies, five among Northern European states (Belgium, Britain, Denmark, France and Germany) and two located in Southern Europe, namely Spain and Italy, we analyse the multicultural citizenship and integration debates developed in these countries. The debates investigated were started in relation to controversial issues such as the headscarf affair and overall legitimization and accommodation of claims by Muslims in Belgium, Britain, France and Germany, the building of new mosques in Italy and Spain, the challenge of citizenship acquisition by Muslims in Germany and the overall acceptance/rejection of the Muslim community in Denmark. The authors contributing to this volume examine what kind of multicultural citizenship claims were raised in the countries studied, how these were framed in the national public and political debate and what type of measures, institutions or regimes of integration were proposed to accommodate these claims in each case. Special attention is paid to the ways in which the national ideology, national political culture, tradition and past experience of each country shape both the debates and their outcomes.

Belgium, France and Britain have a relatively long experience in developing institutions and policies related to immigrant integration. This process has also involved, in differing degrees and directions, a re-elaboration of national identity with a view to incorporating cultural and religious diversity. France and Britain may be considered ideal–typical cases of different models of immigrant integration. The former privileges individual integration into a civic culture, leaving religion and ethnicity to the private realm and following a relatively open citizenship policy. The latter has also adopted a relatively liberal citizenship policy but followed a community-based integration model where not only individual but also collective rights and claims of ethnic and religious groups are recognized and accommodated. The case of Belgium, however, is complicated by its internal divisions and federal structure. Immigrant claims and rights are enmeshed in a complicated federal politics and risk disturbing the sensitive balance between the two Belgian communities, the Francophones and the Flemish.

Denmark and Germany have taken more time to develop deliberate processes of integration despite their strong welfare system models. In Denmark the relevant public and political discourses emphasize a universalistic public self-conception as a highly egalitarian welfare state, at the expense of Muslim immigrants' claims framed as particularistic and ethically inferior. Germany's closure to long-term immigrant residents has been related to its predominant understanding of German society as mono-national and monocultural despite a large immigrant population present in the country for several decades. Although citizenship laws and naturalization processes have recently been liberalized, many are worried about cultural and political changes related to a growing number of naturalized immigrant residents. Such changes are seen to threaten the cultural 'authenticity' of German society as well as the established power structures.

The two Southern European cases presented in this volume examine two 'new' immigration hosts, Italy and Spain, which have been transformed from sending to receiving societies in the course of the last two decades. Even if the immigration population in these countries still amounts to less than 5 per cent of the resident population, a percentage clearly lower than that registered in France, Britain or Belgium, immigration has been a 'hot' public issue in both. The arrival of legal and undocumented immigrant workers has been given high visibility in the Italian and Spanish media (see, for example, Penamarin, 1998; Perez Diaz *et al.*, 2001; Zapata-Barrero, 2003; ter Wal, 1996; 2002a; 2002b), becoming a contested issue in the political debate. The newcomers have largely been perceived by both lay people and politicians as threats to the host country's security, cultural authenticity and affluence. Only in the last few years has the issue of immigrant integration, and more particularly the accommodation of cultural and religious claims raised by Muslims, acquired more prominence as a legitimate and important objective of national immigration policy. The case studies presented here show how multicultural citizenship claims are framed and debated in Italy and Spain and link these debates to the more advanced claims for multiculturalism made in Northern European countries and elaborated in multiculturalism theories.

Although this volume has a wider interest in multiculturalism challenges, particular attention is paid here to the question of religion and more particularly to the claims made by Muslim residents/citizens in the countries studied. Indeed, there is a widespread perception that Muslims are making politically exceptional, culturally unreasonable or theologically alien demands upon European states. It is our contention that the logic of Muslim claims-making is contemporary but also particularly European. Their challenges expose the taken-for-grantedness of secularism in most European countries. They press politicians and intellectuals to rethink what is secularism, whether it has ever truly characterized modern European societies and most importantly why and in what versions it is still desirable. These questions lie at the heart of the philosophical and political discourses of European modernity and may as such be considered as peculiarly European even if generally modern.

The relation between Muslims and the European societies in which they live has to be seen in terms of rising agendas of multiculturalism where Muslims have become central to these agendas as an exemplary 'problem case'. However, a focus on Muslims exposes and contests the narrow definitions of racism and equality and the secular bias of the discourse and policies of multiculturalism in Europe.

These debates and challenges acquire increased salience in the post-9/11 context where security issues and representations of Muslim immigrants as potential terrorists tend to overshadow the everyday experience of millions of

Muslims living and working in European countries and their just claims to difference, recognition and multicultural citizenship rights.

Limitations of the multicultural citizenship literature

While in some countries a policy discourse of multiculturalism emerged in the 1970s, it was only in the 1990s, led by scholars in Canada and the United States, that a political theory of multiculturalism emerged. In the first instance it was seen as an extension of debates around liberal democratic citizenship, concerned as it was with the impact of multiculturalism on the legitimating principles of democracy and liberalism. Since then, the relationship between citizenship and multiculturalism has become one of the dominant topics of theoretical–political research programmes today, especially in the anglophone world.[1]

This book shares this dominant unit of analysis and follows two premises beforehand. First, it is a debate *within* our society and not *among* societies. That is, it is an internal debate forming part of the liberal democratic tradition, and not a debate on cultural models of societies or civilizations (Wieviorka, 2001: 22, 67). The authors share the view that to interpret the citizenship–multicultural debate as along the lines of the 'clash of civilizations' discourse but within states is not only a logical fallacy, but politically damaging. Second, it is a debate on how to manage the public space, and not the private realm. That is, it is concerned with so-called process of the multiculturalization of the public sphere.

Both premises are at the basis of most of the arguments in this book. The first premise concentrates more on the change in cultural traditions and value systems that is taking place.[2] Almost the entire body of existing literature assumes that the theoretical challenge produced by the growing presence of immigrants forces us to re-examine almost all the traditional categories that have helped to describe and explain our liberal democratic tradition. When applied to *circumstances of multiculturalism* (Kelly, 2002) the main pillars of our political thought paradigm lose their solid cores.

The second premise is concerned with how our *public sphere* is structured, who decides its nature and limits, and how and why such limits are politically imposed. It is based on the belief that the way such public spheres are structured is directly related to a type of citizenship attitude, behaviour and practice that on many occasions lead to conflict with immigrants. That is why one must assume that the limits and nature of citizenship's area of action need to change.

To sum up, these normative and institutional effects confront political scientists with new scenarios in a twofold way. First, their interest has been incorporated into what are understood as normative challenges that cultural plurality poses for a liberal theory of justice (Favell and Modood, 2003). The plurality can be understood as a value heterogeneity (Rawls, 1993), as groups oppressed on the basis of their 'difference' (Young, 1990), as historic cultural communities (Taylor, 1994) or as indigenous peoples and nations in multinational states (Kymlicka, 1995). While the conceptualization varies in North American discourse, it is generally understood that the presence of new, especially non-white, ethnic and religious groups formed by migration is one of the constituent elements in contemporary plurality that is challenging liberalism and existing notions of citizenship.

The second political science development is a cross-national focus on the national regimes and institutions that shape the socio-political context, which facilitates or impedes the integration of immigrants and the second generation. Again, initially led by some North Americans (especially Brubaker, 1992), this approach has focused much more on European states and has given rise to a number of studies and research networks, gradually including since the mid-1990s not only Western but also Central and Eastern European countries (see, for instance, Brubaker, 1996). Some of these studies have focused on the ideological aspects of citizenship and nationalism: for example, that there is an *ius soli* and ethnic conceptions of citizenship with their own distinctive characteristics operating in different countries. Moreover, some countries see migrants as sojourners; others insist on assimilation and actively promote naturalization; yet others are more tolerant of group difference but treat some forms of group (for example, racial) differently to other kinds (for example, religious). Thus different countries can be said to have different 'philosophies of integration' and these have become the topic of some studies (Favell, 1998a; Joppke, 1996). Others have focused, increasingly, on a comparative institutional and mobilization analysis. They show how the political framework has developed in different countries, trying to explain why different legislation, institutions and policies have emerged in different countries and why different kinds and intensities of migrant mobilization have occurred. They also show how these factors have shaped the self-proclaimed identities and political strategies of migrant ethnic groups (Kastoryano, 1997; Koopmans and Statham, 2000).

One important shortcoming of the existing political science literature is that the normative and the institutionalist enquiries have so far been conducted quite separately from each other. While the latter are not typically institutionally reductionist and include fine examples, including those mentioned above, of conceptions and norms of citizenship and other ideas implicit in various state responses to immigration and multiculturalism, they rarely connect such ideas-in-institutions with the political philosophy of multiculturalism.

Similarly, the normative analysis of multiculturalism works at the abstract conceptual level of autonomy, recognition, group rights and so on, and, with its North American framing of questions, has some limited influence on European societies. The assumption within this literature is that philosophical reflection alone will provide philosophical solutions to the apparent problems of liberal multiculturalism. Yet this is a frame whose terms and reasoning delimit and restrict what can be seen through it (Favell, 1998c; Parekh, 1994; 2000). Theoretical arguments are sustained by an eclectic appeal to illustrative empirical examples, which pay little attention to issues of interpretation and comparative method (Favell, 1998b).

The type of analysis that is undertaken in this book tends to shun the predominant deductivist and universalist method and takes up induction as one of the most suitable methodological resources to test and develop new arguments. In this framework, the contextual and pluralistic perspectives (Carens, 2000; Parekh, 2000) have only just begun to yield their first results. Both are undoubtedly contributing to new research lines within the dominant programmes of citizenship and multiculturalism, mainly stressing that theoretical arguments cannot be valid unless they take the contextual framework into account (Zapata-Barrero, 2004b). We can even say that this context-oriented approach shares the Rortian conviction that it is not possible to find an 'Archimedean point' that would enable us to position ourselves outside specific contexts and at the same time evaluate political systems or mediate between conflictive values (Rorty, 1989).

One of the main arguments of the book is, then, that multiculturalism in Europe has its own distinctive elements which the theoretical debate, mainly stemming from North American authors, does not take into account. By highlighting European contextual aspects we will be able to specify more easily the arguments to put forward to interpret multicultural challenge to citizenship. What are the distinctive aspects of multiculturalism in Europe? The following list is not intended to be exhaustive but, rather, illustrative. The basic idea is that by using these differentiating aspects we can build 'European' arguments on how to manage multiculturalism. There are at least five main ways for answering this question: the emergence of populist parties; transnational citizenship and the link between two multicultural processes: multinationality and immigration; secularism and Islam, or the political management of religious pluralism; the differentiating features of the process of multiculturality in Mediterranean Europe; and lastly, the colonial past which constantly enters the debate when dealing with *membership procedure* or criteria for deciding *who enters* (Zapata-Barrero, 2004a). This book deals with one way of answering the European multicultural citizenship question: that of secularism and the public presence of Muslims in our societies.

It is quite common for political philosophers to refer to Muslim-related controversies and practices, such as the *Satanic Verses* affair, *l'affaire du foulard*, female circumcision, religious schools funding, and so on. Typically, however, the issues are glossed over in a few sentences in a superficial, journalistic way, relying on pre-existing assumptions and sometimes prejudices of readers to convey meaning (Modood, 1993; 1998: 390–2). But such a non-contextual approach oversimplifies and distorts issues, making minority behaviour serve as exemplars for vices and virtues to which, on a more context-informed reading, they would not be seen as unambiguous cases.

A more context-sensitive approach would bring out how certain issues of liberal principles become quite different from what they appear when the dimensions of racialized exclusion, socio-economic equality and essentialized categorization are taken into account (Modood and Werbner, 1997). Moreover, conceptual tools forged in one place are treated as universal theoretical tools and thus may hide and occlude other distinctions and categories more central to the politics of other parts of the world. Notably, Kymlicka's distinction between national minorities and ethnic immigrant groups may be appropriate for Canada and to a certain extent for 'strange' European cases such as Belgium, Switzerland or Catalunya (Jacobs, 2000), but it is unhelpful regarding the integration of post-colonial immigrants and former 'guest-workers' into traditional European nation-states. Problems of this sort can be avoided if, as we propose, one builds multicultural theory from the ground upwards rather than deontologically or from first principles, and approaches the normative from substantial case studies within a comparative European framework.

'New' and 'old' migrations

Our criticism of the above-mentioned theoretical debates examines both the specific national and local context in which claims are raised, but also the larger European and global environment and its socio-economic and political implications for the development of multiculturalism debates and policies. The investigation of multicultural citizenship and integration debates in Northern and Southern Europe has to recognize the fundamentally different nature of immigration flows that the two sets of countries have experienced.

The immediate post-war period in Europe was characterized by large South to North flows originating in the northern Mediterranean countries (Portugal, Spain, Italy and Greece). Western and Northern European countries like Belgium, Britain, France, Germany or Sweden have also experienced incoming flows from African, Caribbean and Asian countries. The post-war years were a period of reconstruction and industrial growth in a Europe that was short of labour after the disastrous Second World War. Thus, foreign workers came to meet domestic labour market needs and were often seen as temporary sojourners. The flows originating from outside Europe had largely to do with the colonial legacy of the receiving countries, especially as regards countries such as Britain, France, Belgium or the Netherlands. Immigrants from former colonies could take advantage of an open policy towards labour migration and special rights (including in some cases full citizenship rights). These migrations were inscribed in the industrial Fordist system of production, and were often channelled through active recruitment policies of companies in the receiving societies and bilateral agreements between sending and receiving countries. Eventually, most of the immigrant workers settled in the receiving societies raising important social and political challenges for integration.

In this volume we take up two cases of classical post-colonial migration, namely Britain and France, but also the deviant case of Belgium where former colonial subjects were not granted right of residence or work in the 'mother country'. We also include the case of Germany as it is central to the European landscape both for the size of its immigrant population and for its reluctance to incorporate it. Last but not least, we have chosen a Scandinavian country, Denmark, as an additional case of interest. Although less studied than Sweden for instance, Denmark has faced similar immigrant integration challenges that it has sought to accommodate through a strong egalitarian welfare model and discourse. However, this has led to effective inequality as the only logic acceptable in and by the system is that of the dominant, presumably secular, Danish political culture while minority and especially Muslim claims are de-legitimized as particularistic and anti-modern.

The migration dynamics in Europe changed in the early 1970s after the oil price shocks. Already economic growth was slower in Western Europe, structural change in labour markets was evident, and unemployment was growing, especially in the older industrial economies of Britain and Belgium. As the European Communities pursued policies of economic integration, migration between Southern and Northern Europe actually declined. By the time that Greece, Portugal and Spain joined the EEC, there were few migrants travelling to work in the northern member states as the latter had put a stop to labour migration from the early 1970s onwards. At the same time, a certain level of industrial development accompanied by a wide expansion of the service sector helped to keep Southern European citizens at home. The policies put in place by European countries aiming at 'zero immigration' reduced also the flows from Asian and African countries to continental Europe and Britain. Restrictive immigration policies were seen in many countries, including Britain and France, as a prerequisite for the successful integration of those already admitted. In other cases, like Belgium, Denmark or Germany, admissions were restricted in line with the domestic labour market needs while integration remained a non-issue until the 1980s.

Since the 1980s, however, the situation has been changing again. The integration of the world economy through world trade and service agreements (GATT and GATS), the globalization of capital and labour, and the rapid development of transport and communication networks have contributed to new types of population movements. The migrations of the last fifteen years are different in nature from those of the 1950s–1970s. They are characterized by their fragmented nature: they include new forms of flexible labour, insecure legal status (often undocumented), variable duration, new gender roles and multiple destinations.

These new flows meet the needs of post-industrial labour markets where portfolios have replaced machines and investments ignore borders in a way that factories never could. The labour force has become much less substitutable and much more specialized, less homogeneous and less hierarchically organized, with growing marginalization and segmentation in labour markets. Trade unions have lost their control over the supply of labour and governments have lost much of their control of capital. In the new emerging order of flexible labour markets, low-wage foreign workers are in demand for public or private service jobs to which it is difficult to recruit domestic workers. They suit nicely the demands of post-industrial societies with increased standards of consumption of goods and services. Additionally, high-wage foreign employees are demanded for jobs which require specific competence and where, again, the domestic supply is insufficient.

The implosion of the communist regimes in Central and Eastern Europe (CEE) in 1989 has made the new context even more volatile and dynamic. The closed borders between Eastern and Western European countries were suddenly opened and many CEE citizens, faced with the dismantling of the production system and welfare state in their countries of origin, started seeking better life chances and work opportunities in Western and Southern Europe. Just like citizens from Third World countries, people from CEE were integrated into specific niches of domestic labour markets in the European Union. Moreover, the opening of the borders has led to diverse forms of population mobility that involve Eastern, Central and Western/Southern European countries in complex patterns (Favell and Hansen, 2002; Wallace and Stola, 2001).

These changes have subverted, if not openly at least tacitly, the proclaimed policy of zero migration in most European countries. Large numbers of migrants have arrived, worked and stayed, in various guises. They have either entered clandestinely, or as asylum-seekers; but most commonly they have simply come via the pathways of globalization itself – with tourist or student visas which they then overstayed or abused, and at times even as business people (Jordan and Vogel, 1997). Neither the more 'flexible', pro-globalization regimes of Britain and Ireland, nor the more social protectionist regimes of France, Germany, the Netherlands or Denmark, have been able or willing to do much about this, while the governments of Southern Europe have been quite unprepared for it, reacting to immigration through repeated regularization programmes of undocumented workers.

While in the Northern and Western European countries the new migrants may integrate into pre-existing institutions and policies of cultural pluralism and socio-political inclusion, those arriving at the Southern European states are usually faced with societies that perceive themselves as largely monocultural and mono-religious. The new migrants raise thus important and unexpected challenges in Southern Europe. Although it might perhaps seem premature to talk about multicultural citizenship rights as such, Southern European societies have slowly reacted to the presence of immigrants with a view to integrating them not only economically but also culturally. Incidents of social unrest, highly visible cases of racism and ethnic prejudice, have triggered a public debate on the cultural and political rights of immigrants. The former have been largely recognized even if institutionalized only to a limited extent, while the latter still loom far behind, almost a taboo topic for Southern European societies.

The beginning of the new century, however, has been characterized by further developments. Notably, both the European Commission and a number of the EU member states have announced explicitly this time a major shift in policy over recruitment of skilled and unskilled workers from outside the EU. This has come at a time when unemployment among EU citizens is still high – some 15.7 million (or 9.2 per cent of the labour force) in 2001 (Eurostat, 2001) – and social policies are still focused on retraining and inclusion. This shift reflects growing concerns about bottlenecks and shortages, and the overall flexibility of the European Social Model (see Jordan *et al.*, 2003). Although the emphasis is different among the various member states, there is no doubt that an important change is taking place over recruitment from outside the EU. For example, both Italy and Greece had unemployment rates of around 11 per cent in 1999 whereas Spain's unemployment rate exceeded 15 per cent in the same year. Yet Italy admitted 2.5 million, Spain about 2 million and Greece nearly 1 million immigrant workers in the last ten to fifteen years, predominantly in agriculture, tourism, private care, catering and construction, and in Italy also in small and medium-sized productive enterprises. These workers, although initially admitted through illegal channels, were regularized through several 'amnesty' programmes.

The second change has followed from the attack on the World Trade Center and the Pentagon in the United States on 11 September 2001. Immediately, concerns about security that are closely related to migration became an urgent priority. Already the fear that irregular migration was beginning to run out of control had been voiced by politicians and the media. But the policy implications of the events of 9/11 were complex. They signalled that migration, and even globalization itself, concealed a potential for terror attacks, and a threat to security. Yet (as far as can be ascertained) the perpetrators were *legal* migrants. Indeed their profiles – computer experts, technicians, diligent students – were stereotypical of the types of immigrant that the United States and the EU member states are now seeking (even competing) to attract.

Meanwhile, the flexible and cheap labour provided by immigrants from CEE, Asia and Africa in West European societies has been contributing to growth in an increasingly deregulated economic environment of global cities, flexible forms of work, reduced welfare contributions and services, and high competitiveness. Recent studies (Reyneri *et al.*, 1999) have shown that undocumented immigrant labour has had a positive economic impact, at least in the short term, on Southern European countries (Greece and Italy, in particular). In this new environment, immigrant integration, especially in those countries with a short experience as hosts, risks becoming a luxury new receiving states and new immigrants cannot afford.

The contemporary European context

This complex picture of old and new migrations in Europe has to be seen also in the context of European integration. A unique feature of the EU as a socio-political entity is the fluidity of its boundaries. The EU has no fixed external frontiers: as Article O of the Treaty of the European Union (TEU) states: 'Any European state may apply to become a member of the Union.' In other words, it is in a continuous process of constituting itself: it is a community of inclusion rather than exclusion, or so it is stated in the TEU. In any case, the very recent enlargement of the EU to the East makes this in-the-state-of-becoming nature salient.

The inclusive nature of the EU, however, raises a number of identity questions, which relate to both the notion of Europeanness or a European identity and to the national identities of member states or of minorities within them. The process of constituting the EU opens up a tripolar identity space in which existing forms of collective identification have to be renegotiated and re-defined. This space is characterized by the simultaneous existence of three levels of identity and governance: the transnational or European level, the national or member state sphere and the local–regional context, which includes minorities and immigrant communities. Within this context, the dominance of the nation-state as a political agent and of national identity as the primary form of collective identification is put into question (Zapata-Barrero, 2001). Having said this, we are not predicting the demise or dismantling of nations and national or multinational states within Europe. On the contrary, it is our contention that national identities are redefined in response to this double challenge, from above and from below. This process of adaptation and change has to be seen in its transnational and subnational context, that is in relation to the end of the Cold War and the new international environment and also with reference to the revival/survival of minority identities and peripheral nationalisms.

The process of Europeanization affects immigrant communities and minorities living in Europe both directly and through the channels of national states. First and foremost, the Amsterdam Treaty (AT) has incorporated migration policies into the Treaty of the European Communities (TEC) as Title IV on 'Visas, Asylum, Immigration and Other Policies related to the Free Movement of Persons' (Hailbronner, 1998). Following the AT, the TEU states (Article 2) that it is the objective of the EU 'to maintain and develop the Union as an area of freedom, security and justice, in which the free movement of persons is assured in conjunction with appropriate measures with respect to external border controls, asylum, [and] immigration'. Thus, what was previously charac-terized as an area of common interest among member states has become a policy objective of the EU. None the less, the AT has guaranteed a balance between national control and supranational governance by introducing a limit to the jurisdiction of the European Court of Justice (ECJ) on migration policies, a limit that does not exist in other areas (Article 68 TEC; also Stetter, 2000: 95). Discussing the legal and institutional details of the AT provisions concerning migration goes beyond the scope of this volume. It is, however, worth noting that the AT moved the focus from intergovernmental co-operation to protect a common interest to supranational governance. The Directorate General for Justice and Home Affairs has actively engaged in preparing the ground for the development of a common EU immigration policy, issuing a series of rele-vant Communications and Council Directive proposals in recent years (http://europa.eu.int/pol/justice/index_en.htm) and negotiations among the member states have been intense. Taking into account that immigration is linked to citizenship and hence to the very essence of the nation-state (Zapata-Barrero, 2002), the concession of significant powers on this level from the member states to the EU may be expected to have an impact on both national majority and ethnic minority identities in the member states.

Apart from policy effects, the relationship between European integration and immigration regards identity categorizations too. Member state nationals acquire the same rights as citizens of other member states by means of their common European citizenship. Immigrants from Southern Europe residing in Northern European countries are thus fully integrated into the host society and distinguished from third-country nationals, the famous '*extracomunitari*' (literally 'people from outside the Community'). The role of the immigrant Other is delegated to labourers coming from outside the EU, notably Asia, Africa and Latin America, whose cultural, religious and physical difference makes them a suitable target for racism and discrimination (see, for instance, Kastoryano, 1998; Triandafyllidou, 2000; 2001; 2002; Triandafyllidou and Veikou, 2002).

Matters become more complicated by East–West migration within Europe. The post-1989 period has been characterized by a dramatic population influx from the former communist countries to Western Europe, including to Southern European countries that had no previous experience as hosts. Hundreds of thousands of Albanians, Poles, Romanians or Ukrainians, just to name some of the most 'mobile' nationalities, have entered, with or without adequate documentation, a number of EU countries in search of a job and/or better life chances. Xenophobic and racist reactions towards these people have been registered in a number of EU countries, especially in Southern Europe (Eurobarometer, 1997). National stereotype images have developed towards specific nationalities (see, for example, Palidda 1996; Triandafyllidou, 1999) and immigrants have been subjected to a process of racialization and exclusion.

The identity dynamics involved in the Othering of immigrants have to be seen within their international context, that is the end of the Cold War and the Eastern enlargement of the EU. Constructing immigrants and ethnic minorities as national Others has a double function for national identity: it provides a means for affirming the unity and superiority of the in-group while, at the same time, it allows for and justifies the exploitation of immigrant labour in conditions that would be unacceptable for fellow nationals (Triandafyllidou, 2001). These types of dynamics acquire new impetus after the disappearance of Western Europe's main threatening Other,[3] namely the 'Eastern bloc'. Immigrants from non-EU countries provide for the new threatening internal Other: the negative image against which the in-group identity is constructed.

The situation of immigrants coming from CEE countries has, however, become ambivalent given that a number of these countries recently became member states (May *et al.*, 2004). The example of Polish immigrants, for instance, is particularly interesting. Poles are subject to exploitation and ethnic prejudice in a number of countries of Northern and Southern Europe (for example, Germany, Greece or Italy) despite the accession of Poland to the EU. The political and symbolic boundary between immigrants from EU countries and Others is likely to be reorganized. Hence citizens of the ten new member states and/or Romania and Bulgaria (to join in 2007) will be gradually integrated into the European in-group while Others from countries further East and South risk becoming ever more isolated and excluded. Turkey is also the obvious challenge here both for its pivotal position between Europe and Asia and for its large Muslim population. However, while the European future of Turkey – as politicians call it – is being debated (December 2004), ethnic and religious prejudice finds suitable targets among immigrants from Asia and Africa or people originating from the Balkan countries, such as Albania for instance. Coincidentally a majority of these people are of Muslim faith.

The role of religion in this respect is worth particular attention. Muslims have been more often than not the subject of discriminatory and racist practices even if traditionally racism and anti-racist discourses and policies were organized in terms of 'colour'. Countries with relatively large Muslim communities, such as those included in this volume (Britain, Belgium, Denmark, France and Germany, and to a lesser extent Italy and Spain), have adopted different policies to deal with cultural and religious diversity. Their 'regimes of integration' are today mutually confronted and in the context of the EU, member states are required to adopt common standards, as happened for instance with the Anti-discrimination Directive (Council Directive, 2000).

The process of European integration also changes the parameters of the fundamental opposition between the nationalist ideal of a homogeneous and 'pure' national culture and population and the existence of minorities. The ever-closer EU involves the reorganization of national identity so as to accommodate for political and cultural loyalties parallel to the nation. The European dimension may thus open identity and institutional space for minorities and provide for alternative dimensions for inclusion. This inclusive process, of course, will be characterized by the dominant Western European cultural framework. Even though this framework is characterized by internal diversity, it may be discriminating for minorities that have historically been represented as threatening Others for Europe, such as Muslims and Jews.

The case studies presented in this volume engage with the culture, religion and identity, scholarly and political debates considering to what extent the process of European integration has become part of national debates and policies. We thus seek to uncover if and how specific definitions of 'European values', 'European standards' or a presumed homogeneous 'European culture' may be used in national discourses to advocate or deny multicultural citizenship rights for immigrant communities.

The contents of this volume

In order to remedy the limitations of multiculturalism research outlined earlier and explore the complexities of contemporary European reality, the contributors to this volume have undertaken a set of case studies that seek to describe empirically the politics of multiculturalism in their countries, including the claims-making by minorities, their forms of mobilization and the creation of alternative public spheres, the wider public discourses and debates around national and European identities, and the state responses in terms of statements/rhetorics, legislation and institutional modification. The individual contributions analyse how these different debates, concepts and actions are similar to and different from each other, and to what extent their differences relate to the political or national context, and to the type of minority involved. Moreover, we examine how the national and local debates relate to wider normative principles and ideas of equality, liberalism and citizenship. In the latter part of the book, Tariq Modood and Riva Kastoryano bring the analytical threads together concerning what is the state of secularism in Europe today. Bhikhu Parekh, in the concluding chapter, deconstructs the question of European Muslims and their presumed 'inadaptability' to European values and political systems. He discusses Muslim claims through a liberal and rationalist lens and argues that through dialogue all sides can recognize the cultural specificity of their claims and accommodate each other's needs.

In the second chapter of this volume, Hassan Bousetta and Dirk Jacobs analyse the idea of multiculturalism in the Belgian context. They discuss the contours of the disputed concept of multiculturalism, consider the controversies that it raised in Belgium and its difficult encounter with the issues raised by the Islamic presence. They point to the fact that in the Belgian context, the question of dealing with ethnic diversity – at least when being considered independently from the linguistic divide in the country – was initially conceived as an issue limited to handling the consequences of recruitment of a temporary foreign labour force in an ad hoc manner. In the course of the 1970s and 1980s the issue of multiculturalism gradually came to be seen independently from issues of migration and mobility. If today the management of cultural diversity in the public space can no longer be considered within the framework of earlier migration waves alone, it can neither be taken as a matter to be merely dealt with in the private sphere. It is still, however, being handled in an ad hoc way. The authors focus on the headscarf issue as an example of the tensions and challenges of multiculturalism in Belgium and the policies adopted to deal with them.

The issue of Muslim contribution to European politics and society is analysed more deeply by Tariq Modood in his chapter on British Muslims and the politics of difference. Modood emphasizes that the logic of Muslim claims-making is European and contemporary and takes up the case of Britain to illustrate his argument. The relation between Muslims and the wider British society and British state, Modood argues, has to be seen in terms of a development and rising agendas of racial equality and multiculturalism. Muslims, indeed, have become central to these agendas even while they have contested important aspects of multiculturalism – especially, the primacy of racial identities, narrow definitions of racism and equality, and the secular bias of the discourse and policies of multiculturalism. While there are now emergent Muslim discourses of equality, of difference, and of, to use the title of the newsletter of the Muslim Council of Britain, 'the common good', they have to be understood as appropriations and modulations of contemporary discourses and initiatives whose provenance lies in anti-racism and feminism. While one result of this is to throw advocates of multiculturalism into theoretical and practical disarray, another is to stimulate accusations of cultural separatism and revive a discourse of 'integration'. While we should not ignore the critics of Muslim activism, we need to recognize that at least some of the latter is a politics of 'catching up' with racial equality and feminism. In this way, religion in Britain is assuming a renewed political importance. After a long period of hegemony, political secularism can no longer be taken for granted but is having to answer its critics as there is a growing understanding that the incorporation of Muslims has become the most important challenge of egalitarian multiculturalism.

In Chapter 4, the new agendas of multiculturalism and the challenge that religion poses to predominantly secular views of diversity is discussed by Riva Kastoryano in relation to French secularism and Islam. Secularism, long considered to be a 'given' and internalized in French society as a 'reasonable' approach to diversity, has re-emerged at the centre of public debate in the last twenty years with new issues raised by Muslim migrants. Kastoryano concentrates on the arguments, policies and mobilizations that have taken place in France in relation to – and in reaction to – the headscarf 'affair'. The headscarf issue, she argues, involves national history, the place of religion, the principle of *laïcité* (France's form of secularism) and its limits, and the role of schools in 'assimilating' immigrants' children. It leads to the question of integration of Muslim and other immigrants, and Islam as a culture, religion and as a political force in and beyond its countries of origin. The arguments raised in the public debate relate to moral principles such as tolerance, the right to difference, individual liberty, religious freedom, human rights and especially the emancipation of women and equality of the sexes. And finally, the issue leads to questions about the effects of multiculturalism in practice, the re-establishment of public order, the redefinition of the social contract and of equal citizenship. Kastoryano considers the debate on this issue and the underlying phenomenon it addresses as part of globalization. She argues that globalization leads to identity anxiety within both states and communities, which now compete for the loyalty and allegiance of their members within the same geographical space. Therefore, one of the important aspects of multiculturalism that scholars and policy makers need to consider is the transnational scope of community identification, which gives new impetus to expressions of identity within and beyond national territories.

Chapter 5 also features discourses on the wearing of headscarves but additionally a recent analysis of the public debates of two other issues: curriculum and teaching methods in Islamic free schools, and future church–state relations in Denmark, which has a Protestant state church. The author, Per Mouritsen, uses these findings to discuss the ambiguity of dominant universalistic public self-conceptions of a highly egalitarian welfare state, which is also, significantly, an 'old' *nation*-state, as it encounters cultural diversity. First, the debates suggest the peculiar ease with which solemn ideals of liberal universalism can exist alongside calls for cultural assimilation, or at least the legitimacy of a nationalized public–cultural space. The Danish debate thus takes the form of communitarian liberalism arguing that tolerance and respect for diversity positively *require* a dominant official culture ('Danishness', 'our Christian cultural heritage'). It also includes the unstated assumption that Danish political culture simply incarnates universal values, whereas Muslim migrant claims do not. Second, the specific national framing of the headscarf and free school debates indicates ways in which a strongly integrated egalitarian and democratic–universalist public philosophy may be *a fortiori* less 'colour-blind' and more reflecting of national particularities: Hence the emphases on *sexual* equality and a *liberated* (body) culture in the public space, and hence the construction of autonomy as a comprehensive, reflective and anti-authoritarian democratic practice of a specific kind. Such instances of national particularity-masquerading-as-universalism cast critical light on contemporary philosophical doctrines of 'liberal nationalism'. But they also highlight – as indicated in debates over the very phenomenological meaning of practices such as wearing a scarf and teaching in a religious school – the politically contested perfectionism of *deep* liberal doctrines, which emphasize the non-negotiability of private autonomy, democratic participation and comprehensive application of egalitarian ideals. Per Mouritsen thus discusses critically the presumed secularity of policy responses to Muslim claims in Denmark and the oft-hidden nationalist and Christian rationales of liberal democracies.

Werner Schiffauer, in his chapter on naturalized immigrants and moral panics, studies recent developments in German policies and debates concerning immigrant integration. The growing number of naturalization processes which turn '*Ausländer*' into citizens changes the power structure between the 'established' and the 'outsiders'. The '*Ausländer*' were conceived to be different and unequal. They were associated with (rather than integrated into) German society mainly through patron–client relationships. With a growing number of German citizens of foreign descent, German society has now to cope with citizens who fight for their right to difference as an integral part of their citizen status. This new situation creates considerable irritation, especially with regard to conservative Muslims who symbolize the quintessential other for a great part of the German public. The irritation leads to considerable efforts of boundary drawing.

The chapter analyses three areas in which the politics of boundary drawing takes place. First, access to the judiciary: several court decisions in which Muslims were quite successful in gaining legal recognition for their cause stirred intensive reactions by the German public. It was declared to be an abuse of the courts if migrants turned to them with regard to minority rights. The uneasiness was particularly reflected in the 'demonization' of Fereshta Ludin who had fought for her right to wear the headscarf as a teacher in public schools. Second, the sphere of citizenship rights: the quest for citizenship was answered by an attempt to draw a clear classificatory line between 'religious' Muslims and fundamentalists who presumably abuse religion for political purposes. It was observed with suspicion that the conservative Milli Görüs community had made an appeal to its followers to apply for German citizenship. Their applications were interpreted as an attempt to infiltrate the country and abuse the

German legal system; members of the community have thus been regularly denied the status. Third, in relation to public funding, the case of the Muslim Youth is a telling one. The organization used public funds to do projects in schools with Muslim students until a press campaign attacked the organization because of alleged links to the Muslim brotherhood. Although nothing was proven, public support was stopped immediately. The three case studies throw light on different techniques of boundary drawing: demonization, classificatory exercises and recourse to conspiracy theory.

The five chapters presented above discuss advanced versions of multicultural citizenship and particularly concentrate on how Muslim claims can be accommodated in democratic states. The remaining two contributions (Chapters 7 and 8) concentrate on two recent immigration countries, Italy and Spain, and explore the multiculturalism debates that take place there even if still in embryonic forms.

The chapter on Italy, authored by Anna Triandafyllidou, analyses the 'Italian mosque debate' with a view to testing how new migration hosts deal with the cultural and religious diversity challenges that immigration brings. The controversy over the construction of two new mosques in and around Milan, in October 2000, offers a suitable example for the study of attitudes and views on religious diversity in Italy, its recognition, acceptance or rejection. The first part of the chapter puts the specific case in its national context reviewing the size and composition of the immigrant population in Italy, the socio-economic position of immigrants and the legal provisions for naturalization. In the second part, Triandafyllidou concentrates on the 'mosque issue' and the dubious emergence of views and practices favouring a multicultural society and citizenship. The analysis is based on material collected from four major newspapers with both a regional and national circulation. The analysis highlights the main 'voices' involved in the debate and the thematic dimensions that organize it. A qualitative methodology of discourse analysis is used to identify the prevailing discourse(s) and to show how the different positions put forward by the dominant social and political actors are linked with specific features of the Italian political and party system. In the concluding section, Triandafyllidou discusses how Muslim claims put to the test an emerging Italian version of multicultural citizenship.

Ricard Zapata-Barrero takes up the question of multiculturalism in Spain. His core argument is that the analysis of the Spanish context teaches us that tradition matters in orientating public discourse. This tradition has as its main element a *Maurophobia* that has been constructed throughout history. Zapata-Barrero argues that this picture is a substantive element of the process of Spanish identity building. From this focus, basic questions arise such as: how can Spain fight against this deep-rooted negative perception of the Moors without threatening its national identity as expressed through its citizens? How should Muslims express their self-identity in a Spanish society and polity which has a public discourse that refuses to recognize its own Islamic tradition and assumes that Islam belongs to 'a historical anomaly'? After describing the main 'conflict zones' and summarizing the main legal framework regulating the relationship between Muslims and the state, he discusses the main elements that characterize the Spanish discourse and argues, by way of conclusion, for the need to think of impartiality as a criterion of justice and as the main approach to treating Muslims from a European perspective.

In the latter part of the book, Modood and Kastoryano bring together the analytical threads of the seven country cases in their chapter on secularism and religious pluralism. The two authors challenge the fact that *laïcité* has been considered as a 'given' in Western societies. Established with the construction of the nation-state, internalized as a 'reasonable' approach to religion, according to which the individual is freed from the hegemony of the Church, the concept and the principle of secularism,[4] as well as its practice, came into public debate in the last 20 years when the same Western societies have faced Islam on their territory and in their society. Muslims, established citizens in the West, nevertheless external to the long fight between State and Church that made Western national histories, have emerged in the public space through their demand for recognition and institutional representation. Muslim claims have brought to the surface the ambivalence of the secularist concept as well as its unresolved aspects, notably its fundamentally ambiguous character. Kastoryano and Modood argue that in modern Western nation-states, religion becomes a legitimate source for incorporation of immigrants as it constitutes their main element of difference and the core of a politics of recognition.

In the concluding chapter, Bhikhu Parekh explores some of the bases of anti-Muslim discourses in European thought, paying particular attention to the internal tensions and limitations of European liberalism. He argues that while it is clear that there is a European-wide anxiety that Muslim immigrants and their descendants have failed to integrate, do not respect democracy and are sympathetic to terrorism, this anxiety is not empirically informed. Muslims indeed are law-abiding, enthusiastic participants in the democratic process when they are given the chance and are loyal to the states in which they are resident or citizens. This anxiety is based on the false view that political unity is not possible without cultural unity. Even liberals share this false assumption, though they, unlike conservatives, confine the area of cultural uniformity to a public sphere. This confinement of cultural difference to the private sphere is particularly strongly pursued in relation to religion and so particularly leads to conflict with some Muslims. European polities, however, are not secular in a throughgoing sense but make adjustments to maintain the historical accommodation of religion. They rightly do not make citizenship conditional on a membership of a religion but they allow religion its proper place in political life, though the actual provisions and the public–private boundaries varies from country to country.

Parekh goes on to identify a further factor that generates European anxiety about Muslims which has its roots in European rationalism. Rationalist liberals exaggerate the degree to which values, and the number of values, are universal and purely rational, such that they can and should be subscribed to by all rational persons, regardless of their cultural and social commitments. Most values in fact are culturally specific; good reasons can be given for them but these are not so compelling or convincing as to make those disagreeing irrational or intellectually obtuse. Hence many of the reasons for the primacy of liberal values, such as freedom of expression, that the liberal gives to Muslims are not accepted as decisive by the latter. This generates annoyance, self-doubt and moral panic amongst European liberals and is targeted at Muslims. Liberals often have right on their side but not in a monopolistic way and if they arrogantly act as if they do, this will only generate resentment, mutual suspicion, hostility and unnecessary conflict. What is needed is dialogue. But this is possible only if liberals recognize their own cultural specificity – that they are not a universal civilisation – and approach Muslims and other minorities with respect and a willingness to listen and learn, as well as persuade. Parekh concludes on an optimistic note, instancing the example of how the vast majority of Muslim schoolgirls and their families accept the restrictions of *laïcité* on the wearing of the *hijab*, not because they agree with them but out of respect for French culture. He – and we – are confident that Muslims have started becoming an integral part of Europe, seeing themselves as bearers of a proud, historic world faith but intertwined with national identities and liberal values. This process is not without resistance on the part of a small minority of Muslims but will continue best if integration takes a dialogical form.

Notes

1 Zapata-Barrero (2004b). This would explain the influence still exerted by the works of Kymlicka (1995, for example), who succeeded in linking the two main driving forces of the political theory debates in the 1980s and 1990s, liberal democratic citizenship and multiculturalism respectively.
2 Among an extensive list of relevant works, see: Taylor (ed., 1992), Frankel *et al.* (1994), Kymlicka (1995a; 1995b), Glazer (1997), Martiniello (1997), Joppke and Lukes (1999), Kymlicka and Norman (2000, especially the chapters by J. Waldron and T. Modood), the recent work of Carens (2000) and Parekh (2000), Zapata-Barrero (2001b), Barry (2001), Kelly (2002), Joppke and Morawska (2003).
3 Cf. Mehan (1997) with regard to a similar process taking place in the United States.
4 Secularism here stands for the English translation of *laïcité*. In this chapter but also in Kastoryano's chapter on France (see above) the authors discuss the difference between the two terms and highlight the contextual and specific historical connotations of both concepts.

References

Barry, B. (2001) *Culture and Equality*, Cambridge: Polity Press.
Brubaker, R. W. (1992) *Citizenship and Nationhood in France and Germany*, Cambridge, MA: Harvard University Press.
——— (1996) *Nationalism reframed. Nationhood and the national question in the New Europe*, Cambridge and New York: Cambridge University Press.
Carens, J. (2000) *Culture, Citizenship, and Community*, New York: Oxford University Press.

Council Directive (2000) 'Implementing the principle of equal treatment between persons irrespective of racial or ethnic origin', Council Directive 2000/43/EC, 29 June 2000.

Eurobarometer (1997) Racism and Xenophobia in Europe, *Eurobarometer*, opinion poll, No. 47.1, Luxembourg.

Eurostat (2001) *The Social Situation in the European Union*, Luxembourg: Office for the Official Publications of the European Communities.

—— (1998b) 'Multicultureel theorie in theorie en pratijk: empirische analyses in de toegepaste politieke filosofie', in *Krisis: tijdschrift voor filosofie*, No. 72 Herfst (English language version attached to this proposal).

—— (1998c) 'Applied political philosophy at the Rubicon: Will Kymlicka's Multicultural Citizenship', *Ethical Theory and Moral Practice*, 1(2).

—— (2000) 'Immigration politics in Europe', *ECPR News*, Spring.

Favell, A. and Hansen, R. (eds) (2002) 'EU enlargement and East-West migration', *Journal of Ethnic and Migration Studies*, Special Issue, 28(4): October.

Favell, A. and Modood, T. (2003) 'The philosophy of multiculturalism: the theory and practice of normative political theory', in A. Finlayson (ed.) *Contemporary Political Thought: A Reader and Guide*, Edinburgh: Edinburgh University Press.

Frankel, P. E., Miller, F. and Jeffrey, P. (eds) (1994) *Cultural pluralism and moral knowledge*, Cambridge: Cambridge University Press.

Glazer, N. (1997) *We are all Multiculturalist Now*, Cambridge, MA: Harvard University Press.

Hailbronner, K. (1998) 'European immigration and asylum law under the Amsterdam Treaty', *Common Market Law Review*, 35(5): 1047–1067.

Jacobs, D. (2000) 'Multinational and polyethnic politics entwined: minority representation in the region of Brussels-Capital', *Journal of Ethnic and Migration Studies*, 26(2): 289–304.

Joppke, C. (1996) 'Multiculturalism and immigration: a comparison of the United States, Germany, and Great Britain', *Theory and Society* 25: 449–500.

Joppke, C. and Lukes, S. (eds) (1999) *Multicultural Questions*, Oxford: Oxford University Press.

Joppke, C. and Morawska, M. (2003) *Toward Assimilation and Citizenship. Immigrants in Liberal Nation-states*, Basingstoke: Palgrave Macmillan.

Jordan, B. and Vogel, D. (1997) 'Which policies influence migration decisions? A comparative analysis of interviews with undocumented Brazilian immigrants in London and Berlin', *Arbeitspapier*, No. 14/97, University of Bremen.

Jordan, B., Vogel, D., Stråth, B. and Triandafyllidou, A. (eds) (2003) 'From guardians to managers: immigration policy implementation in Europe', *Journal of Ethnicity and Migration Studies*, Special Issue, 29(2): Spring.

Kastoryano, R. (1997) *La France, l'Allemagne et leurs immigrés. Négocier l'identité*, Paris: Armand Colin.

—— (ed.) (1998) *Quelle identité pour l'Europe. Le multiculturalisme a l'épreuve*, Paris: Presses de Sciences Pô.

Kelly, P. (2002) 'Introduction: between culture and equality', in P. Kelly (ed.) *Multiculturalism Reconsidered*, Cambridge: Polity Press.

Koopmans, R. and Statham, P. (eds) (2000) *Challenging and Defending the Fortress: Political Mobilisation over Ethnic Difference in Comparative and Transnational Perspective*, Oxford: Oxford University Press.

Kymlicka, W. (1995) *Multicultural Citizenship: A Liberal Theory of Minority Rights*, Oxford: Oxford University Press.

Kymlicka, W. and Norman, W. (eds) (2000) *Citizenship in Diverse Societies*, New York: Oxford University Press.

Martiniello, M. (1997) *Sortir des guettos culturels*, Paris: Presses de la Fondation Nationales des Sciences Polítiques.

May, S., Modood, T. and Squires, J. (eds) (2004) *Ethnicity, Nationalism and Minority Rights*, Cambridge: Cambridge University Press.

Mehan, H. (1997) 'The discourse of the illegal immigration debate: a case study in the politics of representation', *Discourse and Society*, 8(2): 249–270.

Modood, T. (1998) 'Anti-essentialism, multiculturalism and the 'recognition' of religious minorities', *Journal of Political Philosophy*, 6(4); reproduced in W. Kymlicka, W. and W. Norman (eds) (2000) *Citizenship in Diverse Societies*, Oxford: Oxford University Press.

——— (2000) 'Anti-essentialism, multiculturalism, and the "recognition" of religious groups', in W. Kymlicka, W. and W. Norman (eds) *Citizenship in Diverse Societies*, Oxford: Oxford University Press.

Modood, T. and Werbner, P. (eds) (1997) *The Politics of Multiculturalism in the New Europe*, London: Zed Books.

Palidda, S. (ed.) (1996) *La construction sociale de la deviance et de la criminalite parmi les immigres en Europe*, Bruxelles, COST Communauté Européenne.

Parekh, B. (1994) 'Cultural diversity and liberal democracy', in D. Beetham, *Defining and Measuring Democracy*, London: Sage.

——— (2000) *Rethinking Multiculturalism: Cultural Diversity and Political Theory*, Basingstoke: Macmillan.

Penamarin, C. (1998) 'El analisis de textos en una nueva clave. Discursos e imagenes sobre la inmigracion en El Pais', *Cuadernos de Informacion y Comunicacion*, 3. Online. Available HTTP:

http://www.ucm.es/info/per3/cic/index.htm (accessed 3 November 1998).

Perez Diaz, V., Berta Alvarez, M. and Gonzalez Enriquez, C. (2001) *Espana ante la inmigracion*, Barcelona: Fundacion La Caixa. Online. Available in Spanish and English:

http:www.estudis.lacaixa.comunicacions.com/webes/estudis.nsf/wurl/pfes008cos_esp (accessed 22 April 2002).

Rawls, J. (1993) *Political Liberalism*, Oxford: Oxford University Press.

Reyneri, E., Baganha, M., Dal Lago, A., Laacher, S., Palidda, S., Papantoniou, A., Papantoniou, M., Solé, C. and Wilpert, C. (1999) *Migrants' Insertion in the Informal Economy. Deviant Behaviour and the Impact on Receiving Societies (MIGRINF)*, Comparative Reports, Brussels: TSER Programme (Contract No. SOE2-CT95–3005), unpublished project report.

Rorty, R. (1989) *Contingency, Irony, and Solidarity*, Cambridge: Cambridge University Press.

Stetter, S. (2000) 'Regulating migration: authority delegation in justice and home affairs', *Journal of European Public Policy*, 7(1): 81–103.

Taylor, C. (ed.) (1992) *Multiculturalism and 'The Politics of Recognition'*, Princeton, NJ: Princeton University Press.

——— (1994) 'Multiculturalism and 'The Politics of Recognition', in A. Gutmann, (ed.) *Multiculturalism: Examining the Politics of Recognition*, Princeton, NJ: Princeton University Press.

ter Wal, J. (1996) 'The social representation of immigrants: the Pantanella issue in the pages of La Repubblica', *New Community*, 22(1): 39–66.

────── (2002a) 'Attitudes towards Albanian refugees in political news discourse', in D. Melossi (ed.) *Migrants, Interactions and Conflicts in the Making of a European Democracy*, Milan: Giuffre editore.

────── (2002b) 'The representation of immigrants and ethnic minorities in Italian mass media', *Project Tuning into Diversity*, Rome, April, CENSIS. Online. Available: www.multicultural.net/tuning_results.htm (accessed 15 June 2004).

Triandafyllidou, A. (1999) 'Racists? Us? Are you joking? The discourse of social exclusion of immigrants in Greece and Italy', in R. King, G. Lazaridis and C. Tsardanidis (eds) *Eldorado or Fortress? Migration in southern Europe*, London: Macmillan.

────── (2000) 'The political discourse on immigration in Southern Europe: a critical analysis', *Journal of Community and Applied Social Psychology*, 10(5): 373–389.

────── (2001) *Immigrants and National Identity in Europe*, London: Routledge.

────── (2002) *Negotiating Nationhood in a Changing Europe: Views from the Press*, Ceredigion, Wales and Washington DC: Edwin Mellen.

Triandafyllidou, A. and Veikou, M. (2002) 'The hierarchy of Greekness: ethnic and national identity considerations in Greek immigration policy', *Ethnicities*, 2(2): 189–208.

Wallace, C. and Stola, D. (eds) (2001) *Patterns of Migration in Central Europe*, London: Palgrave.

Wieviorka, M. (2001) *La différence*, Paris: Éditions Balland.

Young, I. M. (1990) *Justice and the Politics of Difference*, Princeton, NJ: Princeton University Press.

Zapata-Barrero, R. (2001) 'The limits of a multinational Europe: democracy and immigration in the European Union', in F. Requejo (ed.) *Democracy and National Pluralism*, London: Routledge.

────── (2002) 'State-based logic versus EU-based logic towards immigrants: evidences and dilemmas', *Asian and Pacific Journal*, 11(4).

────── (2003) 'Spain', in J. Niessen and Y. Schibel (eds) *EU and US Approaches to the Management of Immigration*, Brussels: Migration Policy Group.

────── (2004a) *Inmigración y multiculturalidad*, Madrid: Ed. Síntesis.

────── (2004b) 'Political theory today: political innovation and the management of structural change', *European Political Science*, Issue 3.3: 39–50.

2 Multiculturalism, citizenship and Islam in problematic encounters in Belgium*

Hassan Bousetta and Dirk Jacobs

Introduction

One of the consequences of 9/11 in Belgium is without any doubt that the issue of multiculturalism and the position of Islam within Belgian society have been put centre stage in political and public debate. Any observer who undertakes a quick scan of the focus of contemporary Belgian media attention would have to conclude that the issue of cultural diversity – and in particular the position of immigrant Muslim minority groups – is currently seen to be at the core of public life. The preoccupation of managing ethnic, cultural and religious diversity in the public space did not suddenly appear with the tragic events in New York and Washington. Indeed, it has been a recurring issue, albeit fragmented, for debate in Belgium ever since the mid-1970s (Jacobs and Swyngedouw, 2002).

What is new in the content of the debate, however, is the peremptory negative character of the arguments produced. The most radical opponents of multiculturalism have shaped a space of dialogue in which the claim for identity difference and recognition of minority groups is deeply questioned. Authoritative arguments *vis-à-vis* ethnic and religious minorities have heavily challenged the discourse and ideal of a society where difference is mutually enriching. In many such debates, the incorporation of Islam and Muslims is central, both implicitly and explicitly.

In the Belgian context, the question of dealing with ethnic diversity – at least when being considered independently from the linguistic divide in the country – was initially conceived as an issue that was limited to handling the consequences of recruitment of a temporary foreign labour force on an ad hoc basis. In the course of the 1970s and 1980s the issue of multiculturalism gradually came to be seen independently from issues of migration and mobility. If the management of cultural diversity in the public space can today no longer be thought of in the framework of earlier migration waves alone, it can neither be understood as a matter to be merely dealt with in the private sphere. It is still, however, handled in an ad hoc way.

Fundamentally, the issue at stake is how to define a public space capable of welcoming and organizing a peaceful coexistence of culturally and religiously different minority and majority groups. Such a challenge raises the question of the principles along which we need to reorganize the public space in an accommodating way for all involved groups. Just as the nineteenth-century struggles of the working class were articulated in terms of social justice, the contemporary claims of minority groups manifesting themselves in multicultural societies need to be read as a quest for what political philosophers have called a principle of ethno-cultural justice (Kymlicka, 2001).

One would wish for a serene climate for pursuing the debate on multiculturalism, but this is far from being a readily available condition. These debates are, on the contrary, developing in an increasingly nervous atmosphere. In Belgium, the context is marked by the fact that the question has reached a high level of political centrality, especially in Flanders (the Dutch-speaking part of Belgium) where the extreme right-wing party the Vlaams Blok – which changed its name to 'Vlaams Belang' in November 2004 following a conviction for its racist propaganda – has obtained no less than 25 per cent of the popular vote in the June 2004 federal elections. Pushed in the back by this strong xenophobic far-right movement, the government and political parties are ceaselessly led to comment and make political statements about the perceived failures of multicultural coexistence. Consequently, public deliberations on the issue of dealing with ethnic diversity take place against a backdrop of political manoeuvres seeking to woo either ethnic minority voters – especially in Brussels (see Jacobs et al., 2002) – or, more often, the anti-multiculturalism and/or xenophobic voters (Jacobs and Rummens, 2003). Not surprisingly, the tensions generated by international developments also shape the debate. In 2005, the war in Iraq, the Israeli–Palestinian conflict and the unstable situation in Afghanistan all contributed to a mutual lack of confidence between 'the West' and 'the Arab–Muslim world'. The consequences are not merely diplomatic, but equally impact on domestic politics in Belgium as much as in other European countries. The relationship between Arab and Muslim minorities on the one hand, and the majority groups of the European societies where these minorities live and reside on the other, bear the repercussions of these tensions. The worries raised in mainstream public opinion by acts of political violence happening in the world in the name of Islam raise open questions about the nature of European Islam and the degree of loyalty of European Muslims. This was only exacerbated in Belgium in November 2004, following the murder in Amsterdam of the controversial Dutch cineaste and publicist Theo Van Gogh by a young Dutch Muslim extremist of Moroccan origin.

Interestingly, the focus on Islam and the pressure on multicultural discourse in Belgium have, however, not directly led to an overall change in actual policy. As has been the case in the past, policy is still often of a pragmatic nature and a wide variety of (sometimes contradicting) policy practices coexist in Belgium. At some instances a crude assimilationist line is taken, while at other instances ethnic diversity is stimulated to prosper. Ethnic difference can be both neglected and denied or accommodated depending on the issues and actors involved. On the ground, policy may be *de facto* of a multicultural nature, while all those involved will vigorously deny that it has anything to do with the idea of multiculturalism. Or a strict assimilationist policy scheme may be announced, but in the end it might not be implemented so strictly.

This contribution aims to discuss the particular fortune of the idea of multiculturalism in the Belgian context. After discussing some of the contours of the disputed concept of multiculturalism, we consider the controversies that it raised in Belgium and its difficult encounter with the issues raised by the Islamic presence, taking the topic of the headscarf (or the *hijab*) as a case in point.

Multiculturalism in Europe: rhetoric and politics

The notion of multiculturalism is quite recent. Nearly unknown in the 1970s, it grew in significance and has become omnipresent in every discussion on cultural diversity since the 1990s. For quite a while, multiculturalism predominantly had a positive connotation until it came under heavy attack after the events of 9/11. One can observe that multiculturalism is at the centre of a very passionate debate in both the academic literature and policy communities alike. The notion tends to be presented either as a sort of panacea or as a red herring in the context of the public management of identity differences. Multiculturalism is used as an analytical framework for very different kinds of policy issues ranging from immigrant incorporation to autonomist claims of national minorities, gender equality claims, etc. It also refers to a theoretical position of a higher order concerning the notion of the self, the individual and modernity (Semprini, 1997). Our interest here concerns the philosophies underlying public policies.

In the European context, the notion of multiculturalism was explicitly adopted by the Swedish government at the end of the 1970s in order to deal with the inflow and settlement of immigrant workers (Runblom, 1994). The Dutch were also influenced by this approach but defined their creed as that of the 'minority policy' (Entzinger, 1993). Britain, which perceives itself as a multicultural country, has historically articulated a policy approach hinged on the idea of 'racial equality', an approach where the accent is rather placed on the struggle against discrimination than on the recognition of minority cultures (Modood, 1993). Other countries have experienced types of public policies coming close to multiculturalism. More exactly, some countries have implemented multicultural policies sometimes unwittingly and at other times simply without labelling them multicultural. This is for instance the case of France, where the republican tradition is opposed to the principles of multiculturalism, but which in many accounts is open to multicultural policies locally (Bousetta, 1997; 2001; Kastoryano, this volume). This idea needs to be emphasized in so far as it is not evident to find in Europe models of public policies inspired by multiculturalism which would be as coherent as the outline proposed by normative political philosophers (Taylor, 1992; Kymlicka, 1995) and as explicit as those found in the Canadian or Australian contexts (Vermeulen and Slijper, 2003). In the European context, multiculturalism refers to a wide variety of post-migration and post-colonial circumstances. This is not necessarily done in a clear-cut or consistent way, as is clearly shown by the Belgian case.

At the theoretical level, multiculturalism represents a distinctive model for the management of cultural diversity. In so far as the notion is associated with different meanings depending on the context, it is important to define briefly what we are discussing in this chapter. In its elementary definition, multiculturalism refers to a *de facto* situation marked by the coexistence of groups associated to culturally distinct heritages. This first approach is merely descriptive and lacks analytical incisiveness. In so far as monocultural states are the exception rather than the rule, multiculturalism is a reality for most countries in the world.

It is therefore necessary to envisage more complex definitions of the phenomena that allow us to differentiate multicultural states from what Parekh (2000) calls multiculturalist states. The case in point refers at the same time to public discourses on cultural diversity, an ideology, norms and public policies implemented by the state. By all accounts, the key question posed by the multiculturalist perspective and which is our interest here is that of public recognition – that is to say, recognition in the public space – of particular identity differences of minority groups. The point then is to know how such recognition is bestowed and to what extent.

For multicultural theorists, the starting point is a challenge to the internal organization of nation-states which are seldom, if ever, able to demonstrate their neutrality in cultural terms. The symbols, norms and values embodied in the structures of state power, although having an aspiration to universalism, emanate from particular cultures of majority groups and are playing to their advantage to varying degrees. In the name of what they call the principle of ethno-cultural justice, multiculturalists call for the recognition of minority identities and cultures, not simply in the private, but also in the public sphere. The ideal of the multicultural society starts off from the principle that it is essential to extend recognition and equal respect to minority cultures.

But the legitimacy of these claims cannot be evaluated *ex ante*. As Parekh recommends, they need to be subjected to an intercultural evaluation – which is a precondition for breaking off with ethnocentrism – in the framework of public democratic deliberation. These elements brought in by contemporary political philosophers have facilitated criticism of the classical logic of thinking of a large stream of European political actors. These politicians have tended to define 'integration' as a balance between rights and duties. In their arguing, the founding elements of the public space and the inequalities it generates are, however, almost never questioned.

The Canadian philosopher Kymlicka offers another principle for solving multicultural tensions and for drawing the limits of recognition. He holds the position that minority groups may legitimately claim forms of external protection from the state allowing them to reproduce themselves as distinct cultural groups as long as no internal restriction to the rights and liberties of the individual members of these communities is imposed at the same time. Even though the philosophical debate need not necessarily be grounded in a particular context, the concrete issues raised by Islam and Muslims in the Western world are never far from the discussion.

The Belgian models

In Belgium, the debate on multiculturalism has not been as systematic as in other European countries such as the Netherlands (that is, before the death of the populist leader Pim Fortuyn), Denmark or Britain (Jacobs and Swyngedouw, 2002; Bousetta, 2002). It is fragmented along a double perspective: from a material and a linguistic point of view. The debate is posed differently in Flanders on the one side and Brussels–Wallonia on the other, but on both sides what is discussed are specific multicultural questions such as the headscarf, voting rights and citizenship, anti-discrimination, the institutionalization of Islam, etc., rather than a general principle of diversity management at policy level. An overarching debate occurred only once, between 1989 and 1993, when the Belgian federal government seconded a Royal Commissioner on immigrant policy. Since then, Belgium has been characterized by a lack of a comprehensive political analysis of the conditions under which a viable and coherent multicultural society is possible. It should, however, be mentioned that in recent years several attempts have been undertaken to relaunch an all-encompassing debate.

It is at the turn of the 1990s that Belgium sought (with partial success) to clarify its position concerning the policy management of ethnic diversity. Faced with a variety of identity claims, Belgian authorities have sought to define some principles, if not a model, which permit the state to judge the legitimacy of these demands. This first attempt to elaborate a coherent policy framework came from the Royal Commissioner on immigrant policy through their concept of integration, a concept that was discussed and debated in Parliament. It should be stressed that the institution of the Royal Commissioner was created in direct response to the rise of the Flemish extreme right-wing and racist party Vlaams Blok, which had been able to score its first major successes, notably in local elections in Antwerp where it obtained 18 per cent of the votes in 1988. In its 1989 report, the Royal Commissioner proposed a definition of the concept of integration hinging on three dimensions. On that account, the integration strategy of public authorities should promote:

- assimilation where public order makes it compulsory;
- a consequent promotion of the highest degree of insertion in line with the fundamental social principles underpinning the culture of the host society and which correspond to 'modernity', 'emancipation' and pluralism in the sense given by modern western States;
- unequivocal respect for cultural diversity as a process of mutual enrichment in all other domains of social life.

(CRPI, 1989: 38–39)

What is important to note, however, is that the definition was intrinsically a political compromise. It constituted the formalization of an intellectual approach which consisted of seeking a balance between rights and duties. It also implied the idea that there would be a founding sphere of the public space vested to a difference-blind sort of universalism and a secondary sphere, cross-cutting the public and the private, where all forms of cultural particularisms may coexist as long as they respect public order.

This definition stemmed neither from a truly multicultural logic of thinking nor from a rigid assimilationist conception. It was actually willingly located at the crossroads of both traditions, for political rather than intellectual reasons. As is the *modus operandi* in federal Belgium, the notion was elaborated by both the Flemish and francophone advisers of the Royal Commissioner. However, the intellectual framework of reference was not identical on both sides of the language divide. Whereas the francophones were inspired by the French repub-lican tradition, the Flemish were more prone to follow what was then seen as the successful Dutch model (Jacobs, 2001; Verlot, 2001). Since then, the philo-sophical divergence between Flanders and Walloonia has been amplified among others because most multicultural policy instruments have been decentralized to the regions. Interestingly, in Brussels two contradictory policy visions coexist (Jacobs, 2001; 2001; 2004a; 2004b).

The Belgian situation – more than any other European country – illustrates the idea that the management of cultural and religious differences may be envis-aged in terms of distinctive 'models of incorporation', even though such models have more discursive and ideological coherence than empirical. Since the early 1990s, it has become common sense to talk of the two distinctive Belgian models coexisting within the federal state. However, if one moves from the content to the style of policy making, there is actually a rather overlooked driving force behind the development of the multicultural debate in Belgium, namely the logic of pragmatism and consensus. The underdevelopment of an overarching Belgian vision of multiculturalism is largely prevented by the multi-national character of the country and the complex decision-making procedures devised to pacify the tensions between the two dominant communities. As a matter of consequence, when consensus between the Flemish and francophones is out of reach, non-decision becomes the most likely perspective. Without prej-udice to existing divergence on the issue within each linguistic community, many crucial questions are not adjudicated through democratic public delibera-tions but are abandoned to civil society actors or even to the judiciary. In this sense, the mosaic nature of the country deeply impacts on the course of the multicultural debate. One obvious example of non-decision is the headscarf issue, which we consider further on. More generally, the pragmatic and compro-mising Belgian approach has carefully avoided any debate on the possible limits to the public recognition of minority cultural and religious practices in the public sphere and that is particularly the case with Muslim demands.

Are there limits to the public recognition of minority cultures and, if so, what are they? Belgian social and political actors are confronted on a daily basis with these types of questions, and are often not prepared for them. For instance, should we accept the introduction of Islamic norms in the Belgian legal order regarding personal status – as several judges have done – by issuing decisions accepting a correspondence between repudiation and divorce, which were regularly translated by local administrators into the official documents of Muslim women under the heading 'repudiated'? Should we tolerate, encourage or prevent the tendency to create Islamic primary and secondary schools? What attitude should we adopt when Muslims claim specific provisions from the state when using public infrastructures or when they are patients in hospitals, prisoners, pupils and students and so on?

The various groups acting in the name of Islam, beyond their heterogeneity, present Belgium's multiculturalism with a challenge which is more difficult to solve practically than theoretically. For social and political actors, the emergence in the public space of these types of questions raises obvious difficulties. But the responses are often uncertain, contingent and dependent on the particular socio-political climate. One will consider within one public institution that the observance of religious dietary requirements, the creation of prayer rooms, the separate use of public infrastructure for men and women, or any other claim to reshape the (physical) public space, do not pose any difficulty while the same issues will raise passionate debates within another institution or locality. This situation is well illustrated by the headscarf debate which has followed in the footsteps of the French controversy.

Public Islam and the headscarf debate in Belgium

Religious practice has been a significant dimension of the social practices of Muslims in Belgium since the onset of labour migration to the country. In the 1960s and 1970s, it was characterized by its public invisibility. Muslims opted for self-organization. They started setting up mosques, improvised solutions to the management and funding of their worship, negotiated very soberly prayer rooms in their working place without causing any commotion in public opinion.

The context evolved towards increased dramatization and alarmism in the second half of the 1980s (1986–1989) after a series of events which were widely covered by the media including: the first massive electoral success of the extreme right in Antwerp; the first headscarf affair in France; the *Satanic Verses* controversy; the assassination of the imam director of the great mosque of Brussels and of his collaborator; the controversy around the first large Muslim demonstration in Brussels after the American attacks on Libya. These events have introduced Muslims in the public space as an object of discourse produced by others much before they have been able to manifest themselves consistently as actors in public debate.

The religious factor among immigrant workers was for long perceived as a temporary survival of the pre-migration condition. Integration within society, time and the succession of generations were deemed to promote the alignment of the religious practice of immigrants along the pattern of nationals. A generation later, the religious identification of immigrants and their offspring is, however, more vivid than ever. Furthermore, their religious identity has progressively moved towards a communitarian identity. Taking into account the diversity of the Muslim minority communities in Belgium, Muslims express a range of claims for public recognition. Their particularity is that they simultaneously seek the inclusiveness of certain social structures in order to accommodate specific practices (for example, wearing the headscarf at school and in the workplace) but also the segmentation of the public space in other respects (for example, organization of Islamic schools).

The issue of the headscarf in Belgium is a good example of the politics of recognition pursued by Muslims and of the nature of the policy response in the context of Belgian multiculturalism. The heated debate in France concerning the headscarf in 2003–2004 did not leave Belgium unaffected (see Kastoryano, this volume). To be entirely precise, it should be stressed, however, that the discussion mainly took place in Brussels and the francophone part of Belgium and only to a lesser extent in the Flemish part (where schools take a much more pragmatic position with regard to the headscarf).

As during the first headscarf affair in 1989, there has been a significant resonance of French debates in neighbouring Belgium. This is not entirely surprising. As a local saying goes: it drizzles in Brussels when it rains in Paris. However, although the headscarf has ignited important debates within political circles, civil society and academia, the tone of the argument has been much less passionate than in France and has not led to any political decision comparable to the ban on religious symbols voted by the French Parliament (Kastoryano, *ibid.*).

At the opening of the academic year in 2003 and in 2004, the affair of the Islamic headscarf stood out as one of the most urgent in francophone Belgium. Having reappeared on the media scene during the course of 2002, it still remains a latent issue on the agenda to date. The *modus vivendi* which had been found about fifteen years earlier does not go uncontested any more. The schools in Brussels dependent on the municipal network decided in 2003 to forbid the registration of students wearing the *hijab* by operation of their internal order rules. At the same time, a number of schools affiliated to the network of the French community took the same decision after an internal consultation between the teachers and the management. Very quickly, young Muslim students affected by the ban reacted by setting up a collective called '*Don't touch my headscarf*' which is a reference to the successful anti-racist campaign of SOS Racisme ('*Don't touch my mate*') in France during the 1980s.[1]

The school decisions generated a climate of tension which stretched far beyond the schools and triggered a number of public debates on the matter. It is interesting to note that in comparison to the first outbreak of the headscarf affair at the turn of the 1990s, the configuration of the debate has now changed. At the time, opponents to the wearing of the headscarf insisted on the family constraint undergone by the girls, on the spectre of Islamic radicalism, on the failure of integration or on male domination. Today, it seems that this position is shifting for it is clearer that the headscarf has multiple meanings at the individual level. Young Muslim women are openly claiming their right to wear it precisely in the name of the values of freedom and tolerance dear to the liberal democratic tradition.

Among political actors, two main types of positions were articulated. The first was concerned with avoiding the public expression of religious and philosophical affiliation and the wearing of religious symbols in the name of the neutrality of the state. Others pleaded for a softer approach, tolerating the headscarf for so long as it did not represent either an attempt at *proselytism* or an obstacle to the practical organization of classes. This last argument referred to the idea that the headscarf should be abandoned when security reasons required it (for instance, during chemistry practice or sports) and that pupils could not argue their Islamic heritage to challenge the content of courses which are perceived by the students as contrary to their beliefs (the case most often referred to is *evolutionism* in biology classes). The more pragmatic position was also articulated with reference to the idea that banning the headscarf would lead Muslim girls to face a double exclusion: as women and as pupils or students. The ban on the headscarf would in practice further isolate the girls from mainstream society.

Beyond the nature of the debate which has been going on for more than two years, the interesting point is that no political decision has been taken.[2] Although two French-speaking members of the federal Parliament introduced a bill in the Senate to ban the headscarf, the governmental parties opted for blocking any decision on the matter. The divergence between the Flemish and francophones came on top of internal divergence among the francophones and prevented any official position being adopted on this divisive multicultural question.

The end result of Belgian multicultural pragmatism is that each school has to adopt its own approach to the phenomenon. As a result, the prevalent situation in 2005 is one in which a school may implement a ban on religious symbols while another school, situated on the same block, can remain open and welcoming to veiled Muslim girls.

Multiculturalism, citizenship and Islam: real-world issues and normative considerations

Many European liberals, be they multiculturalists or assimilationists, adhere to the idea that cultural diversity is a source of richness. The question of religion, and even more so of Islam, is generally more difficult to answer. An overview of the European press coverage of multicultural tensions during the last couple of years leads to the conclusion that the question of Islam is perceived in nearly all EU member states as the most pressing and threatening question of the time. The claims articulated by Muslims are seen as divisive and threatening for the idea of a common citizenship based on shared loyalties.

In theory, the questioning of the notion of citizenship engendered by the presence of Muslims is not radically different from that brought about by the presence of other minority cultures. There is a difference of degree in the salience of the topic but not necessarily a difference of nature. What is at stake remains the question: to what extent do we need similar values, norms and

symbols to form a harmonious society? One could also ask whether diverse identities are a threat to the stability and cohesion of modern societies or whether
they constitute an opportunity. In practice, however, Islam and Muslims raise
one of the most difficult questions for multiculturalism. Authors such as Parekh
and Modood have very well captured this challenge and have attempted to
move the issue to centre stage in multicultural theory.

One should, however, note that Islam and the claims formulated by Muslims
are seen by some multiculturalists as a source of worry for two main reasons.
First, it is assumed that a number of – not necessarily religiously inspired –
Muslim practices are at odds with Western values. The problems of polygamy,
forced and arranged marriages are some of the debated issues. Second, Islam is
seen as conflicting with the values of secularism and the separation of Church
and state, an essential value of the EU but which is, as shown by Modood,
implemented in ways that do not always match the ideal (Modood, 2003).

The public and political interest for Muslim issues provoked an intellectual
interest among researchers. What is interesting to observe is that even the best
specialists of Islam in the West have generally had no interest in theories of
multiculturalism. Islam was usually studied by academics who had an interest in
the sociology of religion or by those who initially focused their work on Islamic
states and societies. This is a serious handicap facing the emerging multicultural
literature dealing with Islam and Muslims.

One cannot reasonably discuss the incorporation of Islam in the public space
of Western democracies by restricting the analytical focus to the accommodation of specific religious practices. There is a contextual background against
which the increased public visibility of Islam needs to be read. Public spaces are
to a varying extent structured by collective narratives which represent Islam in
terms of fear, distrust and hostility. Hence, the emergence of Islam as a
contentious issue in the public space unavoidably provokes internal consequences for both the classical boundary between state and Church and the
identity of Muslims and their conception of citizenship. To a large extent individual and social identities are shaped through dialogical processes and the
encounter with the *Other*. The current context is certainly prone to lead a
number of Muslims to dissociative identifications. What is not yet well
perceived in the mainstream is the opposite dynamic: the internal debate that Muslims are feeding about citizenship, political participation,
transnationalism and the accommodations of Islamic orthodoxy as a result of
their minority position, a debate which is notably symmetrical to the Western
multicultural debate.

These developments are at work in several parts of Europe and are occasionally visible during moments of mobilization such as during the last two
European Social Forums in Paris and London in 2003 and 2004 respectively.
The positive dynamic beneath the surface and contradicting the more dramatic
developments, such as the murder of Theo Van Gogh in November 2004, is not
yet fully discernible and audible for the public at large. Paradoxically, the radi-
cality of the *djihadist* discourse of Bin Laden and his followers is to stimulate a

form of civic consciousness among Muslims. It should be recalled here that in nearly all European countries, Muslims have clearly denounced the use of terrorist violence on behalf of Islam. These very moderate reactions tend to indicate that both ordinary Muslim citizens and leaders are more concerned with citizenship than what is assumed in some media accounts.

In light of the debate raised by the Islamic and Muslim presence in the Belgian and European contexts, it becomes increasingly difficult to argue that religious particularism needs to be rejected and managed in the private sphere. It is, however, an argument that has come back under the argument that multiculturalism has not reached its objectives. The difficulty to find convincing practical solutions to the problems raised by the Islamic presence has opened the way to a radical challenge against multiculturalism as a relevant model of policy management.

The challenge to Belgian multiculturalism – although most often of a pragmatic nature – is as acute as in the other European countries which are most advanced in this area. The arguments which are used to cast doubt on multiculturalism are multiple. For the most radical voices, multiculturalism has evolved from an inclusionary project aimed at meeting the needs of ethnic minorities in an aggressive ideology opposed to essential Western values. The extreme cultural relativism that is attributed to multiculturalists would only be instrumental to an enterprise aimed at challenging and deconstructing the West. It is also a reproach to certain minorities to use the framework of liberal democracy to promote practices which are not very liberal and respectful of individual autonomy.

Although 9/11 had an important impact, we should not forget that the uneasy feelings that are being expressed about multiculturalism are not its direct consequence. In the European context, it is in the Netherlands, a country where tolerance is lived as a historical tradition, and where integration public policies have been inspired by a form of multiculturalism since 1981, that the first sign of a challenge appeared. In January 2001, a few months before the populist party of Pim Fortuyn was set up, the journalist and writer Paul Scheffer, known until then as a progressive leftist intellectual, published a newspaper article that marked the Dutch debate for good. Under the title 'The multicultural drama', Scheffer argued that the multicultural minorities policy of the Netherlands has led to segregation and has failed to tackle socio-economic differences between groups. The Dutch, so argues Scheffer, have mistakenly opted for a model of integration based on the principal recognition of collective cultural identities. In his view, this policy model has led to a situation in which every group only caters and cares for itself and social cohesion within society at large is being sacrificed. Strikingly, a very similar debate has been surfacing in Britain. Journalists and public intellectuals in publications such as the *Guardian* or *The New Statesmen* have talked of the end of multiculturalism. Even figures such as Yasmin Alibhai–Brown, a journalist and essayist known for her engagement for minority groups, now invites us to think beyond multiculturalism (Modood, 2003: 101).

In Belgium, the debate has not (yet) been tackled in a head-on manner as in the Netherlands. Nevertheless, similar arguments have been made and debates in neighbouring countries have received quite some attention. As elsewhere in Europe, the idea of multiculturalism is under severe pressure in Belgium. This does not mean that forms of multicultural policy are no longer present nor that they will quickly disappear (on Flanders, see Jacobs, 2004c), but in the long run it seems to be unavoidable that sustained negativism about multiculturalism will have consequences.

Concluding remarks

When discussing Belgium's version of multiculturalism, we argue that there is a significant difference between the debates on multicultural issues on the one hand and the practice of multicultural policy on the other. The practice is marked by pragmatism and compromise which are generic features of the Belgian political system and which have very little to do with the ideal of multiculturalism. The question remains open, in our view, about the validity of the same reasoning for other multicultural countries like the Netherlands or the Nordic countries.

In defence of multiculturalism, one should recall that the disqualification of the normative theoretical outline proposed by multicultural writers is challenged on the grounds of empirical experiences which do not match the expectations of the model. Multiculturalism – although often not even really implemented – is being blamed for not having sufficiently contributed to the resolution of the main societal problems (such as socio-economic arrears, criminality, etc.) involving citizens of immigrant origin. When analysing the obstacles and difficulties facing immigrant and ethnic minorities in European societies, one could, however, well stigmatize the lack of adequate multicultural strategies. Paraphrasing Jacques Lacan, everything happens as if a non-existing multicultural model was condemned for errors that it did not generate.

We need urgently to envisage intermediary solutions, an open multicultural model articulated on the basis of public policies favouring channels of communication and dialogue between all groups in society whatever their ethnic origins. Because, if we eventually get rid of multiculturalism as a model, it will remain necessary to conceive of an alternative way by which cultures need to coexist and be respected in our public spaces which remain de facto multicultural.

Notes

* The authors wish to thank Anna Triandafyllidou, Tariq Modood, Ricard Zapata, Rainer Bauböck, Adrian Favell, Judith Squires and Riva Kastoryano for their comments on earlier versions of this chapter.
1 What was initially a small group of Muslim girls later in 2004 turned into a larger coalition involving anti-racist organizations such as COIFE (Collectif d'Associations Opposées à l'Interdiction du foulard à l'école). The acronym COIFE means head-

dress in French and stands for Collective of associations opposed to the ban of the headscarf in schools.

2 Compare with Kastoryano's contribution on France in the same volume.

References

Boussetta, H. (ed.) (1997) 'Citizenship and political participation in France and the Netherlands: some comparative reflections on two local cases', *New Community*, 23(2): 215–231.

—— (2001) 'Immigration, post-immigration politics and the political mobilisation of ethnic minorities: a comparative case-study of Moroccans in four European cities', PhD dissertation, KUBrussel.

—— (2002) *Rompre le silence. 11 septembre 2001 – 11 septembre 2002*, Brussels: Labor.

CRPI (1989) *L'intégration: une politique de longue haleine*, Brussels: Inbel.

Entzinger, H. (1993) 'L'immigration aux Pays-Bas: du pluriculturalisme à l'intégration', in M. Wieviorka (ed.) *Racisme et modernité*, Paris: Editions la découverte.

Jacobs, D. (2000) 'Multinational and polyethnic politics entwined: minority representation in the region of Brussels-Capital', *Journal of Ethnic and Migration Studies*, 26(2): 289–304.

—— (2001) 'Immigrants in a multinational political sphere: the case of Brussels', in A. Rogers and J. Tillie (eds) *Multicultural Policies and Modes of Citizenship in European Cities*, Aldershot: Ashgate.

—— (2004a) 'Pacifying national majorities in the Brussels Capital Region: what about the immigrant minority groups?', in E. Lantschner and A. Morawa (eds) *European Yearbook of Minority Issues*, Volume 2, 2002/3: 309–329. Leiden: Martinus Nijhoff.

—— (2004b) 'The challenge of minority representation in Brussels', in G. Aubarell, A. Nicolau Coll and A. Ros (eds) *Immigració i qüestió nacional. Minories subestatals i immigració a Europa*, Barcelona: Editorial Mediterrània.

—— (2004c) 'Alive and kicking? Multiculturalism in Flanders', *International Journal on Multicultural Societies*, 6(2): 189–208.

Jacobs, D. and Rummens, S. (2003) 'Wij zeggen wat ù denkt: Extreem-rechts in Vlaanderen en nieuw radicaal-rechts in Europe', *Krisis, tijdschrift voor empirische filosofie*, 4(2): 41–59.

Jacobs, D. and Swyngedouw, M. (2002) 'The extreme-right and enfranchisement of immigrants: main issues in the public debate on integration in Belgium', *Journal of International Migration and Integration/Revue de l'intégration et de la migration internationale*, 3(3–4): 329–344.

Jacobs, D., Martiniello, M. and Rea, A. (2002) 'Changing patterns of political participation of citizens of immigrant origin in the Brussels Capital Region: the October 2000 elections', *Journal of International Migration and Integration/Revue de l'intégration et de la migration internationale*, 3(2): 201–221.

Kymlicka, W. (1995) *Multicultural Citizenship. A Liberal Theory of Minority Rights*, Oxford: Clarendon Press.

—— (2001) *Politics in the Vernacular: Nationalism, Multiculturalism and Citizenship*, Oxford: Clarendon Press.

Modood, T. (1993) 'Muslim views on religious identity and racial equality', *New Community*, 19(3): 513–519.

——— (2003), 'Muslims and the politics of difference', *Political Quarterly*, 74(s-1): 100–115.

Parekh, B. (2000) *Rethinking Multiculturalism: Cultural Diversity and Political Theory*, Basingstoke: Macmillan.

Runblom, H. (1994) 'Swedish multiculturalism in a comparative European perspective', *Sociological Forum*, 9(4): 623–640.

Semprini, A. (1997) *Le multiculturalisme*, Paris: PUF.

Taylor, C. (1992) *Multiculturalism and 'The Politics of Recognition'*, Princeton, NJ: Princeton University Press.

Verlot, M. (2001) *Werken aan integratie. Het minderheden en onderwijsbeleid in Vlaanderen en de Franse Gemeenschap van België (1988–1998)*, Leuven/Amersfoort: Acco.

Vermeulen, H. and Slijper, B. (2003) *Multiculturalisme in Canada, Australië en de Verenigde Staten. Ideologie en Beleid, 1950–2000*. Amsterdam: Aksant.

3 British Muslims and the politics of multiculturalism*

Tariq Modood

Introduction

Following the 9/11 terrorist attacks in the US, Madrid and msot recently in London (7/7 and 21/7), Western societies are in fear of international, Islamist groups. The concern of this chapter, as of the book as a whole, is on the domestic politics of civic multiculturalism. Independently of and predating these attacks, there is a widespread perception that Muslims are making politically exceptional, culturally unreasonable or theologically alien demands upon European states. My contention is that the logic of Muslim claims-making is European and contemporary. The case of Britain is illustrative. The relation between Muslims and the wider British society and British State has to be seen in terms of a development and rising agendas of racial equality and multiculturalism. Muslims, indeed, have become central to these agendas even while they have contested important aspects of it – especially, the primacy of racial identities, narrow definitions of racism and equality and the secular bias of the discourse and policies of multiculturalism. While there are now emergent Muslim discourses of equality, of difference, and of, to use the motto of the newsletter of the Muslim Council of Britain, 'the common good', they have to be understood as appropriations and modulations of contemporary discourses and initiatives whose provenance lies in anti-racism and feminism. While one result of this is to throw advocates of multiculturalism into theoretical and practical disarray, another is to stimulate accusations of cultural separatism and revive a discourse of 'integration'. While we should not ignore the critics of Muslim activism, we need to recognize that at least some of the latter is a politics of 'catching up' with racial equality and feminism. In this way, religion in Britain is assuming a renewed political importance. After a long period of hegemony, political secularism can no longer be taken for granted but is having to answer its critics as there is a growing understanding that the incorporation of Muslims has become the most important challenge of egalitarian multiculturalism.

After France and Germany, Britain is home to the greatest number of Muslims in an EU country (1.6 million in the 2001 Census, more than half of South Asian, primarily Pakistani, origin). This is a result of Commonwealth immigration from the 1950s onwards. Initially, this was in the form of male labour from rural small-farm-owning and artisan backgrounds seeking to meet the demand for unskilled and semi-skilled industrial workers in the British economy, with wives and children arriving from about the 1970s. The proportion of urban professionals among South Asian Muslims was small, though it increased with the arrival of political refugees from East Africa in the late 1960s and 1970s (though the majority of this group were Hindus and Sikhs). Britain, especially London, as a cosmopolitan centre, has been very attractive for some of the rich and the professional classes from the Middle East, particularly from the 1970s onwards, and many of them have large investments in property in the city. During this period, there have also been waves of political refugees from other parts of the Muslim world, notably from Somalia, Bosnia, Afghanistan and Iraq. In the last decade, Britain and especially London have been a magnet for all kinds of migrants, many of whom are Muslims.

Racial equality movements

The presence of new population groups such as these has made manifest certain kinds of racism in Britain. As a result, anti-discrimination laws and policies began to be put into place from the 1960s. These laws and policies, initially influenced by contemporary thinking and practice in relation to anti-black racism in the United States, assume that the grounds of discrimination are 'colour' and ethnicity. Not only is it in the last decade or so that Muslim assertiveness has become a feature of majority–minority relations, but indeed prior to this, racial equality discourse and politics was dominated by the idea that the dominant post-immigration issue was 'colour racism' (Rex and Moore, 1967; CCCS, 1982; Sivanandan, 1985; Gilroy, 1987). This perspective was epigramatically expressed by the writer, Salman Rushdie: 'Britain is now two entirely different worlds and the one you inherit is determined by the colour of your skin' (Rushdie, 1982). He, together with most anti-racists, later came to adopt a more pluralistic perspective, and one in which the Muslim presence is seen as a fact to be ignored at one's peril. Nevertheless, in a pure or in a mixed form, the US-derived racial dualism continues to be an influential force in British social science and radical politics (Luthra, 1997; Alexander, 2002). One consequence of this is that the legal and policy framework still reflects the conceptualization and priorities of racial dualism.

Until December 2003, it was lawful to discriminate against Muslims as Muslims because the courts did not accept that Muslims are an ethnic group (though oddly, Jews and Sikhs are recognized as ethnic groups within the meaning of the law); on that date an offence of religious discrimination was created but confined to employment. Before the advent of the offence of religious discrimination, the exclusive focus on race and ethnicity, and the exclusion of Muslims but not Jews and Sikhs, increasingly came to be a source of resentment amongst Muslims. Muslims did, however, enjoy some limited indirect legal protection *qua* members of ethnic groups such as Pakistanis, Arabs and so on. Over time, groups such as Pakistanis have become an active constituency within British 'race relations' (Middle Easterners tend to classify themselves as 'white', as in the 1991 and 2001 Censuses, and only recently and gradually have become involved in political activism of this sort, or in domestic politics generally). One of the effects of this politics was to highlight 'race'.

The initial development of anti-racism in Britain followed the US pattern, and indeed was directly influenced by US personalities and events. Just as in the United States the colour-blind humanism of Martin Luther King Jr came to be mixed with an emphasis on black pride, black autonomy and black nationalism as typified by Malcolm X, so also in Britain (both these inspirational leaders visited Britain). A key measure/indicator of racial discrimination and inequality has been numerical under-representation in prestigious jobs, public office, etc. Hence people have had to be (self-)classified and counted, and so group labels, and arguments about which labels are authentic, have become a common feature of certain political discourses. Over the years it has also become apparent that by these inequality measures it is Asian Muslims, and not Afro-Caribbeans, as policy makers had originally expected, who have emerged as the most disadvantaged and poorest groups in the country (Modood *et al.*, 1997). To many Muslim activists the misplacing of Muslims into race categories and the belatedness with which the severe disadvantages of the Pakistanis and Bangladeshis has come to be recognized by policy makers means, at best, that race relations are an inappropriate policy niche for Muslims (UKACIA, 1993) and, at worst, a conspiracy to prevent the emergence of a specifically Muslim socio-political formation (Muslim Parliament of Great Britain, 1992). Such thinking, however, was itself a product of minority identity assertiveness which characterizes the contemporary period.

Indeed, it is best to see the development of racial explicitness and Muslim assertiveness as part of a wider socio-political climate which is not confined to race and culture or non-white minorities. Feminism, gay pride, Quebecois nationalism and the revival of Scottishness are some prominent examples of these new identity movements which have come to be an important feature in many countries, especially those in which class politics has declined. This means that our basic concept of civil rights or civic equality has been supplemented by the concept of equality as 'difference', by the right to have one's 'difference' recognized and supported in the public sphere.

Beyond a liberal politics

This new, emergent notion of equality creates some dissonance with pre-existing political concepts. It does not fit in easily, for example, with a Tory British nationalism. But, more to the point, it is at odds with some of the centre-left ideas that underpinned the earlier notion of racial equality (Goulbourne, 1991a; 1991b). The politicization of 'racial' and ethnic groups (but also women and homosexuals) is taken to introduce 'particularism' into 'universalistic' conceptions of justice defined by meritocratic individualism, liberal citizenship or socialist equality. The success of the new concept of multicultural equality, at least on the Left, has, however, been made possible because it was not anomalous but fitted in with wider challenges to liberal individualism. For example, it fitted in with feminist arguments that ostensible gender-neutral conceptions of the political, of citizenship, of the domain of law and of legal norms, as well as a host of substantive laws and policies, were in fact covert but systematic expressions of male perspectives and ignored the needs and capacities of women (Pateman, 1988; Young, 1990). On the one hand, the abstract, rational individual of liberal politics and jurisprudence was a man (as evidenced by the fact that this individual did not seem to have any domestic or child-rearing obligations). On the other hand, the definition of the political, the activities appropriate for public discourse, political campaigns and legal control favour male interests, leaving unchallenged male power in domestic and sexual relations. Hence, the alternative politics born out of the slogan 'the personal is the political'.

The politics that I have just mentioned is both a theoretical, discursive politics as well as a politics of institutional reform, competition for office and social policies. My concern here – as a way of coming to approach the political–normative climate of opinion in which British Muslims can and are mounting a case for Muslim rights – is particularly with the theoretical dimension of the politics of 'difference' as a critique of the 1960s' notions of liberal equality. It is therefore worth mentioning some other theoretical sources of this politics in order to emphasize how important it has become amongst centre-left egalitarians, especially in book-writing and book-reading circles, in Britain and elsewhere. It is a politics that gets considerable underpinning from the rise of philosophical anti-essentialism in the social sciences (Modood, 1998). Originating from the very different work of thinkers such as Nietzsche, Heidegger and Wittgenstein, given a certain indeterminate radicalism in the hands of more recent theorists like Foucault and Derrida, anti-essentialism in one form or another has been used to critique hegemonic ideas such as nation-state, community, class, and even counter-hegemonic notions such as woman, black and so on (Fuss, 1989). This has been taken to such an extent that an appreciation of perspectivism, of the essentially contested nature of concepts, of fluidity and multiplicity of meanings, of cultural pluralism and perhaps even aporia, has quickly established itself as an orthodoxy in social theory.

Of relevance here is how this anti-essentialism, when married to a theory of political equality as participation in a discursive public space (Arendt, 1963; 1968; Habermas, 1984; 1987), can define inclusion in a political community not in terms of (as many European politicians do as regards Muslims) accepting the rules of the existing polity and its hallowed public–private boundary lines, but the opposite. Public space is defined as essentially contested and indeed created through on-going discursive contestation and political struggles, where the rules of what are appropriate concerns, and the terms of politics, far from being fixed in advance, are an object of political discourse (Benhabib, 1992; Fraser, 1992). Typically, on these accounts, the public–private distinction works as a 'gag-rule' to exclude matters of concern to marginalized and subordinated groups, and the political integration of these minorities on terms of equality inevitably involves their challenging the existing boundaries of publicity. Integration flows from the process of discursive engagement as marginal groups begin to assert themselves confidently in the public space, and others begin to argue and reach some agreement with them, as well as with the enactment of new laws, policies and so on.

Indeed, laws and policies may be of lesser importance, for these theories explicitly repudiate the classical liberal identification of the political with the realms of law and the state. A more expansive understanding of the political is more compatible with the idea of shifting boundaries and politics as debate. This understanding allows for the changing of certain attitudes, stereotypes, stigmatizations, media images and national symbols as primary political goals. Thus, it should now be clear why I believe that today we are dealing with a new concept of equality, one in which the issues of 'representation' are to do not just with the numbers of various categories of people in certain jobs or positions of power, but with 'representation' as the public imagining of groups *qua* groups (Hall, 1992).

Racialization and identity

The issues raised above may seem quite abstract, little more than the preoccupations of a few academics and their students. It is, in my opinion, an important part of the story of the emergent politics of Muslim identity in Britain. In any case, it is time to mention briefly some of the events that had been taking place 'on the ground'. The 'minorities' politics, the cutting-edge anti-racism that developed in Britain in the 1970s and early 1980s, first in radical activism and ultra-left corpuscles then, following the Brixton riots of 1981, in some local government, trade unions, radical public sector professional associations and the Labour Party, was based on a concept of political blackness. The British population was divided into two groups, black and white. The former consisted of all those people who were potential victims of colour racism though, in both theory and practice, they were assumed disproportionately to have the characteristics of the Afro-Caribbean population (Modood, 1994).

This political movement has played an important part in opening up the question of 'race' in Britain and has come to define the identity of many people (less so now than at its height in the mid- to late 1980s). Whether at any point this political identity was embraced by the majority of South Asians or Muslims is an open question (personally, I think not). Two things, however, are clear. First, this identity was embraced by Asian political activists in the 1980s, especially those whose activism was concerned with mainstream British society rather than the organization of their own communities. Second, that from the late 1980s onwards, if not earlier, most Asians were emphasizing a more particular ethnic or religious identity rather than this all-inclusive non-whiteness.

Political blackness was, therefore, unravelling at a grassroots level at the very time when it was becoming hegemonic as a minority discourse in British public life (1980s). The single event that illustrated this most dramatically was the battle over *The Satanic Verses* that broke out in 1988–1989, when many Muslims complained that the novel by Salman Rushdie was offensive (Modood, 1990; 2005). This was seen by all concerned as a Muslim versus the West battle. Confining ourselves to the protests of British Muslims and leaving aside the international row caused by the intervention of Ayatollah Khomeini, it can be safely said that it generated an impassioned Muslim activism and mobilization that no previous campaign against racism had been remotely able to stir. Many 'lapsed' or 'passive' Muslims (especially non-religious Muslims, for whom hitherto their Muslim background was not particularly important) (re)discovered a new sense of community solidarity. What was striking was that when the public rage against Muslims was at its most intense, Muslims neither sought nor were offered any special solidarity by any non-white minority. It was in fact some white liberal Anglicans that tried to moderate the hostility against the angry Muslims, and it was inter-faith fora rather than political black organizations that tried to create space where Muslims could state their case without being vilified. Political blackness – seen up to then as the key formation in the politics of post-immigration ethnicity – was seen as irrelevant to an issue which many Muslims insisted was fundamental to defining the kind of 'respect' or 'civility' appropriate to a peaceful multicultural society, that is to say, to the political constitution of 'difference' in Britain (Modood, 1994).

The black identity movement, in a growing climate of opinion favourable to identity politics of various kinds, was successful in shifting the terms of the debate from colour-blind individualistic assimilation to questions about how white British society had to change to accommodate new groups. It thus paved the way for a plural ethnic assertiveness, as Asian groups, including Muslims, borrowed the logic of ethnic pride and tried to catch up with the success of a newly legitimized black public identity.

Since getting out, the genie has not been re-corked. In a very short space of time 'Muslim' became a key political minority identity, acknowledged by Right and Left, bigots and the open-minded, the media and the government. It has become integral to local community politics and yet thrives through romantic, global solidarities as wars and massacres in Palestine, Bosnia, Kosovo, Iraq, Chechnya, Kashmir, India and so on, fill our newspapers and television screens and led some young British-born Muslims to reinvent the concept of the Ummah as global victims. This politics has meant not just a recognition of a new religious diversity in Britain but a new or renewed policy importance for religion.

Religious equality

So, one of the current conceptions of equality is a difference-affirming equality, with related notions of respect, recognition and identity – in short, what I understand by political multiculturalism. What kinds of specific policy demands, then, are being made by or on behalf of religious groups and Muslim identity politics in particular, when these terms are deployed?

I suggest that these demands have three dimensions, which get progressively 'thicker' – and are progressively less acceptable to radical secularists.

No religious discrimination

One Muslim organization concerned with these issues is the Forum Against Islamophobia and Racism (FAIR). Set up in 2000 'for the purpose of raising awareness of and combating Islamophobia and racism, monitoring specific incidents of Islamophobia and racism, working towards eliminating religious and racial discrimination, campaigning and lobbying on issues relevant to Muslim and other multi-ethnic communities in Britain', its mission statement sets out this first dimension of equality.

The very basic demand is that religious people, no less than people defined by 'race' or gender, should not suffer discrimination in job and other opportunities. So, for example, a person who is trying to dress in accordance with their religion or who projects a religious identity (such as a Muslim woman wearing a headscarf, a *hijab*) should not be discriminated against in employment. Up to the end of 2003 there was no legal ban on such discrimination in Britain, and the government argued that the case for it was not proven.

The legal system thus left Muslims particularly vulnerable because, while discrimination against *yarmulke*-wearing Jews and turban-wearing Sikhs was deemed to be unlawful *racial* discrimination, Muslims, unlike these other faith communities, were not deemed to be a racial or ethnic group. Nor were they protected by the legislation against religious discrimination that did exist in one part of Britain: being explicitly designed to protect Catholics, it covers only Northern Ireland. The best that Muslims were able to achieve was to prove that the discrimination against them was indirectly against their ethnic characteristics: that they suffered discrimination by virtue of being, say, a Pakistani or an Iraqi.

While it is indeed the case that the discrimination against Muslims is mixed up with forms of colour racism and cultural racism, the charge of race discrimination will provide no protection if it is clearly the individual's religion, not the individual's race, that has led to the discrimination. Moreover, some Muslims are white and so do not enjoy this second-class protection; and many Muslim activists argue that religious freedom, being a fundamental right, should not be legally and politically dependent on dubious concepts of race and ethnicity. The same argument applies to the demand for a law in Britain (as already exists in Northern Ireland) making incitement to religious hatred unlawful, to parallel the law against incitement to racial hatred. (The latter extends protection to certain forms of anti-Jewish literature, but not anti-Muslim literature – though see note 1.)

After some years of arguing that there was insufficient evidence of religious discrimination, the hand of the British government was forced by Article 13 of the Amsterdam Treaty (1999), which includes religious discrimination in the list of the forms of discrimination that all member states are expected to eliminate. Accordingly, the British government, following a European Commission directive (that, incidentally, not all member states have rushed to implement), outlawed religious discrimination in employment, with effect from December 2003. This is, however, only a partial 'catching up' with the existing anti-discrimination provisions in relation to race and gender. It does not extend to discrimination in the provision of goods and services, and will not create a duty upon employers to take steps to promote equality of opportunity.

Even-handedness amongst religions

Many minority faith advocates interpret equality to mean that minority religions should get at least some of the support from the state that longer
established religions do. Muslims have led the way on this argument, and have
made two particular issues politically contentious: the state funding of schools
and the law of blasphemy. After some political battle, the government has
agreed in recent years to fund a few (so far, five) Muslim schools, as well as a
Sikh and a Seventh Day Adventist school, on the same basis enjoyed by thousands of Anglican and Catholic schools and some Methodist and Jewish
schools. (In England and Wales, over a third of state-maintained primary and a
sixth of secondary schools are run by a religious group – but all have to deliver a
centrally determined National Curriculum.)

Some secularists are unhappy about this. They accept the argument for parity
but believe this should be achieved by the state withdrawing its funding from all
religious schools. Most Muslims reject this form of equality in which the privileged lose something but the underprivileged gain nothing. More specifically,
the issue between 'equalizing upwards' and 'equalizing downwards' in this
context is about the legitimacy of religion as a public institutional presence.

Muslims have failed to get the courts to interpret the existing statute on blasphemy to cover offences beyond what Christians hold sacred, but some political
support exists for an offence of incitement to religious hatred, mirroring the
existing one of incitement to racial hatred. The government inserted such a clause
in the post-9/11 security draft legislation, in order to conciliate Muslims, who,
among others, were opposed to the new powers of surveillance, arrest and detention. As it happened, most of the latter was made law, but the provision on
incitement to religious hatred was defeated in Parliament. It was reintroduced in a
Private Member's Bill, which also sought to abolish the laws governing blasphemy,
from a Liberal Democrat, Lord Avebury. Although unsuccessful, in September
2004 the government announced its intention to create an offence of incitement
to religious hatred, though some of its supporters continued to express their opposition. It proved to be part of the raft of legislation that was abandoned to make
way for the General Election of May, 2005, but was reintroduced in Parliament in
June, 2005. In any case, it may be that a recent High Court judgement has created
a form of indirect protection against anti-Muslim incitement.[1]

Positive inclusion of religious groups

The demand here is that religion in general, or at least the category of 'Muslim' in
particular, should be a category by which the inclusiveness of social institutions
may be judged, as they increasingly are in relation to race and gender. For example,
employers should have to demonstrate that they do not discriminate against
Muslims by explicit monitoring of Muslims' position within the workforce, backed
up by appropriate policies, targets, managerial responsibilities, work environments,
staff training, advertisements, outreach and so on. Similarly, public bodies should

provide appropriately sensitive policies and staff in relation to the services they provide, especially in relation to (non-Muslim) schools, social and health services; Muslim community centres or Muslim youth workers should be funded in addition to existing Asian and Caribbean community centres and Asian and black youth workers.

To take another case: the BBC currently believes it is of political importance to review and improve its personnel practices and its output of programmes, including its on-screen 'representation' of the British population, by making provision for and winning the confidence of, say, women, ethnic groups and young people. Why should it not also use religious groups as a criterion of inclusiveness and have to demonstrate that it is doing the same for viewers and staff defined by religious community membership?

In short, Muslims should be treated as a legitimate group in their own right (not because they are, say, Asians), whose presence in British society has to be explicitly reflected in all walks of life and in all institutions; and whether they are so included should become one of the criteria for judging Britain as an egalitarian, inclusive, multicultural society. There is no prospect at present of religious equality catching up with the importance that employers and other organizations give to sex or race. A potentially significant victory, however, was made when the government agreed to include a religion question in the 2001 Census. This was the first time this question had been asked since 1851 and its reintroduction was largely unpopular outside the politically active religionists, among whom Muslims were foremost. Nevertheless, it has the potential to pave the way for widespread 'religious monitoring' in the way that the inclusion of an ethnic question in 1991 has led to the more routine use of 'ethnic monitoring'.

These policy demands no doubt seem odd within the terms of, say, the French or US 'wall of separation' between the state and religion, and may make secularists uncomfortable in Britain too (see Modood and Kastoryano, this volume). But it is clear that they virtually mirror existing anti-discrimination policy provisions in Britain.

In an analysis of some Muslim policy statements in the early 1990s, following the activism stimulated by the *Satanic Verses* affair, I argued that the main lines of arguments were captured by the following three positions:

- a 'colour-blind' human rights and human dignity approach;
- an approach based on extension of the concepts of racial discrimination and racial equality to include anti-Muslim racism;
- a 'Muslim power' approach.

I concluded that these 'reflect not so much obscurantist Islamic interventions into a modern secular discourse, but typical minority options in contemporary Anglo-American equality politics, and employ the rhetorical, conceptual and institutional resources available in that politics' (Modood, 1993: 518).

All three approaches are present today. For example, the Muslim Council of Britain, whose stated aim is to 'make Britain a successful multi-faith and multi-cultural society', has said that its three key domestic policy concerns are 'the need to outlaw religious discrimination; measures to tackle high levels of poverty and social exclusion and concern about the curtailment of civil liberties and the targeting by the authorities of Muslim organisations' (MCB press release, 1 October 2003).[2] At the same time, some high-profile radicals have made a Muslim power approach more prominent, in a manner not dissimilar to the rise of black power activism after the height of the civil rights period in the United States. This approach is mainly nourished by despair at the victimization and humiliation of Muslims in places such as Palestine, Bosnia, Kashmir and Afghanistan. For many British Muslims, such military disasters and humanitarian horrors evoke a strong desire to express solidarity with oppressed Muslims through the political idea of the *Ummah*, the global community of Muslims, which must defend and restore itself as a global player. To take the analogy with US black power a bit further, one can say that as black nationalism and Afro-centrism developed as one ideological expression of black power, so, similarly, we can see political Islamism as a search for Muslim dignity and power.

Muslim assertiveness, then, though triggered and intensified by what are seen as attacks on Muslims, is primarily derived not from Islam or Islamism but from contemporary Western ideas about equality and multiculturalism. While simultaneously reacting to the latter for its failure to distinguish Muslims from the rest of the 'black' population and its uncritical secular bias, Muslims positively use, adapt and extend these contemporary Western ideas in order to join other equality-seeking movements. Political Muslims do, therefore, have an ambivalence in relation to multicultural discourses. On the one hand, as a result of previous misrecognition of their identity, and existing biases, there is distrust of 'the race relations industry' and of 'liberals'; on the other hand, the assertiveness is clearly a product of the positive climate created by liberals and egalitarians.

This ambivalence can tend towards antagonism as the assertiveness is increasingly being joined by Islamic discourses and Islamists. Especially, as has been said, there is a sense that Muslim populations across the world are repeatedly suffering at the hands of their neighbours, aided and abetted by the United States and its allies, and that Muslims must come together to defend themselves. Politically active Muslims in Britain, however, are likely to be part of domestic multicultural and equality currents – emphasizing discrimination in educational and economic opportunities, political representation and the media, and 'Muslim-blindness' in the provision of health, care and social services; and arguing for remedies which mirror existing legislation and policies in relation to sexual and racial equality (Modood and Ahmad, 2005).

After 9/11

Following the riots of summer 2001, when young Asian Muslim men fought with supporters of the racist British National Party and/or the police in some northern cities (Kalra, 2003), positive rhetoric about multiculturalism and plural Britishness (CMEB, 2000) has come to be counter-balanced by an integrationist, anti-Muslim rhetoric. The issues raised were far from new, having already been made prominent during and after the *Satanic Verses* affair. They were, however, considerably reinforced by the reactions to the terrorist attacks in the United States of September 11 and the 'war on terrorism' that has followed, which clearly has had and is having major implications for domestic, political multiculturalism. The military and civil liberties aspects of the 'war against terrorism', even more so than at the time of the *Satanic Verses* affair, has seen a vulnerable and besieged group assert itself publicly, and at times defiantly. The majority of Muslims, whilst condemning the terrorist attacks on the United States, opposed the bombing campaign in Afghanistan and the invasion of Iraq. A significant minority of Muslims, however, voiced support for the Taliban, even for bin Laden, and there were some media reports that some young men had gone to Afghanistan to fight for the Taliban, and that some of them had been killed in the US attacks, though such reports were difficult to confirm. A British Muslim in Pakistan claimed to have helped recruit more than 200 British volunteers to fight for the Taliban (*Telegraph*, 8 January 2002); a British national was convicted in Pakistan for the murder of the American journalist, Daniel Pearl. Three of the first fifty captives brought from Afghanistan to the US prison in Guantanamo Bay, Cuba, were Britons and eventually they were joined by six others (by mid-2004 none had been charged and five were released in February 2005). Moreover, the failed 'shoe bomber', Richard Reid, was a Briton of Caribbean origin on his father's side. Some British Muslims seem to have been involved in a number of other terrorist incidents in various parts of the world, including a 'suicide bombing' in Israel (the *Independent*, 9 March 2004). Under new anti-terrorism legislation, 664 persons, nearly all Muslims, had been taken into detention without trial by September 2004 but only 99 had been charged with an offence, usually a minor one, and over half had been released without charge. The seventeen who had been found guilty of a connection to a terrorist organization were mainly members of the Ulster Defence Association and the Real IRA (BBC TV, 2004). As this book goes to press, terrorist attacks, believed by the police to be carried out by Islamists, have taken place in London with considerable loss of life, creating a climate of fear and suspicion of Muslims.

While some Muslims from a variety of Western countries have been drawn into *jihadi* activities, Britons seem to be quite prominent. This may even be a consequence of the political consciousness and assertiveness that are a feature of struggles for multicultural equality. Several commentators have noted that the young Britons who seem to have got involved in these international networks were not necessarily from the large Muslim underclass in Britain, but were just as or more likely to be students or graduates and professionals (Shaw, 2002). This is not in itself surprising and is not inconsistent with the argument of this book that racism and anti-racism, broadly conceived, are a primary source of Muslim assertiveness in Britain. It is a feature of much contemporary equality movements – such as feminism – that they are led by intellectuals and public sector and media professionals and focus more on glass-ceiling and elite issues than on severe deprivation. There is also a focus on discursive representations and unconscious racism and sexism, the counterparts of which are likely to be acutely felt by educated Muslims and can be a direct or indirect source for oppositional activism. This is particularly relevant because, as had been argued in previous chapters, Muslims acquire/gain self-pride and oppositional energy from their personal faith and collective solidarity. For example, Pnina Werbner has carefully brought out how certain kinds of Islamic millennialism, originating from the Sufism of rural Pakistan, give succour and redemptive hope in the light of contemporary domestic and international humiliations and powerlessness (Werbner, 2001; 2004). Yet she also shows that this discourse, popular amongst migrants, is not meant to be taken militantly; indeed it does not offer a political agenda. The latter can of course be found in a militant Islamism – journalistically known as 'Islamic fundamentalism' – which was absent amongst Asian Muslim migrants but is increasingly attractive to some of the 'second generation', especially the better educated. Islamism, then, offers an alternative source of political mobilization to egalitarian multiculturalism, or perhaps a complementary one with the former focused on the international and the latter on the national. It is too early to say what effect the emergence of Islamism will have on the discourse of multiculturalism among British Muslims and among Britons generally. A study of 'moderate' Muslim activists and public intellectuals in 2003 found strong support for multiculturalism, as long as it included faith as a dimension of 'difference', with some arguing that the Qur'ān, Islam and Muslim history are powerful sources of multiculturalism and represent a superior form of multiculturalism than has been developed elsewhere or is on offer in the contemporary West (Modood and Ahmad, 2005).[3]

Just as international Islamism and, certainly, terrorism have complicated the case for multicultural equality on the Muslim side, so too on the non-Muslim side. The confused retreat from multiculturalism has of course been given an enormous impetus by post-9/11 events. There has been widespread questioning, echoing the Rushdie affair, about whether Muslims can be and are willing to be integrated into British society and its political values, paralleling discourses in most of the EU. The New Labour government was at the forefront of this debate, as were many others who are prominent on the centre–left and have long-standing anti-racist credentials. For example, the Commission for Racial Equality published an article by the left-wing author Kenan Malik, arguing that 'multiculturalism has helped to segregate communities far more effectively than racism' (Malik, 2001/02). The late Hugo Young, the leading liberal columnist of the centre–left newspaper the *Guardian*, went further and wrote that multiculturalism 'can now be seen as a useful bible for any Muslim who insists that his religious-cultural priorities, including the defence of jihad against America, override his civic duties of loyalty, tolerance, justice and respect for democracy' (*Guardian*, 6 November 2001). More extreme again, Farrukh Dhondy, an Asian who had pioneered multicultural broadcasting on British television, writes of a 'multicultural fifth column' which must be rooted out, and argues that state funding of multiculturalism should be redirected into a defence of the values of freedom and democracy (Dhondy, 2001).[4] Most recently, Trevor Phillips, the Chair of the Commission for Racial Equality

(CRE), has declared that multiculturalism was useful once but is now out of date for it makes a fetish of difference instead of encouraging minorities to be truly British (Baldwin, 2004).[5]

One of the specific issues that has come to be a central element of this debate is 'faith schools'; that is to say, state-funded schools run by religious organizations. While they must teach the National Curriculum and are inspected by a government agency, they can give extra space to religious instruction, though not all do so. They are popular with parents for their ethos, discipline and academic achievements and so can select their pupils, often giving priority to children whose parents can demonstrate a degree of religious observance. Yet the violent disturbances in some northern English cities in summer 2001, in which Asian Muslim men had been among the protagonists, were officially blamed in part on the fact of segregated communities and segregated schools. Some of these were church-run schools and were 90 per cent or more Christian and white. Others were among the most under-resourced and under-achieving in the country and had rolls of 90 per cent or more Muslims. They came to be called, including in official reports (Ouseley, 2001), 'Muslim schools'. In fact, they were nothing of the sort. They were local, bottom-of-the-pile comprehensive schools which had suffered from decades of under-investment and 'white flight' and were run by white teachers according to a secular National Curriculum. 'Muslim schools' then came to be seen as the source of the problem of divided cities, cultural backwardness, riots and lack of Britishness, and a breeding ground for militant Islam. Muslim-run schools were lumped into this category of 'Muslim schools' even though all the evidence suggested that their pupils (mainly juniors and girls) did not engage in riots and terrorism and, despite limited resources, achieved better exam results than local authority 'secular' schools. On the basis of these 'Muslim schools' and 'faith schools' constructions, tirades were launched by prominent columnists in the broadsheet newspapers against allowing state funding to any more Muslim-run schools or even to a church-run school, and demands were made once again that the British state be entirely secular. For example, Polly Toynbee argued in the *Guardian* that a precondition of tackling racial segregation was that 'religion should be kept at home, in the private sphere' (*Guardian*, 12 December 2001), utilizing a public–private distinction the political revival of which is a reaction to Muslim assertiveness and Muslim claims upon a public policy of multiculturalism (see Modood and Kastoryano, this volume).

New developments

As at the time of the Rushdie affair, the media gave massive and disproportionate coverage to Muslim extremists, regardless of the limited support they enjoyed among Muslims. While the same occurred in relation to more recent controversies, there were, however, at least two new features in the media and political debates after 9/11. First, while in the late 1980s there were virtually no self-identified Muslims (as opposed to persons with a Muslim background) with a platform in the national media, by 2001, partly because Muslims had achieved notoriety as a political problem, there were a couple of Muslim broadsheet columnists. They, together, with other occasional Muslim contributors, expressed collective self-criticism. This was absent in the Rushdie affair. While maintaining a strongly anti-US foreign policy stance, they expressed shock at how much anger and latent violence had become part of the Muslim identity in Britain, especially youth culture, arguing that West-hating militant ideologues had 'hijacked' Islam and that the moderates had to denounce them.[6] The following quote from Yusuf Islam (formerly the pop star Cat Stevens before his conversion to Islam, and now the head of the Islamia Educational Trust, who had been wrong-footed by the media in relation to Khomeini's fatwa in 1989) nicely captures this shift in the position of the moderates:

> I was still learning, ill-prepared and lacking in knowledge and confidence to speak out against forms of extremism. ... Today, I am aghast at the horror of recent events and feel it a duty to speak out. Not only did terrorists hijack planes and destroy life, they also hijacked the beautiful religion of Islam.
>
> (*Independent*, 26 October 2001)

Other Muslim intellectuals issued fatwas against the fanatics (Ziauddin Sardar, *Observer*, 23 September 2001), described the Muslim revolutionaries as 'fascists' (Sardar, *Evening Standard*, 5 November 2001) and 'xenophobes' (Yasmin Alibhai-Brown, *Independent*, 5 November 2001), with whom they did not want to be united under the term 'British Muslims'. While in the *Satanic Verses* affair moderate Muslims argued against what they took to be a bias against Muslims – a failure even by liberals to extend the ideas of equality and respect for others to include Muslims – moderates now added to this line of defence an argument about the urgency of reinterpreting Islam. This reinterpretation variously calls for a re-excavation of the Qur'ān as a charter of human rights, which, for example, abolished slavery and gave property rights to women more than a millennium before either of these was achieved in the West; a restoration of the thirst for knowledge and rational enquiry which characterized medieval Muslim societies; a re-centring of Islam around piety and spirituality, not political ideology; a 'reformation' that would make Islam compatible with individual conscience, science and secularism. Sardar, one of the most prominent of the moderate Muslim intellectuals, said that the failure of the Islamist movements of the 1960s and 1970s was partly responsible for the contemporary distortions of Islam by the militants. Such movements, he argued, had started off with an ethical and intellectual idealism, but had become intellectually closed, fanatical and violent. Just as today's middle-aged moderates had encouraged the earlier Islamic renewal, they must now take some responsibility for what has come to pass and do something about it (Sardar, *Observer*, 21 October 2001).

A second difference from the *Satanic Verses* affair was that Muslims found that many of their analyses of international developments were shared by non-

Muslims, often the majority of Britons, especially the politically minded. While Tony Blair's close support for all US initiatives, especially the invasion of Iraq, deeply alienated most Muslims from the government and the Labour Party[7] – the main forum of Asian Muslim mainstream political activity – the same was true of many non-Muslims. While in some countries where US policy, and their governments' support for it, was deeply unpopular, as in Italy and Spain, Muslim protests were marginal because Muslims lacked a political presence, British Muslims were prominent and much more voluble (except for those bound by Labour Party constraints) than their better resourced counterparts in the United States. There was a greater political maturity amongst British Muslims in comparison to the *Satanic Verses* affair. While in terms of elected national politicians and presence in national public bodies and influential nexuses, Muslims continued to be woefully under-represented (Anwar and Baksh, 2003), there was a new embeddedness in the British political structure. The crucial difference, however, was that Muslims were, virtually for the first time, not isolated. Indeed, on some occasions they were part of a broad consensus. For example, there was a near unanimity in the op-ed pages of the national papers that the price for the invasions of Afghanistan and Iraq and the rest of the 'war on terrorism' was a just solution for the Palestinians, a position that Muslims of all stripes heartily endorsed. This meant that alliances and coalition building were possible in a way denied with the Rushdie affair, and which meant that Muslims were on some occasions part of the political mainstream. For example, the Muslim Association of Britain was one of the three partners that organized a series of mass protest marches in London, including one in February 2003, the largest ever held in that city, and in which – in contrast to most Muslim organized action hitherto – Muslims formed only a fraction of the gathering of about 2 million participants.

Reaffirming multiculturalism

As the *Satanic Verses* affair had done earlier, so the events following from 9/11 are turbulent and testing for political multiculturalism. The watchword, however, has to be: Don't Panic. Perhaps, we ought to brace ourselves for some excesses: I am reminded of the Marxist radicalism of my student days in the late 1960s and 1970s; as we know, that passed and many a radical now holds high office (and fulminates against young radicals!). But we must distinguish between criminal actions and militant rhetoric, between radical Islamists and the wider Muslim opinion; for the former, despite the bewitchment of the media, are as representative of Muslims as the Socialist Workers Party is of working-class politics. We must note that despite the special stresses and strains that arise for Muslims, and in relation to Muslims, the situation is not uniquely difficult. It is most likely that Muslims are following the same trajectory as Afro-Caribbeans of making a claim upon Britishness through forms of political self-defence and anti-racism. Hence, it is important that we not give up on the moderate, egalitarian multiculturalism that has been evolving in Britain, and has proved susceptible to gradually accommodating Muslim demands, through a process of campaigning, debate, negotiation and political consensus.

Other than Muslims themselves, a leading actor in bringing Muslim concerns and racial equality thinking into contact with each other has been the Runnymede Trust, recognizing Islamophobia as one of the chief forms of racism today when it set up its Commission on Islamophobia (Runnymede Trust, 1997; 2004). The demand for Muslim schools within the state sector was rejected by the Swann Report on multiculturalism in the 1980s and by the Commission for Racial Equality even in the 1990s (Swann, 1985; CRE, 1990), yet it became government policy in 1997. Adapting the census to measure the extent of socio-economic disadvantage by religious groups has been achieved, and support has been built up for outlawing religious discrimination and incitement to religious hatred. Talk of Muslim identity used to be rejected by racial egalitarians as an irrelevance ('religious not political') and as divisive, but in the last few years Muslim organizations like the Muslim Council of Britain (MCB) and Forum Against Islamophobia and Racism (FAIR), mentioned earlier, have co-organized events and demonstrations with groups such as the National Assembly of Black People and are often supported by the Commission for Racial Equality.

There must, certainly, be an emphasis not just on 'difference' but on commonality too. British anti-racists and multiculturalists have indeed been too prone to ignore this; but to do so is actually less characteristic of Muslims than of the political left (see, for instance, the various statements of MCB from its inception, and its choice of motto, 'Working for the Common Good'). To take up some recent issues, of course wanting to be part of British society means having a facility in the English language, and the state must be protective of the rights of those oppressed within their communities, as in the case of forced marriages. But blaming Muslims alone for segregation ignores how the phenomenon in the northern cities and elsewhere has been shaped by white people's preferences as individuals ('white flight'), and the decisions of local councillors, not least in relation to public housing, and by employers, including local councils. Muslim politics in Britain clearly includes an advocacy for multi-culturalism; indeed, some of this group of Muslims believe that the Qur'ān, Islam and Muslim history are powerful sources of multiculturalism and represent a superior form of multiculturalism than has been developed elsewhere or is on offer in the contemporary West. It is true that for some Muslims the ideal multi-culturalism is faith based in identifying dimensions of 'difference', with other religions not just included but given primacy in terms of respect. It probably also is faith based in terms of limits of recognition with, critically, homosexu-ality more likely to be positioned as what is tolerated rather than respected (Modood and Ahmad, 2005). These are differential emphases that may be open to dialogue and should not be used as reasons to argue against multiculturalism.

It is most regrettable that the emergence of Muslim political agency has thrown British multiculturalism into theoretical and practical disarray. It has led to policy reversals in the Netherlands and elsewhere, and across Europe has strengthened intolerant, exclusive nationalism and secularism. We should in fact be moving the other way. We should be extending to Muslims existing levels of protection from discrimination and incitement to hatred, and the duties on organizations to ensure equality of opportunity, not simply the watered-down versions of legislation proposed by the European Commission and recently effected by the British government. We should target more effectively, in consultation with religious and other representatives, the severe poverty and social exclusion of Muslims. We should also recognize Muslims as a legitimate social partner and include them in the institutional compromises of Church and state, religion and politics, that characterize the evolving, moderate secularism of mainstream Western Europe, resisting the wayward, radical example of France.

Ultimately, we must rethink 'Europe' and its changing nations so that Muslims are not a 'Them' but part of a plural 'Us', not mere sojourners but part of its future. The twentieth century can be seen, as DuBois predicted (1995), as having been dominated by struggles about 'colour', with non-whites resisting the domination of whites. The first years of the new century suggest that similar struggles between non-Muslims and Muslims may define our era. The political integration or incorporation of Muslims – remembering that there are more Muslims in the European Union than the combined populations of Finland, Ireland and Denmark – not only, therefore, has become the most important goal of egalitarian multiculturalism, but is now pivotal in shaping the security, indeed the destiny, of many peoples across the globe.

Notes

* This chapter reworks and updates some previous material of mine, namely 'The place of Muslims in British secular multiculturalism', in N. Alsayyad and M. Castells (eds) (2002) *Muslim Europe or Euro-Islam: Politics, Culture and Citizenship in the Age of Globalisation*, New York: Lexington Books; 'Muslims and the politics of multiculturalism in Britain', in E. Hershberg and K. Moore (2002) *Critical Views of September 11: Analyses from Around the World*, New York: New Press; and, 'Muslims and the politics of difference', in S. Spencer (ed.) (2003) *The Politics of Migration*, Oxford, Blackwell. I am grateful to these publishers for letting me reuse some of the material.

1 Following '9/11' an Anti-Terrorism, Crime and Security Act was quickly passed and extended the phrase 'racially aggravated' to 'racially or religiously aggravated'. In 2003, the High Court upheld the conviction in the *Norwood* case, arguing that displaying a British National Party poster bearing the words 'Islam out of Britain' and 'Protect the British People' accompanied by a picture of the 9/11 attack on the Twin Towers amounted to an offence of causing alarm or distress. The High Court argued that evidence of actual alarm or distress was not necessary if it was determined that 'any right thinking member of society' is likely to be caused harassment, alarm or distress. It concluded, therefore, that the poster was racially insulting and, additionally, religiously aggravated. It seems then – though this is only on the basis of one case – that Muslims in Britain may have some legal protection against a version of incitement to religious hatred (for further details see *Norwood v DPP* 2003, and Runnymede Trust, 2004).

2 For further examples of how a 'catching-up' anti-discrimination and equality agenda has been developing in relation to Muslims, see Runnymede Trust (2004).

3 The study found that the term 'moderate' was not readily embraced. Even those who did not object to it as a divisive term created by the non-Muslim media and

politicians felt that it had unfortunately come to mean 'sell-out' in the Muslim communities (Modood and Ahmad, 2005).

4 For a recantation of his Black Panther radicalism, see his 'A Black Panther Repents', *The Times*, 24 June 2002, T2, pp. 2–4.

5 The timing of Phillips' intervention was puzzling given that only a few weeks earlier he had rubbished David Goodhart's widely supported attack on culturally diverse immigration (Goodhart, 2004) as genteel xenophobia and liberal racism (Phillips, 2004); see also my reply to Phillips (Modood, 2004/05).

6 The 'hijacking' theme was most notably introduced by a charismatic, white US Muslim, Hamza Yusuf (who was also consulted by President Bush), and who was taken up by the magazine of the young Muslim professionals, *Q News* (for example, in the November 2001 issue). Dr Muqtedar Khan, Director of International Studies, Adrian College, Michigan, had an even more uncompromisingly 'moderate' statement in the right-wing tabloid newspaper, the *Sun*, but was not taken up by the British Muslims with a comparable enthusiasm, perhaps because he, unlike Yusuf, did not visit Britain.

7 A poll in March 2004 found that support for New Labour among Muslims had fallen from 76 per cent in 1997 to 38 per cent in 1997 to 38 per cent (Travis, 2004).

References

Alexander, C. (2002) 'Beyond Black: re-thinking the colour/culture divide', *Ethnic and Racial Studies*, 25(4): 552–571.

Anwar, M. and Baksh, Q. (2003) *British Muslims and State Policies*, Warwick: Centre for Research in Ethnic Relations, University of Warwick.

Arendt, H. (1963) *On Revolution*, New York: Viking Press.

—— (1968) *Human Condition*, London: University of Chicago.

Baldwin, T. (2004) 'I want an integrated society with a difference', *The Times*, 3 April.

BBC TV (2004) 'The power of nightmares: the politics of fear', Part 3, BBC 2, 3 November.

Benhabib, S. (1992) *Situating the Self*, New York: Routledge.

CCCS (Centre for Contemporary Cultural Studies) (1982) *The Empire Strikes Back: Race and Racism in 70s Britain*, London: Hutchinson.

CMEB (Commission on Multi-Ethnic Britain) (2000) *The Future of Multi-Ethnic Britain*, London: Profile Books.

CRE (Commission for Racial Equality) (1990) 'Schools of faith', London: CRE

Dhondy, F. (2001) 'Our Islamic Fifth Column', *City Limits*, 11(4).

Du Bois, W. E. B. (1995) *The Souls of Black Folk*, New York: Signet; originally published 1903.

Fraser, N. (1992) 'Rethinking the public sphere', in C. Calhoun (ed.) *Habermas and the Public Sphere*, Cambridge, MA: MIT Press.

Fuss, D. (1989) *Essentially Speaking*, New York: Routledge.

Gilroy, P. (1987) *There Ain't No Black in the Union Jack: The Cultural Politics of Race and Nation*, London: Heinemann.

Goodhart, D. (2004) 'Horns of the liberal dilemma', *Guardian*, 8 February.

Goulbourne, H. (1991a) 'Varieties of pluralism: the notion of a pluralist, post-imperial Britain', *New Community*, 17(2).

—— (1991b) *Ethnicity and Nationalism in Post-imperial Britain*, Cambridge: Cambridge University Press.

Habermas, J. (1984) *The Theory of Communicative Competence*, Volume 1: *Reason and the Rationalization of Society*, Boston: Beacon.

—— (1987) *The Theory of Communicative Competence*, Volume 2: *Lifeworld and System*, Boston: Beacon.

Hall, S. (1992) 'New ethnicites', in J. Donald and A. Rattansi (eds) *'Race', Culture and Difference*, London: Sage.

Kalra, V. (2003) 'Police lore and community disorder: diversity in the criminal justice system', in D. Mason (ed.) *Explaining Ethnic Differences: Changing Patterns of Disadvantage in Britain*, Bristol: The Policy Press.

Luthra, M. (1997) *Britain's Black Population: Social Change, Public Policy and Agenda*, Aldershot: Ashgate.

Malik, K. (2001/02) 'The real value of diversity', *Connections*, Winter, London: Commission of Racial Equality.

Modood, T. (1988) ' "Black", racial equality and Asian identity', *New Community*, 14(3): 397–404.

Political Quarterly, 61(2): 43–160; reproduced in J. Donald and A. Rattansi (eds) *'Race', Culture and Difference*, London: Sage.

—— (1993) 'Muslim views on religious identity and racial equality', *New Community*, 19(3): 513–519.

—— (1994) 'Ethnic difference and racial equality: new challenges for the Left', in D. Miliband (ed.) *Reinventing the Left*, Cambridge: Polity Press.

—— (1998) 'Anti-essentialism, multiculturalism and the "recognition" of religious minorities', *Journal of Political Philosophy*, 6(4): 378–399; reproduced in W. Kymlicka and W. Norman (eds) *Citizenship in Diverse Societies*, Oxford: Oxford University Press.

—— (2004/05) 'Multiculturalism or Britishness: a false debate', *Connections*, Winter, London: Commission for Racial Equality.

—— (2005) *Multicultural Politics: Racism, Ethnicity and Muslims in Britain*, University of Minnesota Press and University of Edinburgh Press.

Modood, T. and Ahmad, F. (2005) *British Muslim Perspectives on Multiculturalism*, forthcoming.

Modood, T., Berthoud, R., Lakey, J., Nazroo, J., Smith, P., Virdee, S. and Beishon, S. (1997) *Ethnic Minorities in Britain: Diversity and Disadvantage*, London: Policy Studies Institute.

—— (1990) 'British Asian Muslims and the Rushdie Affair', The Political Quarterly, vol. 61, no. 2, April 1990, pp. 143–160; reproduced in James Donald and Ali Rattansi (eds) 'Race', Culture and Difference, Sage, 199: 260–277.

Muslim Parliament of Great Britain (1992) 'Race relations and Muslims in Great Britain: a discussion paper', London: The Muslim Parliament.

Norwood v DPP [2003] All ER (D) 59.

Ouseley, H. (2001) 'Community pride, not prejudice: making diversity work in Bradford', Bradford Vision, Bradford City Council.

Pateman, C. (1988) The Sexual Contract, Stanford, CA: University of Stanford Press.

Phillips, T. (2004) 'Genteel xenophobia is as bad as any other kind', *Guardian*, 16 February.

Rex, J. and Moore, R. (1967) *Race, Community and Conflict*, Oxford: Oxford University Press.

Runnymede Trust Commission on British Muslims and Islamophobia (1997) *Islamophobia: A Challenge To Us All*, London: Runnymede Trust.

—— (2004) *Islamophobia: Issues, Challenges and Action*, Stoke-on-Trent: Trentham Books.

Rushdie, S. (1982) 'The new empire within Britain', *New Society*, 9 December.

Shaw, A. (2002) 'Why might young British Muslims support the Taliban?', *Anthropology Today*, 18(1).

Sivanandan, A. (1985) 'RAT and the degradation of the black struggle', *Race and Class*, XXVI(4).

Swann, M. (1985) *Education for All*, Cmnd. 9457, London: HMSO.

Travis, A. (2004) 'Desire to integrate on the wane as Muslims resent "War on Islam" ', *Guardian*, March 16.

UKACIA (UK Action Committee on Islamic Affairs) (1993) 'Muslims and the law in multi-faith Britain: need for reform', London: UKACIA.

Werbner, P. (2001) 'Divided loyalties', *Times Higher Education Supplement*, 14 December.

——— (2004) 'The predicament of diaspora and millennial Islam: reflections on September 11, 2001', *Ethnicities*, 4(4): 451–476.

Young, I. M. (1990) *Justice and the Politics of Difference*, Princeton, NJ: Princeton University Press.

4 French secularism and Islam

France's headscarf affair*

Riva Kastoryano

Introduction

Few social issues cover so many various areas of society and the social sciences as the 'headscarf affair' in France. The 'affair' involves national history, the place of religion, the principle of *laïcité* (France's form of secularism) and its limits as well as the role of schools in 'assimilating' immigrants' children. It leads to the question of integration of Muslim and other immigrants, and Islam as a culture, religion and as a political force in and beyond its countries of origin. The arguments relate to moral principles such as tolerance, the right to difference, individual liberty, religious freedom, human rights and especially the emancipation of women and equality of the sexes. And finally, the issue leads to questions about the effects of multiculturalism in practice, the re-establishment of public order, the redefinition of the social contract and of equal citizenship. The debate on this issue and the underlying phenomenon it addresses are part of the globalization that leads to identity anxiety within both states and communities, which now compete for the loyalty and allegiance of their members within the same geographical space. Therefore one of the important aspects of multiculturalism is related to the transnational scope of community identification, which gives new impetus to expressions of identity within and beyond national territories (Kastoryano, 2002a).

History of the headscarf affair

The story begins in November 1989 when three girls wore headscarves to their public school in Creil, a suburb in the north of Paris. The event unleashed a flood of commentary on identity: the identity of the latest wave of immigrants, but also that of national identity. The emphasis lay on Islam and, of course, its compatibility with the secular principles of French society. More than that, the issue made *laïcité* (secularism) a French exception different from the secularism prevalent in other Western states. The issue came back to the political arena in October 1994 when the right-wing government, in the person of the recently appointed Minister of Education, François Bayrou, issued a circular to public schools forbidding any ostentatious religious signs in public schools, an institution that is *par excellence* the very embodiment of national ideology as being 'egalitarian, *laïque*, inclusive'. Since then every once in a while there has been a local 'headscarf affair' commented on, condemned and defended by public opinion, the political class, the media and intellectuals. The political class and certain intellectuals, torn between a defensive republicanism and a pluralistic liberalism, took it upon themselves to remind society of the basic principles of the Republic, principles that constitute the 'core of national identity' and to Muslim migrants 'a way of life' in a country that has made secularism – *laïcité* – its 'state religion'. At the same time the headscarf issue thus led to a re-evaluation of the principles of the Republic and of secularism considered to be the pillar of social cohesion that had to be maintained as a constitutive value of the nation-state.

In the eyes of some, this was confirmation that Islam was 'incompatible with the West', or that it was 'impossible for Muslims to assimilate universal values and/or integrate into French society', or 'Islam rejects secularism'. On the other hand, in the classic interpretations, the state was being weakened, or the values of the Republic were eroding. The crisis of the welfare state was invoked as well. Sociologists noted the obsolescence of schools and other mechanisms such as the school, Church or a political party – more precisely the Communist Party (PCF) – for integrating or assimilating immigrants. Others saw it as 'the end of national societies', emphasizing the separation between culture and society.

It is interesting to note that the 1989 'headscarf affair' occurred shortly after the hearing commission studying France's citizenship code published its report *Être français aujourd'hui et demain* (Being French today and tomorrow), which discussed at length questions of access to citizenship and the relationship between citizenship and identity – whether so-called 'identity of origin', religious identity or other (see Commission de la nationalité, 1988). The public debate on citizenship was followed by an avalanche of books and reports on 'the French model' which in simplistic terms evoked republican political traditions that reject any representation of communities in a state that recognizes only the individual as an interlocutor (see Haut Conseil à l'Intégration, 1991).

The affair also occurred just as the impact of voluntary associations in the social and cultural realm was losing its force. The politics of recognition formulated as the 'right to be different' has led to the proliferation of voluntary associations since 1981 when the law for associations was liberated and allowed foreigners to create their own organization. Spontaneous gatherings based on interpersonal relations in concentrated areas such as in the *banlieues* found therefore an institutional and formal structure through associations. These associations of formalized and institutionalized *de facto* communities aimed at defining an identity that intended to be collective, drawing its boundaries, creating new solidarities and asserting a 'permanent difference' with reference to Islam. Such associations situated themselves as playing an intermediary role between the marginalized groups and the state.

It was believed that voluntary associations had taken over from families and schools in socializing children, whose integration into French society was being left to social workers, community organizers and cultural institutions instead of to teachers, the privileged agents of the Republic. In short, the affair happened at a time when people were increasingly accustomed to hearing about 'communities' (immigrant or religious) and becoming resigned to a social reality that contradicted republican rhetoric.

To quell emotions, the Minister of National Education, Lionel Jospin (Socialist Party), submitted the matter to the State Council (Conseil d'Etat), France's highest administrative court, which rendered its opinion on 27 November 1989. The Council emphasized the freedom of pupils 'to express and manifest their religious beliefs within public institutions with respect for pluralism, without infringing on educational activities of the curriculum, and the obligation to attend class'.

The Council sought to articulate the international and national rules protecting freedom of conscience on the one hand, and the constitutional principle of the *laïcité* of the state on the other. It concluded that religious symbols should not be outlawed unless they were '*ostentatoires*' (ostentatious) or '*revendicatifs*' (expressing a demand). The question would be treated on a case-by-case basis under the supervision of a judge.

After a period of at least verbal 'indifference', the headscarf became a public issue again in 1994, when girls wearing headscarves were expelled from a public school and new guidelines were issued to supplement the Council's decision. Minister Bayrou (right wing) had a more radical attitude. Through the issuance of a circular, he forbade the wearing of the headscarf (actually any ostentatious religious sign) in public schools and asked for the exclusion of girls if they resisted this rule. The circular and expulsion suggested that the headscarf should be managed on a local basis and gave teachers the power to decide. This emphasis on the local level was no accident, as both associations and schools exercise their power at the local level. It was also on a local level that the government tried to encourage the establishment of socio-cultural associations as a counterweight to the Islamic associations active in certain areas of high Muslim presence. In this way, it contributed to the creation of a community perceived by the political class as 'dissident' in which jockeying for power and influence was paramount. Thus, the headscarf issue brought into the open the tensions that existed between national institutions and immigrant Muslim populations and established a kind of power relationship between the 'law of the Republican state' and the Qur'ān, between a sort of 'society's law' and the 'community's law'.

In 2003, President Chirac appointed a commission to consider the question of religious signs in public schools, the *Commission de réflexion sur l'application du principe de laïcité*, chaired by Bernard Stasi (a former minister). The Stasi Commission suggested in its report, delivered in 2003, that wearing conspicuous religious symbols should be banned in public schools. Once again, the legislation passed by the French Parliament on 3 February 2004 has been the subject of extensive comment. Some have rightly emphasized the dangers and limits of such legislation, or of a dogmatic approach to *laïcité* that would be inconsistent with the liberal spirit in which it was conceived. Others – also rightly – have insisted on the urgent need for such legislation to restore public order, or to redefine the social contract, or to bring the meaning of *laïcité* up to date since the meaning that it had in the early twentieth century no longer corresponds to contemporary reality. Its target is no longer Catholicism but rather Islam, and the issue no longer takes the form of overt religious conflict but rather of disguised religious conflict around issues such as girls' headscarves in school – the institution that most clearly embodies the national ideology.

It may be true that there are dangers of stigmatizing Islam with legislation of this sort. It may be true that there is a risk of intensifying the primary loyalty to community – with undeniable transnational connections – that is already well established in the *banlieues*, the suburban neighbourhoods surrounding major cities that have taken on the character of ethnic, more precisely Muslim ghettos. And there may be some truth in the comments that the behaviour of some of these girls may have been guided by individual choice and freedom of belief. Despite all this, is it still not possible to think that a law could have an 'emancipating' function, especially in the *banlieues* where individualism is regarded as a sin? The idea of 'emancipation' had led to the repression of belief in the private space, and the new political involvement as a new encompassing value in the name of individual autonomy. The result is an internal tension where freedom in the civil society is ensured by the state. The report of the Stasi Commission on *laïcité*

> ensures that groups or communities of any kind cannot impose on individuals a belonging or a religious identity. *Laïcité* protects everyone from any pressure, physical or moral, justified by a religious prescription. The defence of individual freedom against any proselytise action completes today the notion of separation and neutrality that at the core of the concept of *laïcité*.
> (Rapport au Président de la république, 2004)

Patrick Weil, who was a member of the Stasi Commission, points out that the wearing of the headscarf or imposing it upon others has become an issue not of individual freedom but one of national strategy involving fundamentalist groups using public schools as their battleground. Banning the headscarf at the local level would have created a permanent tension between principals and these national groups who would have targeted schools one after the other in order to attract, every week, the attention of the public and of the national press (Weil, 2004).

Therefore, might not a voice coming from 'on high' (from the state) speak louder than the voice of the *muezzin* in the mosque and provide support for families seeking to free themselves from the social pressure within each community that bears especially heavily on women? The phenomenon of exclusion, expressed by young people and analysed by researchers, is often linked to the Islamic associations as a refuge and escape route. But for families the real escape route for their children is still the school. Even if confidence in the school system is no longer widespread, there is still hope.

Laïcité

In response to the headscarf, French society is redefining *laïcité*. Until November 1989, this republican principle was self-explanatory. Since then, there have been innumerable interpretations of it, although no final version has been agreed on. Perhaps the only firm conclusion is that *laïcité* is clearly the 'official religion' of France. The law enshrining the principle was passed in 1905 and marked the separation of Church and state after nearly a century of conflict. According to this law, 'The Republic assures freedom of conscience. It guarantees the free exercise of religious worship, limited only by the exceptions enumerated below in the interest of public order' (Article 1). *Laïcité* was enshrined again in the Constitution of the Fifth Republic in 1958. According to Article 2, 'France is an indivisible, *laïque*, democratic and social Republic. It assures equality among all its citizens without distinction according to origin, race or religion.'

Nevertheless, secularism, or rather *laïcité*, is ambiguous about the boundary between culture and religion. Culture refers to religious identity and religion to belief or practice. Research on French religious expression shows a constant decline of practice, which is easily measured, unlike the cultural reference which remains abstract and hard to measure, but which appears whenever it confronts another religion, like Islam today.

Yet, the idea of *laïcité* is inseparable from the 'indoctrination' implemented by the public schools under the Third Republic. It is not surprising that its contemporary challenge was triggered when some young Muslim girls wore their headscarves in school.[1] And it is principally at schools that Jules Ferry introduced a radical change in 1882 by making the public, secular (*laïque*) free primary school compulsory for everyone, including girls. The school then became the instrument for propagating secularism and equality between girls and boys. The centralization of instruction, the creation of secular teachers' training schools, conferred upon the school the role of unifying the nation. Of course, seeking national unity and social order in the republican school amounts to obscuring the educational wars that preceded the law of 1882 which consists of 'getting God out of school' (see for more details Déloye, 1994). The moral vacuum produced by the abolition of religious instruction in curricula was filled by civic instruction. The school became the bearer of new moral values which, Mona Ozouf maintained, were 'the virtues of order and obedience [that] make up the portrait of the French as economical, hard-working, honest, and disciplined'. With the creation of the public school, relations between public schools and private schools (understood to a large extent as denominational establishments) were defined by the 1959 Debré law which directed that private schools were to be of general instruction under a contract with the state.[2] But it is with the republican school instituted by Jules Ferry that the question of 'national unity and social order' arose, which led Minister Bayrou to declare in the parliamentary debates of October 1994 on the headscarf at school that 'French national identity is inseparable from its schools'.

In practice, the principle of *laïcité* is translated into the neutrality of the state towards religious denominations. This neutrality becomes synonymous with tolerance because it presupposes freedom of conscience in private and personal life. As a result, *laïcité* becomes defined as the main factor of social cohesion, the pillar of republican France. It acts as a foil, in much the same way as Catholicism did for the definition of *laïcité* in the early twentieth century.

Laïcité, Islam and republicanism

Thus, *laïcité* is an integral part of the institutional, legal and intellectual history of the Republic, and has even taken on the role of its founding principle. However, this principle is no longer self-explanatory. Islam represents a twofold challenge to it. First of all, it constitutes a minority, and a religious one at that. Secondly, this minority has a public expression. Both contradict the ideological representation of the French republicanism expressed in terms of 'model'. According to this 'model' France is represented as the very example of a nation-state: unitarian, universalist and egalitarian. It sees assimilation as a basis for equality and points to the United States as an 'anti-model', represented as practising racial segregation. The elective and political perception of the French nation also contrasts with Germany's emphasis on common ancestors and membership in the same cultural community. In the United States, as in France, citizenship is placed at the centre of the theory and practice shaping the nation-state, but the doctrine of the 'French model', based on republican individualism, would be the assimilation of individuals who have made a political choice to become citizens (as in the United States), while the 'American model' is represented by the French view as one based on the recognition of communities that express their cultural membership in public life. However, neither of those two models refers to origins or ancestors as in the 'German model' (regarding the construction of models see also Dumont, 1991; Schnapper, 1991; Brubaker, 1992).

Of course, these models find a justification in 'remembered history'; they crystallize a self-perception as a nation-state, its construction, its values, its founding principles, in short its ideology. They constitute an anchor that allows for the development of a coherent discourse connecting a representation of political traditions with the treatment of modern realities. They establish the role of national institutions in the maintenance and perpetuation of those principles, and indirectly define the place granted to newcomers and develop public discourses on 'intégration à la française' as the title of the 1993 Report of the High Committee on Integration recalls. In big black letters on a white cover, this title seems to be an appeal to the collective memory, evoking French uniqueness and its importance in the assimilation of foreigners. The authors of the report claim that the French model of integration, 'based on a principle of equality, contrasts with the "logic of minorities" that confers a specific status on national or ethnic minorities'. The report emphasizes 'the profound calling of our country which, inspired by the principles of the Declaration of the Rights of Man, asserts the equality of men across the diversity of their cultures'.

This is the idea developed by Ernest Renan in *Qu'est-ce qu'une nation?* (What Is a Nation?), an excerpt from a lecture he delivered at the Sorbonne on 11 March 1882. Renan defined the nation as a 'soul' composed of common memories and plans expressing the desire to live together. He refers to a collective will shared among individuals and groups speaking different languages or belonging to different religions; in short, to groups with different cultural references, but united by one single political reference concerning the general will of individuals, beyond cultural, linguistic or religious affiliations. According to Renan, 'making politics rest on ethnographic analysis turns it into a chimera'. He thus rejected a political representation of separate identities of minorities or communities that would endanger the integrity of the nation. He repudiated community bonds and regional or local allegiances that accompanied the republican state. Maintaining the integrity of the nation is inherent in its elective conception, formulated as an 'everyday plebiscite'. These were the principles that played a vital role in the *invention* of the nation of France.

The reference of French literature in social sciences to Renan's speech has become systematic since the 1980s. This is not accidental. It is sign of a crisis atmosphere that affects the idea of a national unity directly or indirectly, and affirms the need to recall traditions and 'memories'. Renan's political and legal concept of the nation was a reaction to Germany's arguments of organic bonds to justify the annexation of Alsace and Lorraine. History seems to have proved him right. In 1918, after the defeat of the Germans, the region was returned to France. It was not language, hence not a common culture with the people across the Rhine, that was decisive, but the political experience of the revolution that presumably moved the Alsatians closer to France. Thus, national consciousness originates in a (subjective) political identification, to continue Max Weber's thinking, and not in a linguistic identity (which claims to be objective).

The appeal to Renan today is obviously not a reaction to Germany – now an ally in the construction of the European Union. It is no longer the territorial definition of the country that is at issue neither, but its identity. Lately, Renan's lecture has been reintroduced into French public and scientific discussion as a reaction to expressions of ethnic or religious identities expressed by migrants mostly from North Africa, therefore Muslims. One partial explanation for this is the feeling that the political nation has been neglected and the idea of state sovereignty weakened for the sake of economic interests that favoured immigration. Their settlement and claim for cultural rights is perceived as a challenge to the national community, the only community that counts, and its unity.

In this way, Islam challenges France's long national history of relations between religion and the state, starting with the emancipation of the individual from community constraints that were largely religious in nature. The private sphere was separated from the public sphere, where the principle of '*raison publique*' would reign. Islam, however, challenges public neutrality, which has become a source of ambiguity as the boundary between private and public has become increasingly fuzzy. Religious tolerance comes up against the question of cultural diversity, which is expressed in ways that are tied to religion and blur the boundary between the private world and public space.

The place that Islam should be accorded in France raises once again the old duality of religion and state. The separation of Church and state in France effectively grants legal institutional status to the Catholic clergy, the *Fédération Protestante de France* and the Consistory, established under Napoleon, is the representative body for French Jews. This 'recognition' is intended as an expression of respect for freedom of worship and the neutrality of the *laïque* state. In the French government, responsibility for *cultes* – that is, religion, falls to the Minister of the Interior (not religious institutions). Since the first headscarf affair, successive Interior Ministers have tried to establish a representative institution for Islam on the model of the institutions representing other religions. In this way, the government has sought to structure the mobilization of its 'adversary' and bring French Muslims together, transcending national and even religious difference.[3]

In April 2003, the Conseil Français du Culte Musulman (CFCM) was established to give institutional legitimacy to French Muslims. The establishment of the CFCM is also viewed by Muslims as a form of religious legitimacy (Sevaiste, 2004). The process has been denounced as authoritarian, and the artificial and pragmatic nature of the procedure for choosing the official representative of Islam in France has been subject to criticism. Nevertheless the most important is that such a structure now situates Islam, institutionally, on an equal footing with other religions in France as well as other countries in Europe such as Britain, the Netherlands and Belgium. Its creation is a way of orchestrating a shift from Islam in France to Islam of France, from a simple presence of Muslims and their practices visible in France to an Islam that is expressed and developed within national institutions, assuming its freedom from 'foreign' influences, especially those of the homeland. In effect, the CFCM has brought into the open the tensions and power struggles among Muslims seeking representation, as well as the external influences that weigh on the choice of representatives.

The institutionalization of Islam is a response to a demand for recognition by the Muslim population. In this perspective, it leads to treatment of Islam by the state on an equal footing with other religions in France. Of course, this development raises a number of normative questions. In particular, there is the question of whether recognition can be limited to institutional representation when other institutions, such as schools, are not fulfilling their function of 'assimilation' and the promotion of social, cultural and religious equality. At the same time, if religion appears as the main cleavage in European countries today, then perhaps its recognition can be seen as a path towards integration. This kind of 'institutional assimilation' may be the only form of assimilation possible in countries that are, *de facto*, multicultural.[4] And it could encourage Muslims to identify with national institutions and thus help them to break free of external political forces – their countries of origin and international Islamic organizations seeking to promote Islam in Europe. These forces weigh on the choices of individuals, families and local communities in France as in other European countries.

Transnational Islam?

It can perhaps be hoped that institutionalization of this kind, a step towards the nationalization of Islam, will succeed in halting the penetration of networks that seek to reconstitute transnational Islam, a re-imagined *Ummah*, in Europe. Such a *Ummah* could become a non-territorial nation, and people's sense of belonging to it would be constructed under external influence over which states would have no control.

Of course, it is impossible to imagine one unified Islam in Europe. Muslims in Europe are as diverse as Christians in origin, language, nationality, ethnicity and even denomination (Sunnites, Shiites or Alawites). Their identity boundaries are drawn by their loyalties to their state of origin, therefore to national identities of home countries. Within the national groups, sects, brotherhood and regional allegiances and political ideologies provide identity repertoires for community organizations specialized in language teaching, folklore or religion. Such organizations, subject to immigration policies and to legislation concerning social activities of migrants in host countries, have proliferated since the 1980s in all European countries.

Even if Islam also appears fragmented from within by national identities, it represents a unifying force among Muslim immigrants in so far as collective interests are concerned. In some minor cases a broader network initiated by international Muslim organizations aims at promoting Islam in Europe as a cultural existence as well as a political force that can act back in the country of origin. Official or unofficial institutions in the countries of origin, or international Islamic organizations, or both, finance activities that transcend national, ethnic, linguistic cleavages and religious divergences with the goal to promote a common identification, that is to be Muslim in Europe and the construction of a Muslim community in Europe as a part of the 're-imagined *Ummah*', associating the French Islam or the Islam of France to the Islam of Britain, the Netherlands or of the countries of origin of many Muslims such as Morocco or Turkey or even to some imaginary belonging expressed through an indentification with the Israeli–Palestinian conflict or the war in Iraq.

It may not be a coincidence, then, that soon after the establishment of the CFCM, which brought into the open the internal power struggles and external influences that involve a portion of the Muslim community and whose effects include the politicization of Islam in France, President Chirac appointed his commission on *laïcité* along the lines of the commission on citizenship set up in the 1980s. In an era when the international context is becoming increasingly globalized, can the proclamation of a law be separated from its political environment?

The first headscarf affair in 1989 occurred just after the Rushdie affair in Britain. After an interlude of relative quiet, the Stasi Report was delivered in 2003. The Report emphasized the connection between a law banning the headscarf and the increase in acts of violence in France's *banlieues* since 2000, attributed to the second Intifada in Israel–Palestine that began in

September 2000. These developments show that questions of ethnicity and the position of minorities, which on one level are subject to classical analyses of cultural diversity as a phenomenon faced by liberal democratic multicultural states, are also increasingly linked to new expressions of identity that are taking shape outside national territories. This is a consequence of the emergence of so-called transnational communities, which connect local experience with external developments that take place in other territories but are felt as an extension of life in the *banlieues*, the best example of these spaces of resistance. The emergence of these communities leads to an upsurge of what could be called transnational nationalism, for which Islam constitutes the source of global identification (Kastoryano, 2002a).

In the *banlieues*, Islam is becoming an element in people's identity that affects the way they act and react, the main element in their 'self-enchantment' in the Weberian sense of the term. It is a feeling of being part of a community whose elements are drawn from Islamic practice, traditions and rituals, but also from Islam's moral values and social utility. Islam thus gives a 'romantic' sense to the conception of the community. It serves as a justification for internal cohesion and ethnic pride, providing a means of recovering 'lost' youth and reaching out to the 'victims of immigration'. The terms of belonging are not expressed as a matter of 'blood' or kinship. The goal may be to restore the 'moral community' in which religion – Islam – becomes the element of internal cohesion, distinction and unification across national boundaries.

Such communities have established religion as the major criterion, in place of the social criteria that bring people together in the *banlieues*. The Muslim community's resistance to their environment and its institutions comes out of their social immobility and the permanence of their being grouped together, which no longer appears to be the result of individual choice but rather of the failure of the project of immigration, failure of both state policies on the subject and the failure of the immigrants themselves as the main agents of the immigration project that aimed at a social mobility in the country of immigration as well as in the country of origin. This failure is confirmed by an unemployment rate of more than 20 per cent, with young people being the most heavily affected group. Poverty combined with long-term grouping on an ethnic basis reflects the negative identity of the group and relates to the idea of concentration, which has become synonymous with segregation. Collectively, these groupings constitute zones of exclusion (a term that has become fashionable in France since the 1990s and settled as antipode of citizenship), where those who are 'excluded from assimilation' are concentrated. Of course, this phenomenon has to be seen as a result of housing and relocation policies, as well as of *de facto* discrimination in the job and housing markets. Paradoxically, this closing of the job market has taken place in a society that gives the impression of being more open, if only because of the development of communication networks and the invasion of the media by satellite channels and other new outlets.

The *banlieues* correspond to what Pierre Bourdieu has called 'spatial structures and mental structures'. Rage is becoming prevalent in these spaces, expressed in violence in relations both within the community and between communities. This verbal and sometimes physical violence guides interpersonal relations in public space, which has its own codes including dress codes, and defines the boundaries of the community. In the *banlieues*, violence provides a territorially and ethnically based form of collective expression, a way of ruling by provocation. Since 2000, numerous reports have sought to alert the political class to the social malaise prevailing in the *banlieues*; the increase in ethno-religious conflict, especially between Jews and Muslims (Commission Nationale Consultative des Droits de l'Homme, 2000; 2001; 2002); the verbal and some-times physical violence against girls who choose dress codes similar to those of their peers in the surrounding society; and the symbolic violence represented by the headscarf. Terms such as 'anti-Semitism', 'racism' and 'sexism' are used to describe the motivations of young people in these areas and schools.[5] Such terms attest to the democratic deficit of the Republic, its lack of legitimacy in these 'territories' which have become places that are presented as conflict zones between civil society and the forces of order, between generations and cultures and between national, local and community institutions.

The existence of communities of this kind has led to the questioning of the very concept of communities as spaces for cultural and political socializa-tion, and reflection on the limitations of this concept. The nature of the group, its mechanisms for entry and exit, its internal coherence and its rules of operation and representation constitute the basic principles of its legiti-macy and recognition. Its relations with society and with other cultures and groups and how it is situated within civil society and especially in relation to the state enter into the equation as well. Additional factors include its capacity for 'consensus', how well disposed it is to demonstrate its loyalty to the political community and its principles, and its ability to deal with the state and its ways of negotiating its identity and its interest. Its legitimacy is related to the internal restrictions that are imposed on individuals in the name of the community and solidarity between its members, the conditions of its operation and especially respect for individual freedom within the community.

The normative questions that arise are related to the definition of a common civic space in which people can participate and with which they can identify, and of the common good, justice and equality. If such an approach is to be followed, then the state needs to take responsibility for adapting to reality by adjusting its policies, restructuring its institutions and redefining the terms of citizenship. How can a new balance be struck between emerging community forces and the national interest? How can the foundations of social ties be rein-vented, internal peace ensured, tensions that result from mutual suspicion lessened and violence avoided, all under new democratic norms according to which both differences and equality are valued? How, at the same time, can atti-tudes be changed so that differences are accepted as part of the historical continuity of democratic societies? This leads to re-establishing the role of the state in defining a common identity shared by its citizens and a feeling of solidarity and loyalty to the political community. States still constitute the framework for the individual's citizenship and democratic representation.

The headscarf, then, raises a number of questions, and therefore requires several levels of analysis: how is society evolving, how can it adapt its principles such as *laïcité* to new realities, what role should institutions play in re-establishing social ties, how should the influence of transnational solidarity networks and the new nationalist expressions that they generate be dealt with, how can a state be part of the process of globalization and avoid the effects of globalization on ethnic and religious solidarities and political forces beyond its borders?

Legislation is clearly a means of marking the sovereignty of the state, especially in its function of defining the terms of citizenship and individual emancipation. This is particularly true when the community does not respond to the need for personal development. In this perspective, banning the headscarf in public schools should be understood for its symbolic value of freedom on both sides. In fact, banning it might serve as a 'negative freedom'. But community oppression goes as much against the project of individual emancipation as banning. The state in this case acts as emancipator of women who can find a refuge in a law to reject the social control or religious pressure, giving the opportunity to achieve emancipation through integration into a liberal democratic society even though the prohibition on wearing the headscarf seems to contradict the principle. Much still needs to be done before everyone can enjoy equal citizenship, before both individuals and groups identify with society and its institutions and have more than a merely instrumental relationship with them, and before people can benefit from the opportunities that such a path can offer.

As Philip Resnick states, 'there is no magic solution to the dilemma that liberal democratic societies face when it comes to reconciling shared citizenship on the one hand and respect for cultural diversity on the other' (Resnick, 2004). The fundamental question has to do with the capacity of states to negotiate both inside and outside their borders (Kastoryano, 2002b). Inside their borders, the negotiations have to do with the *de facto* pluralism that characterizes civil society, the terms of recognition of the communities that are emerging within it and the limits of their political legitimacy. In other words, the state needs to negotiate the terms of citizenship. External negotiations have to do with degrees of institutional and decision-making interdependence with other states and especially with NGOs and other supranational institutions.

Notes

* Earlier versions of some sections of this essay have been published in *Inroads. Canadian Journal of Public Opinion*, 15: 63–72, and were translated by R. Chodos from the same journal.
1 This issue is developed also in Chapters 5 and 7.
2 This is why private schools in France are 'schools *sous contrat*'. The subsidies they receive from the state are a way of controlling the curricula. But this arrangement is not applied to Alsace and Lorraine which have a different status for historical reasons relating to their formerly coming under German law (cf. Tremeau, 1996).

3 Different steps in the institutionalization of Islam are discussed in this volume in Chapter 9 by Modood and Kastoryano.
4 See Chapter 3 by Modood, this volume.
5 Public opinion on these developments was significantly influenced by a book written collectively by college and secondary school teachers and edited by Brenner (2002).

References

Brenner, E. (ed.) (2002) *Les territoires perdus de la république: antisémitisme, racisme et sexisme en milieu scolaire*, Paris: Éditions Mille et une nuits.

Brubaker, R. W. (1992) *Citizenship and Nationhood in France and Germany*, Cambridge, MA: Harvard University Press.

Commission de la nationalité (1988) 'Être français aujourd'hui et demain', Paris: Paris Collection.

Commission Nationale Consultative des Droits de l'Homme, 'La lutte contre le racisme et la xénophobie', Reports for 2000, 2001 and 2002, Paris: La documentation française.

Déloye, Y. (1994) *Ecole et citoyenneté. L'individualisme républicain de Jules Ferry à Vichy: controverses*, Paris: Presses de la FNSP.

Dumont, L. (1991) *France-Allemagne et retour*, Paris: Gallimard.

Haut Conseil à l'Intégration (1991) 'Pour un modèle français d'intégration', First annual report, Paris: La documentation française, Collection des rapports officiels.

Kastoryano, R. (2002a) 'The reach of transnationalism', in E. Hershberg and K. W. Moore (eds) *Critical Views of September 11: Analyses from Around the World*, New York: Free Press.

—— (2002b) *Negotiating Identities: States and Immigrants in France and Germany*, Princeton, NJ: Princeton University Press.

Resnick, P. (2004) 'Republicanism, multiculturalism and liberalism', in *Inroads. The Canadian Journal of Opinion*, 5(Summer/Fall): 77–80.

Schnapper, D. (1991) *La France de l'intégration. Sociologie de la nation en 1991*, Paris: Gallimard.

Sevaiste, V. (2004) 'L'islam dans la République: le CFCM', *Regards sur l'actualité*, 298: 33–48.

Tremeau, J. (1996) 'France', in 'L'Ecole, la religion et la Constitution', *Annuaire internationale de justice constitutionnelle*, 12: 244–266.

Weil, P. (2004) 'Lifting the veil of ignorance', *Progressive Politics*, 3(1): 17–22.

5 The particular universalism of a Nordic civic nation

Common values, state religion and Islam in Danish political culture

Per Mouritsen

Introduction

The murder of the film director Theo van Gogh provoked a free speech controversy in Denmark. The Danish Liberal Party decided to give its annual liberty prize to the Dutch politician Ayaan Hirsi Ali. Ali wrote the manuscript for the director's recent film *Submission*, which portrayed the sexual domination of Muslim women in a controversial manner. While – almost – unanimously condemning the murder, a number of Danish Muslims criticized the party and called for stricter legislation on religious blasphemy, arguing that freedom of speech was regularly misused to slander Islamic religion and the Prophet. Their timing was bad. It invariably linked the discussion of freedom of speech with the assumed condolence of murder. Also, the choice of van Gogh's film as a test case was particularly disastrous in Denmark. In a speech the Prime Minister wondered how

> we have come to a point where giving a freedom prize to a person who fights the subjection of women is regarded as a provocation. Those who call it provocative have not understood the core of the Danish freedom of speech. Freedom of speech in our country means that you can openly and freely criticize anything and anybody.
>
> (Cited in Mortensen, 2004)

Somewhat contrary to Rasmussen's sweeping formulation, Denmark does have a (rarely used) blasphemy law as well as a law against hate speech. The Liberal Party opposes the latter, but curiously has opted (along with the Conservative Party) *not* to support a parliamentary move to abolish the blasphemy law.

The polarized insistence that freedom of speech in the confrontational Danish mode is non-negotiable has now been linked to the alleged failure of Muslims to accept the separation of religion and politics – in fact Denmark has a state church. Politicians insist that Muslims, to qualify as democrats, must confirm that sharia is below Danish democracy, also in the hypothetical future if Muslims were to form a majority in the country. Quite a few Muslims have made ambiguous comments about sharia as a package deal which cannot be negotiated, except that when in Denmark one should accept the supremacy of Danish laws. Yet much antagonism arises from demands that Muslims should declare their opposition to various unsavoury aspects of fundamentalist tradition in public, and from the insistence of some of the latter that sharia means something else and more than critics believe, and that one *can* indeed be religious in a serious way and yet adopt a sufficiently liberal outlook from inside Islam.

The controversy is the most recent manifestation of public agonies before Islam, which arises from what I term the particular universalism of Danish political culture. The chapter argues that Denmark increasingly sees a construction of the parameters of belonging – and the conditions of entry and acceptance of immigrants, particularly Muslims – in terms of a move towards a civic nation, characterized by universalistic values. These values correspond to popular images of Denmark as an inclusive, egalitarian, indeed 'universal' (Esping-Andersen, 1990) welfare state. They tap the image of a people's democracy with a strong emphasis on Parliament as the undivided voice of the people. Above all they denote a shift in public discourse towards an image of the country as custodian and spearhead of human rights, liberty and equality. However, this universalism, as that of any other state, is of a certain brand. The purpose of what follows is to investigate this particularity in the context of Muslim immigration. More specifically, the chapter deals with problems that arise when this particularity is articulated – and sometimes *not* articulated, or even acknowledged – in debates about shared *Danish* values which must be affirmed by newcomers to the nation.

The chapter is organized around an empirical analysis of the Danish common values debate – a series of political statements and arguments, which has involved all the main political parties, and which is framed in the context of concern about the Islamic community in Denmark. Before this analysis, the following section introduces the stakes, political as well as theoretical, of a more general movement in the West towards a more civic discourse of nation and political communality as a response to cultural pluralism. A further section briefly introduces the discursive terrain of Danish nationalism in the framework of political responses and popular attitudes to Muslim immigration. The empirical analysis is followed by a discussion of the normative ambivalence of 'speaking politics to culture', in the particular Danish fashion and more generally, which comments on attempts to conceptualize political community in recent political theory.

Political solutions to cultural diversity in Western politics and political theory

The Danish case typifies a double shift in Western political culture. On the one hand, we witness a certain convergence towards more *civic* understandings of national communities. The preservation of heritage, language and religion certainly continues as vehicle of sub-nation mobilization. Migration pressures fuel defensive nationalist revivals in old nation-states (Hedetoft, 1999), provoking political concessions to a new Right, which, hostile towards cultural pluralism, wishes to preserve the nation as vessel of majority belonging. Even so, the dominant trend is a new discourse, which emphasizes universal, liberal values and citizenship as means towards inclusion of immigrants, and hostility towards comprehensive multiculturalism, which is seen to be in conflict with equal rights.

On the other hand, this shift goes hand in hand with a concern for loyalty, solidarity and cohesion, and for precisely what constitutes, in the absence of deep culture or ethnicity, the stuff of cohesion. What must newcomers be brought to share? Here, affirming democracy and human rights may not after all be sufficient. In the French tradition assimilation into aspects of French high culture (seen as a carrier of universal values) as well as an ideology of republican *civisme* have always been regarded as necessary (Favell, 2001). In Germany parts of the old nationalism pop up in arguments about the need for a majority *Leitkultur* – with predictably contested content – and clash with notions of *Verfassungspatriotismus* (Krauel, 2000). And in countries as diverse as Australia, France, Canada and Britain citizenship ceremonies and civic education signal to newcomers that belonging requires a more active type of identification and loyalty (Demaine, 2004).

This development corresponds to a turn in normative theory towards questions of unity and cohesion in culturally pluralist states. Multicultural critics of Rawlsian liberalism have pointed out that liberal states never in fact conformed to the colour-blind ideal, whereby religious and cultural identities remain tucked away in the private sphere. Many liberals now say that while one should remain neutral as to which conceptions of the good are intrinsically worthwhile, they cannot afford neutrality between ways of life in terms of their beneficial effects on liberal institutions themselves. A common language may be necessary for democratic communication; common culture, even a shared religion, may promote harmony and solidarity; or political participation may be necessary for the survival of liberal constitutionalism (Kymlicka, 2002: 343–344).

While this new conceptualization of necessary political culture looks like a paradoxical return to *community*, it tends to transcend, criticize, or at least select specific elements from the deeper culture. Discussions assume several levels and forms of political culture (Bauböck, 2001; Laborde, 2002) – including identity and individual belonging; shared (imagined) political pasts; political values and constitutional principles; civic norms and practices; and different conceptualizations of a somewhat broader, but still 'public', culture. To advocates of *constitutional patriotism* citizens must share allegiance to a set of universal values, enshrined in liberal constitutions, which are rendered legitimate by connection with communicatively sanctioned principles through the representative institutions of a *Rechtstaat* (Habermas, 2001). These principles receive motivational support from within nationally specific traditions in disputed manners (Ingram, 1996; Lacroix, 2002; Markell, 2000). By contrast, David Miller's (1995) position, which we may call *liberal or instrumental nationalism*, is to claim that a sense of nationality is particularly conducive to trust in a society, such trust in turn facilitating participatory democracy and a redistributive welfare state. Nationality to Miller is more than political principles. It also refers to social norms, very important shared cultural ideas (in some societies including religion), language and history. Cécile Laborde, somewhere in between, speaks of *civic patriotism* where citizens must be familiar with political culture understood in a more diluted, but still nationally particular, sense of a shared conversational space, the 'malleable frameworks which sustains our political conversations over time' (Laborde, 2002: 609). Although emphases differ, each perspective notes the deliberative character of political culture and the possibility of criticizing aspects which alienate newcomers. Whereas each view carves out a place for minorities to maintain (hyphenated) identities, the emphasis on dialogue corresponds to a general civic turn in liberalism, which sees ability to compromise and assume an autonomous *public self* (Rawls, 1993) as necessary in pluralist societies, where the most preciously held beliefs may be held up for scrutiny. This tendency, visible also in new dialogical multiculturalism (Parekh, 2000), puts under pressure first-generation multicultural claims about such autonomy being a specifically liberal value, while raising questions about the possibility of demarcating public autonomy from such private religious beliefs which require faith or unquestioning obedience (Kymlicka, 2002: 228–244).

Theoretical positions on the proper thinness of reasonable liberal cohesion are not directly at issue here. I am concerned instead with what happens when the discourses of common values, national culture and citizenship enter debates, which are already polarized, particularly in the context of Islam. That the well-known distinction between ethnic and civic nationalism, conceptually muddled to begin with (Brubaker, 1999), says little per se about the degree of cultural openness, is not news. I argue that civic nationalism is at best a necessary condition of more difference accepting public cultures, not a sufficient one.

Actual debates may tell us more about the difficulties encountered when nations start to speak politics to culture (Mouritsen and Jørgensen, forthcoming, 2006). The point is not so much whether we share specific values, but rather that we often talk about these values *as* shared, as constitutively ours, in specific ways. The West is presently seeing a politicization of culture, not just in the form of new backward-looking nationalisms and essentialist multiculturalisms which repeat logics from the early history of nation-states, but above all in the way that the continuity of the nation-state format under conditions of globalization is predicated by identity projects which present culture in terms of *politically necessary, functional homogeneity* – whereby some forms of culture are beneficial, and others are not (Hedetoft, 2003). However, in this process we also see *a new culturalization of politics*. By this I do not just mean that politics becomes 'filled with culture' when everybody talks about diversity and culture whatever the problem at hand. I have in mind that political values, including universal liberal values, are *talked about* as culture either in the sense of being linked to nationally specific and favourable historical traditions or ways of life (including, in the Danish case, secularized religion), or in the sense of national ownership of, or avant-gardism relative to certain values. Moreover, very often politics is *manifested* as cultural, where culture means those perceptions of political reality and subterranean orderings of value which subtly drive us, while we are busy talking about something else – such as 'our common values'.

Islamophobia and Danish political culture

Denmark began to receive work immigrants from Turkey, Yugoslavia and Pakistan in the late 1960s. Since then it has seen a typical Western European sequence of developments, with a freeze on immigration in 1973, continuing influx through family reunification programmes, and waves of refugees in the 1980s and 1990s, still primarily from Islamic countries including Iran, Iraq, Lebanon, Kosovo and Somalia. The process of incorporation has not been very successful. While electoral political participation is comparatively widespread, particularly at local levels (Togeby, 2002), the country has no formalized consultation between Muslim communities and the state. Most Muslims remain geographically segregated, and unemployment rates for immigrants in Denmark are higher than anywhere else in Western Europe. In the case of new refugees, a comprehensive, paternalist (and expensive) three-year integration programme may well in some ways be counter-productive, in a country where a relatively generous, entitlement-based welfare system, combined with high minimum wages (and corresponding lack of unskilled jobs), perpetuate circles of dependency and labour market marginalization (Tranæs and Zimmermann, 2004). Moreover, the conspicuous inability of so many Muslim immigrants, particularly women and early school leavers, to fulfil the work obligation underlying the universal welfare state may be conducive to a more homogenizing and assimilationist public policy and to lower popular tolerance of cultural diversity (Necef, 2001). The question is constantly asked in what way immigrants, particularly Muslims, must change in order to be able to function in and contribute to Danish society (Hedetoft, 2003), hence lowering the 'price of solidarity' for others to pay (Nannestad, 1999).

Recently, the liberal–conservative government, which relies for its parliamentary majority on the xenophobic Danish People's Party (hereafter the DPP), has adopted very restrictive measures, particularly in the area of family reunification. A 'twenty-four-year rule' is designed to curb arranged transnational marriages between younger (Muslim) individuals, although politicians also defend it simply because it drastically reduces influx per se. This policy, supported by the social democratic opposition, was criticized by the Council of Europe's Human Rights Secretary. Indeed, Denmark's old humanitarian reputation was lost with the 2001 election, where the present government successfully adopted a fear of immigration platform that foreign commentators found difficult to distinguish from that of the far right, and which followed tough measures already put in place under the previous centre coalition.

Yet the picture of Danish intolerance and ethnocentrism is mixed. The country's relative 'performance' depends on who you ask. Denmark, these days (along with Belgium, Germany and Greece), has a high proportion (20 per cent) of 'intolerants' with strongly negative opinions – but it also has the highest number of 'actively tolerants' in the EU, along with Sweden (33 per cent) (EUMC/SORA, 2001: 24–25). It also depends on what you ask about. Principled support for receiving politically persecuted refugees is significantly above the EU average (EUMC/SORA, 2001: 34), and slightly *increasing*, even though 1999–2002 saw a temporary fall (Togeby, 2004: 58). Surveys find high and, since the 1970s and 1980s, increasing support for equal political rights and incorporation of immigrants as welfare state citizens (Togeby, 1998a; 1998b). And compared to other EU countries, few Danes favour forced repatriation, whereas support is relatively high for 'policies improving social coexistence', including active anti-discrimination and particularly the promotion of understanding of different cultures and lifestyles (EUMC/SORA, 2001: 27–31; 46–47).

However, the same research also shows Danes as the most likely in the EU to ascribe social problems (particularly regarding education and crime) to minorities.[1] And whereas Denmark again scores high on *Eurobarometer's* 'multicultural optimism' (that is, regarding presence of minorities as 'enriching'), it hits an EU low, with Greece and Belgium, on measures of personal feelings of 'disturbance in daily life' by the presence of other nationalities, other races and *particularly other religions*. Also, Danes, compared to EU countries and the United States, are rather less supportive of multicultural policies (EUMC/SORA, 2001; Togeby, 1998b: 195). Finally, an increase is visible from the early or mid–1990s in affirmations of national pride and cultural superiority, fear of national culture being threatened by immigration, and support of assimilation (citizenship conditional on 'learning to behave like Danes') (Togeby, 1998b: 190; 2004: 60).

We see, as before (Mouritsen, 1995), a small country with high humanitarian principles of equal citizenship (which are difficult to live up to, once financial burdens and problems are politicized in the media), with a significant segment of the population which worries about, fears or even resents a future life of conspicuous cultural diversity. However, the Danish problem with culture is very much a problem with religion. Only about half the population in 1993 agreed that immigrants should be allowed to 'freely advocate and practise' their religion, and a recent survey showed Danish respondents to be *far* the most likely, in a group of thirty countries, to associate religion with conflict, and strong faith with intolerance. This general Scandinavian phenomenon is even more pronounced in Denmark than in Norway and Sweden (Goul Andersen, 2002: 7, 21). It is also relatively new. Denmark has had no historical contact with the world of Islam and it took a while for people to discover that the early work migrants were actually Muslims and to understand what that meant. Early stereotypes were about anything *but* religion: an ensemble of prejudices about 'Southern' eating habits, sexual conduct, criminal behaviour, laziness and so forth (Jensen, 2001).

Today, debates on immigrants often concern religious aspects, such as the building of a publicly visible mosque or the availability of sites for a burial ground (both of which Danish Muslims lack to this day), religious schools, headscarves, arranged marriages and child education. Moreover, such issues are very often part of an 'us–them', 'Danes–foreigners' frame of discourse (Hervik, 2004; Karpantschof, 2002), widespread since the early 1990s and propelled towards the political centre by the DPP, which tends to frame questions in terms of essentialist culture. It often takes on a harsher tone than in neighbouring countries (Nielsen, 2002). However, the conceptual *content* of this polarized discourse of culture varies.

To anticipate, the Danish case exhibits a specific entanglement of civic state nation and *Kulturnation*. Both the romantic vocabularies that came to Denmark from Germany and the later revolutionary ideologies of popular self-government were conceptualized, in a parallel development in the mid nineteenth century, as a specific understanding of a homogeneous, egalitarian and freedom-loving people reaching maturity from below (Østergaard, 1991; Hansen, 2002). As traditional cultural nationalism is waning, civic nationalism becomes expressed, first, in the value of consensual, small-scale democracy, and, second, in the ideology of the successful welfare state. This type of egalitarianism has deep percussions in discourse about Islam. The Lutheran heritage remains important as facilitating the presentation of Danes as an old Christian people. But religion is particularly important in terms of the contrast between Islam as an overly serious, un-modern religion, which denotes on the one hand authority and inequality and on the other hand 'modern' individualism and secularism, either as scepticism about religion as such, or as religious forms (Danish Lutheranism) which are constitutive of individualism. The current debate on 'our common Danish values' reflects these embedded public codes.[2]

A national right to own (Christian) culture

The first position stresses the right of the nation's first born to a *Kulturnation* and its accompanying values, although the concept of common values is often replaced by words like national heritage, habits, way of life and the like.[3] This is a communitarian idea of privileging the *Leitkultur* of a majority people, because it was there first and thus owns the country for the safe development of this cultural content. It is presented as particular, not universal; as valuable for this distinct people; as threatened for demographic reasons, as the proportion of immigrants and their descendants grows; and as legitimizing cultural assimilation and strict immigration measures. According to one MP, Louise Frevert (DPP), arguing against recognition of Ramadan in schools, 'We live in a Christian country, and when you come here you must conform to Danish norms, laws and habits', not incidentally by being Christian but by accepting those values which have *emerged* from Denmark's Christian past.[4]

A radical version of Denmark as carrier of an old Christian culture brings to mind Charles Taylor's argument about a constitutive *duty to belong* (Taylor, 1989). To the Danish priest, right-wing intellectual and MP Søren Krarup (DPP) (2004a), 'Danish history, happily, has enabled us to be as one family in this country, which for this reason has faith and church in common.' To be a human 'means that there is something that he holds dearly, which binds and constrains him … a guilt, a responsibility, a history, and a historically given context which is reality'. This concrete reality (which, by sleight of hand, gets invested with a selective national content including national literatures, church attendance, unpretentiously decent family life, and folk scepticism of progressive–liberal values) is the historically emerged given, in which God has placed us, and which humans should not question in the name of universalistic ideologies – for example, of human rights – as this would place an abstract humanity in the place of a fatherly God (Krarup, 2000). Yet, despite divine sanction of this concretely given reality (and despite Krarup's defence of official Lutheranism), its *specified content* is more nationalist than Christian, and never Christian in a pious, let alone a fundamentalist, sense.[5] It implies a certain relativism, whereby a people should remain faithful towards their *own* givens, without claiming the moral superiority of this or that set of values (Krarup, 2004b).

The DPP recognizes that Danish society is 'secularized'. Even so 'Christianity … remains inseparable from the life of the people', and hence 'our duty as a nation first and foremost regards Danish culture and its Christian foundation of ideas', or our 'culturally determined [*sic*] faith, norms, traditions and attitudes'.[6] What this secularized Christianity-as-culture consists of is unclear. Newcomers need not become Christian, indeed religious freedom is stressed. But the fact that they typically *are not*, and *never were*, makes integration extremely difficult, because religion is constitutive of culture: Just as our culture is constituted by an old religious heritage, so is theirs – making even secularized Islam perpetually alien.

In this unbridled cultural nationalism deep Danishness is valuable per se and requires constant protection. Such views are not widespread outside the DPP. Weaker forms exist, though, which do not exhibit this sense of besiegement. One version stresses that a liberal right of minorities to live as they please should not be mistaken for a right to equal treatment, as in some version of official (liberal) multiculturalism (Hornbech, 2000) This remnant of cultural nation thinking, *not* as an entry requirement for newcomers but as the comfortable privilege of the majority, now prevails in the Liberal Party. To one prominent member, 'Danes are not just any old ethnic group, which happens to live in Denmark. We are one people. We have a common language and do things our way.' Neither pride in, nor emotional belonging to, a nation should be equated with nationalism (Hornbech, 2001: 10, 12). This majority right is not unchallenged. Indeed its proponents present the argument as targeted against a left-leaning intellectual establishment. Although other markers of deep culture exist (language, history and a national literary canon in schools), the presently dominating element remains religion, albeit typically in the sense of Christian heritage as *shaper* of national culture.

The main conflict of this debate concerns the future of the Danish Lutheran Church, of which four out of five Danes are (passive) members, and which continues to be married to the state.[7] A state church remains supported by the main parties, including the Social Democrats, but recent years have seen criticism from the Left. Arguments concern the unreasonableness of maintaining a privileged position for a religious organization, of which sizeable minorities are not members, both regarding finance and the role of the Church as official childbirth registry. They also concern the instability of a modern state, which ultimately sanctions or even adjudicates doctrinal disputes. Such criticism tends to meet the argument that treating religions (and the non-religious) equally (that is, a standard liberal theory conception of state neutrality) would be misplaced cultural value relativism. Such relativism is contrasted to a notion of *frisind* or 'free-mindedness'. This is a non-neutral fighting creed of respecting and tolerating one's opponent, while maintaining one's own – *and*, here, of expecting the latter to enjoy the unquestioned privileges of the majority creed and its (secularized) cultural manifestations.[8]

Instrumental civic nationalism: solidarity, Lutheran liberalism and democracy as way of life

The theme of a right to dominant culture in the senses just outlined does *not*, however, dominate debates, and when it is heard it often connects to a variety of argumentative figures concerning shared *civic* values where the *Kulturnation* becomes a vehicle of democracy, liberalism and social justice.

Thus, a second and increasingly important theme is the conceptualization of shared national culture as not (only) valuable in itself, but instrumentally necessary for maintaining a well-functioning democratic and liberal society, as well as a society where one may feel safe and have 'external and internal security'. One argument, which stresses homogeneity and shared values, suggests that common culture and values *as such* 'tie together the citizens of the nation' and is a prerequisite for stability and solidarity. Generally speaking, a multicultural society is a society without internal cohesion, and therefore the multicultural societies of this world are characterized by a lack of solidarity, and often also overt conflict. Danish culture is particularly vulnerable to heterogeneity – through immigration by conspicuously different groups – by being both small and relatively unique in its degree of homogeneity.[9] Former Minister of Integration for the Social Democrats, Karen Jespersen, argues in a similar vein that solidarity in a modern welfare state arises from, and in times of globalization must be reinforced by, experiences of national belonging, including its deeper, cultural and symbolic aspects (Jespersen, 2003a; 2003b: 121–129; cf. Pittelkow, 2004: 28–48; Haarder, 2004). The same argument, tied to trust and social transparency through homogeneity, and bringing to mind Miller's argument, may occasionally be found on the Left, when EU-level democracy is presented as impossible, because real democracy requires experience of cultural sameness by co-operating compatriots.[10]

As with Miller, the idea of common culture as an integrating and motivating device often slides into a separate argument (Miller, 1995: 94). Here, homogeneity is only a necessary, not a sufficient, condition of welfare democracy. Values must be of the right kind – namely, a shared support of redistribution and liberal democracy. As we shall see below, the dominant political discourse simply equates Danish common values with these civic values. However, we are concerned here with different notions of a supportive relationship between culture and civic values. Certain elements of Danish national culture are somehow especially conducive to such values.[11] Two articulated positions stand out. One concerns the particular liberty-supporting nature of Danish Lutheranism. The other one concerns democracy and egalitarianism as a cultural *way of life*.

A very important argument presents the Christian state religion as valuable in part because it was and remains conducive to liberal democracy and pluralism. The reference here is to the Calvinist–Lutheran division between the personal realm of (free) faith, organized inside the Church, and the realm of external conduct, regulated by state authority, as established by the Danish Reformation in 1536. Lutheranism, here, facilitated a specific tradition of legal protection from political encroachment on private life, and an ideal of pragmatic politics, unburdened by contentious issues of faith.[12] Liberty and secularization are *constituted* by Lutheranism, and continue to be upheld by it – or at least by a cultural Lutheranism which emphasizes personal autonomy. For Tove Fergo, liberal church minister, 'it is difficult to imagine a state which is not supported by or embedded in a society based on faith' (Fergo, 2003: 3). The type of religion that prevents political culture from becoming illiberal is Danish Lutheranism (Hornbech, 2001). If this suggests the instrumental value for liberalism of Lutheran religion, one may ask why this relationship is facilitated by a *state* religion (over and above the communitarian argument already noted about the legitimately privileged position of the Danish *people's* church). The argument here is that Lutheranism itself can only be kept sufficiently autonomy respecting internally (and hence maintain its watchdog function) by being tied to the state, both locally (to democratically elected parish councils) and nationally (to a Parliament with members of all Christian, non-Christian and even non-religious creeds). This constraining relationship guarantees a non-pious church, which refrains from undue politicizing and moralizing (Fergo, 2004; Hornbech, 2001: 167–168; Krarup, 2002).

This line of argument, prominent in parts of the Liberal Party and in the DPP, employs selective historical records. The Reformation was a heavy-handed inculcation of Protestant subjectivity where the peoples of Danish territories were constituted as Christian under a common king. It only promoted an autonomously confirmed *Lutheran* faith. Toleration did not emanate from the Church and religious freedom was only institutionalized with the 1849 Constitution whereby, for instance, compulsory baptism was abolished (Korsgaard, 2004). To the extent that conscientious issues in parliamentary politics are avoided, this relegation of morality to the private realm is hardly the result of a particular brand of religion (let alone the labours of politicians who embrace it).

Arguments against a state church, according to this discourse, fail to understand the historical dependency of liberal outlooks in Denmark on Lutheranism, even when popular faith may be gone (Fergo, 2003). In the absence of faith or its cultural substitutes (the recognition of Christian traditions and symbols) bad things are in store. 'Without gospel [and its separation of realms] salvation becomes a political task. Political ideologies will reign freely over people's souls' (Hornbech, 2001: 168). Those who believe in nothing will readily believe in anything. Alienation from Danish Christianity, or certainly failure to respect popular religious sentiment, means faltering readiness to stand up for liberal values; that is, an unprincipled neutrality between all cultural groups, including un-liberal ones. It also carries with it an impulse to force the ideology of multicultural relativism on others (Hornbech, 2001; Jespersen, 2003b: 185–186). People who do believe, in a personalized way, or acknowledge their cultural Lutheran heritage, are more able to stand their ground, and because they do so, also more able to tolerate and even respect views with which they disagree, including the views of religious minorities such as Muslims. Liberalism is presented as a confrontational fighting creed of *frisind*, a 'spiritual competition' (Hornbech, 2000). It is in fact a creed, more than a set of universal liberal principles. Historically, autonomy in Danish liberalism was valued in terms of an individual search for (religious) truth, and in terms of a free-spirited *people* doing this – not by reference to pluralism and the fallibility of enlightenment liberalism. But the equation between national Lutheranism and autonomy/tolerance consistently carries the conclusion that atheists, other Christian denominations and *particularly* Muslims are not natural carriers of a truly liberal political culture. Most importantly – and this argument is dominant way beyond the religious circles of its origin – Islam, unlike Lutheran Christianity, is a law-based religion, without a secular division between the private sphere and politics, which had no enlightenment, and did not promote autonomy in matters of faith (Jespersen, 2003b: 162). Muslims, practising or not, by virtue of never having been Lutherans, will be less liberal than native Danes.

A second discourse also trades on the idea of Danish culture as particularly conducive to liberal democracy. Its understanding of democracy often refers to a towering figure in the Danish intellectual past, not Søren Kierkegaard, but the internationally rather less well-known N. F. S. Grundtvig (1783–1872), who played a key role in early Danish nation-building. In his teachings a this-worldly, free-spirited Lutheranism is closely connected to a nationalism of heroes, ancient battles and sentimental depiction of countryside. But this nationalism, though cultural, Christian and romantic, was also egalitarian, democratic and closely connected to the concept of *folkelighed* (literally 'Völkishness'). *Folkelighed* on the one hand denotes a *people* coming into its own with a distinct past, language and character. On the other hand it is tied to ideals of popular enlightenment and destruction of barriers between ordinary country folk and urban elites. In the countryside, it became a backbone of the Danish folk high school movement, the peasant co-operative movement and the early Liberal Party.

As noted already, this 'people' is now predominantly politically conceptualized, denoting egalitarianism, anti-authoritarianism, speaking one's mind, deliberation and consensual decisions. Hal Koch, the main synthesizer of this vision, spoke of democracy as a gradually acquired 'way of life' (*livsform*) (Koch, 1945: 62). Koch was critical of romantic nationalism and presented his vision as a humanistic and European achievement. But reception of Koch's work has invariably regarded this way of life as a nationally peculiar – and particularly outstanding – child of Danish civil society (Korsgaard, 2001).[13] In a similar vein, egalitarianism is linked to solidarity and social justice. The theme of the Danish people's treasured welfare state is popular way beyond its social democratic origins.[14] And often, most directly with the DPP, this way of life is seen as so much more difficult to acquire for those who were never socialized in similar national schools of equality and democracy, and to whom 'the principle of redistribution and the idea of equality behind our welfare model is completely impossible to understand'.[15]

Common values as civic values

The last argument (if, despite its simplicity, it merits this term) is presently dominant. It is often found alongside those already discussed and essentially goes like this: we in Denmark have certain values, on which our society is based, and which we rightly hold dear; these values are *ours* in the sense that they constitute our *culture*. Moreover, these values are described – with certain differences of emphasis according to party ideology – in terms of highly general, indeed 'universal', concepts; they are currently challenged by other cultures with other values; and accepting them is an entry requirement. Talk about Danish identity and culture has become overwhelmingly civic. To a young Social Democrat Vice-Chairman:

> there is a Danish identity, which builds on respect for certain basic values and rights. We should not exclude others or be intolerant, but we must dare to say that to be Danish and to live here is also about saying yes to for instance equal treatment (*ligestilling*) and free-mindedness (*frisind*). It is dangerous if we do not dare affirm Danish values ... such as democracy, freedom of expression and much else, on which we should not compromise.
>
> (Redder, 2004)

And in the 2004 party programme: 'Globalization means that our common values are being challenged, at the same time that immigration means that fundamental values of Danish society are being questioned.' These values, 'freedom, equality and solidarity', are cultural: 'People develop their personality through upbringing and in the meeting with other people and society. As Danes we have Danish culture in common' (Social Democrats, 2004: 7) The liberal Prime Minister's 2003 New Year's speech was also replete with references to common values:

> Emigrants must make an effort to get to understand the values on which Danish society is based. Many of these we consider as a matter of course, because we have developed them over many generations. ... Danish society has been built on some fundamental values, which must be accepted, if you are to live here. In Denmark politics and religion are separated. In Denmark there is inviolable respect for human life. In Denmark, as a matter of course, women are equal to men.
>
> (Rasmussen, 2003b)

The challenge to these values comes from 'religious medieval thinking', the 'darkness of the mullahs' and 'political fanaticism', and is associated, in this speech, with female sexual mutilation, stoning and suicide bombs (Rasmussen, 2003b). To a member of the DPP, Danish *civisme* becomes culturalized racism:

> Just as rooted in our democratic view of society we Danes are, just as rooted Arab Muslims are in their hatred of the Western world and democracy. The world in which these people live – in the Arabic countries or Denmark – is one where human lives do not count.
>
> (Mogens Camre, in Karpantschof, 2002: 53)

Whereas civic values to the Prime Minister and the Social Democrats are *just as* culturally Danish as Danish food ('Danishness is also something else and more than *frikadeller* and brown gravy'), most politicians take pains to specify that the most important elements of Danish culture are *not* a question of lifestyle, such as food or clothes, *or* of religion. Yet in some texts one finds conceptual sliding. This is systematic in the DPP's programmes and speeches. It can be found in the Liberal Party's appeals to Christianity, and in the Social Democrat programme's peculiar link between a list of political values and the need to 'strengthen and develop the understanding of a Danish culture, language and history' (Social Democrats, 2004: 7).

One argument, pervasive outside the DPP, is about 'staying open'. However, the meeting of cultures will only work if we remain safe in our own. In the Social Democrats' version:

> a person with a strong identity dares to meet other people with an open mind. A country with a strong common culture dares to meet the world. ... Culture shapes our values and gives us a point of reference in the world. The better we know ourselves and our own culture, the easier it will be to meet and understand the culture of others.[16]
>
> (Social Democrats, 2004: 7–8)

But this dialogue of cultures, in a subtly familiar way, is asymmetrical. Openness is on 'our' side. In the government's *Action Plan to Promote Equal Treatment and Combat Racism*, it declared that 'it is the government's view that a modern welfare state should be based on liberalism, diversity and inclusiveness. ... We should be true to our own values while remaining open to impulses from outside.' Indeed

> the principle of equal treatment does not mean we should treat everyone the same. The ancient Nordic saying 'freedom for Loke as well as Thor' promotes the principle of equal treatment while conveying the message that we are not the same and should not be forced to be alike. [However,] freedom to differ does not mean that anything goes and everything is equally good.
>
> (Danish Government, 2003)

In other words *Thor*, in Nordic mythology the upright god of thunder, should know his own liberal values, including the duty to tolerate the un-liberal *Loke* – the jealous god who killed the good *Balder*.

The political ambiguity of national public culture and common values

These arguments do not exhaust Danish debates on common values. On the Left and occasionally elsewhere, some politicians will also speak of values as simply universal, social democratic or liberal, and certain commentators (but very few politicians) will praise cultural pluralism. But the debate overwhelmingly connects such civic values to arguments and assumptions about *national* culture, and about immigrants – above all Muslims – as inhabiting an inherently un-civic culture. These forms of political culturalization highlight ambiguities of recent theories of cohesion in pluralist societies, discussed above. To be sure, these theories mix regulative ideals with sociological theories of solidarity, trust and legitimacy at a high level of generality, and cannot simply be 'tested'. Nevertheless, we may be concerned with how common culture and civics get linked up in the real politics of a Nordic nation-state, the general flavour of whose political model each author would find agreeable.

There are several problems with Miller's theory, which assumes that a society with redistributive institutions and democratic participation requires a shared public culture. It assumes a distinction between a pre-political 'nationality', which generates trust and transparency, and the willingness to practise comprehensive liberal democratic values. In this benign liberal–Rousseauan assimilation model, this or that culture is no better or worse than any other per se, at least outside the non-egalitarian Unites States. Newcomers should simply respect that *a* public culture is necessary, and that as latecomers they must accept the dominant one, find room for their private identities outside it, and then gradually, through deliberation, insert suitable culture-launderings into the mainstream (Miller, 1995). But in Danish debates the very distinction between a culture/nationality and the principles, practices and competences it supports is unacknowledged, whereas the more general idea that solidarity requires homogeneity is widespread. On the xenophobic Right, the idea of culture-based cohesion becomes widened, falling out of liberal bounds in two ways. On the one hand, 'national culture' becomes a flexible marker, capable of picking up anything from religion to sexual norms. It trades on the idea of Danish culture as particularly vulnerable, because especially dependent on a homogeneity which is very ancient, very distinct and very important for a form of welfare democracy, which is presented in turn as almost unique in the world. On the other hand, the instrumentality of culture comes to support not just democracy and distribution, but also the 'security' – real and psychological – of what is presented as a fragile social order. In place of arguments for trust for political purposes we have a management of cultural fear.

Even more pervasive is an assumed specific supporting relation which constructs Danish identity (Christian, democratic way of life) as *particularly* conducive, indeed organically linked, not to trust and transparency, but to the values of redistribution, democracy – and liberal tolerance – themselves. This becomes dramatically exclusive when the common public culture is described as either very old and habitual or very dependent on religion – that is, on cultural Lutheranism. The emphasis on perceived genesis over validity of liberal and democratic norms is very damaging in the context of a clash between a re-emerging cultural Lutheranism in a secularized society and a predominantly Islamic immigration influx. The threshold of inclusion in an increasingly civic nation is hardly lower (Eisenstadt and Giesen, 1995), when civicness is tied to the old ways of life of an inherently democratic nation. Moreover, whereas theorists such as Miller are comfortable with the imagined nature of identities and pasts – and hence their future malleability – this feature is invariably lost in public discourse, where essentialism and authenticity is not just an assumption, but also a stake in arguments.

The analysis outlined above indicates that the dominant discourse in fact stays on the high ground of 'universal' values and emphasizes that the condition of membership in the Danish polity is simple adherence to these values. Is Denmark on the road towards constitutional patriotism? Details of the debate suggest our caution here, in ways that come out clearly when we distinguish different interpretations of Habermas's idea. If it denotes an appropriation of a particular national past, which mixes justified pride in a specific road to liberal democracy with self-critical interpretation of shadier aspects of this past and its hold on the present (Markell, 2000), our analysis suggests the existence of emphasis on the former aspect. Second, and in contrast to a more Kantian view of constitutional patriotism, where allegiance and solidarity come from simple recognition of participating in *a* functioning co-operation of justice (Lacroix, 2002), we saw that universal values were simply assumed to be intrinsically Danish, or universal *qua* Danish in a Nordic version of the French–Jacobin short circuit.[17] Here, adherence to these values was often presented as the give-and-take of self-confident cultures, where the giving turned out to be all on one side (the Danish). Finally, if *constitutional* patriotism denotes the more pluralist idea of *different* versions of liberal universalism, each mobilizing the distinct loyalties of peoples adhering to one national form (Ingram, 1996), the idea of

Danish liberal universalism is hardly ever in the form of a reasonable pluralism (Rawls, 1993); that is, some sense of admissible variation of constitutional content with correspondingly different flavours of political culture. Instead, the particularity of the Danish model invariably denotes particularly *superior*, or *genuinely* liberal and democratic, as in appeals to Lutheran secularism, Grundtvig-style *frisind*, and democracy or welfare equality as way of life.

This predicament, incidentally, highlights limitations of the Habermasian model. Most populations have nothing approaching a consensus on a specific national form of constitutional values; indeed internal divisions may often be greater than between some states. The Danish case exactly highlights the phenomenon of politicians speaking in the name of 'us' and 'the people', while simply forwarding specific ideological versions of very general principles. Moreover, in appeals to the particularity of a liberal democratic tradition, the illusion of a monolithic consensus becomes a substitute for arguments. 'Our' model is non-negotiable, simply because of its assumed shared character, because of the culturalism of 'what we do around here'.

In Laborde's *civic patriotism*, which no doubt reflects the more sophisticated French traditions of debate, the common stuff is defined somewhere between Miller's relatively thick idea of common public culture and versions of constitutional patriotism, as shared patterns of political conversation. This conception of political communality may be more helpful. In the Danish case debates are clearly influenced by a limited set of discourses, which have certain common references and assumptions, which use certain types of arguments, and which refer to specific Danish experiences and symbols – smallness, Lutheranism, Grundtvig and the welfare state. The ability of immigrants to translate their concerns effectively seems obviously dependent on the ability to navigate political culture in this way.

But this raises a final problem. It is a paradox that contemporary discussions focus so much on culture and political values, *without* explicating and confronting political culture at Laborde's level. On the one hand, fascination with abstract common values takes up so much space, in the type of political discourse I have analysed, relative to attempts to formulate the agony points of the Danish predicament with reference to history and shared political experiences that they serve as a shield protecting participants from confronting the latter critically. On the other hand, even debates that *do* refer to 'the Danish way' hardly scratch the surface of what actually constitutes those 'accumulated habits and expectations' of Danish political culture which *are* quite dominant, but which influence the debate as barriers of entry in an unacknowledged way. Tariq Modood, in a British context, has noted the frustration of immigrants who find it difficult to pinpoint exactly *what* is expected of them – the target moving from political values to love of cricket (Modood, 1994). I contend that much of the *real* particularism of Danish universalism consists of a species of liberalism, which emphasizes personal autonomy, egalitarianism and democratic participation as comprehensive values which penetrate all aspects of personal and social life, but, not surprisingly, does so in a specific way, which is rarely specified and never discussed critically in the way that Laborde holds up as an ideal. Moreover, some of it is a type of political culture, which often influences, not what we talk about (abstract common values), but the *way* we talk – or remain silent – about it. Let us briefly look at a few manifestations of this comprehensive liberalism in debates on multicultural issues.

The particular liberalisms of Danish political culture

The Danish headscarves debate began as a discussion of the right to wear religious head garments in shops and private firms. Arguments against concerned the rights of employers to decide details of uniforms; the idea that headscarves were 'cultural' and hence not covered by constitutional freedom of religion provisions (or that the latter did not extend to the 'private' workplace); and the need to stand firm on Danish dress codes. But one of the most important arguments voiced by feminists and the nationalist Right alike concerned gender equality and women's (sexual) autonomy. Again the issue was typically framed as a *Kulturkampf* against 'spiritual darkness' and religiously motivated discrimination and dominance of women (Rudolf, 2003: 65–66). In Denmark, equality and individual autonomy are often interpreted as valuable ways of life, which people should affirm. They get politicized, *vis-à-vis* Muslims, not merely as political principles (Rawls, 1993), but as comprehensive interpretations of the right organization of schools, and the proper relation between the sexes or between parents and children. The welfare state is the institutional carrier of this modern project of liberation. Wearing headscarves, for many, is a way to deny its achievements, as is of course arranged marriages, differentiated education of girls and boys, and the practice of sending children to homeland Islamic schools for 'de-westernization', all of which are highly politicized issues in Denmark. Equality and liberation even refer to a political culture of the body, as in discussions over whether religious minorities should be given special bathing facilities in connection with public school swimming education. Such problems are generally dealt with – often sensibly – at local levels, but conflicts occasionally arise and reach public debate, when institutions refuse to provide any 'special treatment'. In a country where beach nudity is not a big deal, and where first- and second-grade boys and girls will sometimes shower together in certain schools, many regard bodily shyness and modesty as an old-fashioned, un-natural hypersensitivity which children (and their parents) should grow out of.

However, the comprehensive liberal values appear to point more than one way, except that they only rarely do so in the debate. Muslim women have argued that wearing (or not wearing) the scarf is an individual choice, which takes on an even more 'autonomous' meaning in a secular society. They have argued that the scarf is a way to break free from the sexual marketplace to participate in public life and escape the scrutiny of fathers and brothers (Mørk, 1998). It is simply indeterminate what may be construed as autonomous here, in a society characterized by increasing sexualization of public space, where minorities believe

Danish parents have taken leave of their senses when accepting G-strings, piercing and the world's highest alcohol consumption among young teenagers.

The free speech controversy following the murder of Theo van Gogh, with which we began this chapter, indicates another particularity of Danish political culture. In a TV debate (*DR-Deadline*, 14 December 2004) Shadow Cabinet member Frank Jensen's repeated argument against blasphemy legislation was the need to have a more 'open' debate. By contrast the imam Abu Laban, commenting on the depiction of 'a naked woman who performed the most sacred act of Islam – submission in front of God', thought that

> freedom of expression is not sacred, and it is wrong to use it to overstep all limits of respect for the values of others. Therefore there should be limits to how far you can go, and these limits should be discussed in open debate.
>
> (Mortensen, 2004)

The reinvigoration of the blasphemy law in fact was connected, by many Muslims, to a more general hope for a more moderate tone of debate (Krusell, 2004). Whether a rarely used law would help here may be doubted. At any rate reverence for religious symbols and sensitivities – including Christian piety – have become ridiculed non-starters. The decline of traditional (doctrinary) religion has led to 'a general dislike of religion as such, whenever it is taken seriously' (Goul Andersen, 2002: 22).

No doubt much of Western Islam assumes non-liberal versions. In Denmark as elsewhere in Europe intergenerational struggles go on about being a 'good' Muslim versus degrees of apostasy, sexual liberation and so on. My point is not that liberal states should be neutral. They should certainly tolerate, indeed respect, individual choice. However, they should also firmly facilitate the right of young people *to* choose – against patriarchal authority, traditional honour codes and new fundamentalism alike – and accept the conflicts. But the debates above nevertheless raise serious questions about parameters of belonging to a political community, about what you are allowed to do, or even forward as arguments in debate, and still be one of us.

First, it is one thing for liberal states to be non-neutral, say, in education and social policy, and quite another to adopt a discourse, let alone legislation, which holds acceptance of comprehensive liberalism to be a strict entry requirement to the political community. Even bracketing whether such standards should be met and tested in the case of old and new members alike, attempts to enforce them are not uncontroversial to liberals (Bauböck, 2001). Second, and more important, liberal values, including comprehensive interpretations of individual autonomy and free debate, are not cut in stone. Here, the framing of discourse in terms of 'our' liberal values suggests reflection on the notion of political culture advanced by Cécile Laborde, who argues that

> no more can be asked of newcomers than that they become familiar with the country's political culture in such a way as to be 'functioning' citizens'.

The very malleability of this culture entails that 'the political culture itself be one of the objects of democratic deliberation'.

(Laborde, 2002: 608–610)

In light of this appealing regulative ideal, the Danish case looks bleak. The mere existence of civic ideals as conditions of belonging is no guarantee of a non-exclusive discourse. Such ideals, when presented as tied to a particularly favourable Danish history, to Lutheran Christianity, or simply to a non-negotiable Danishness which they allegedly incarnate, can be employed as a contrast to un-liberal Islam, and constitute formidable barriers. This happens, in part, because of unwillingness to enter public interpretations about reasonable plural meanings of this quintessentially Danish 'culture'.

Conclusion

In all of Europe, Islam has become the un-liberal other. Islamic traditionalism often conflicts with liberalism, and certainly with the particular comprehensiveness of a strong egalitarianism, which emphasizes autonomy, free speech and sexual liberation. However, presenting Islam as *inherently* anti-liberal further stigmatizes large, mainly young populations, including members of emerging elites, who frame identities by presenting democratic and liberal credentials as part and parcel of a religious outlook – and who may come to resent the double standards of those native liberals who do so themselves, be it in the form of a cultural Christianity or the real thing.

Moreover, the Danish case does not raise much hope for deliberative contestation of the specific particularity of liberal political cultures, indeed for the very acceptance of alternative views as reasonable in a debate. The historical and malleable nature of political cultures tends to be denied exactly when we speak politics to culture in the name of common values. It is *not* generally the case that political culture in Laborde's sense, unlike 'wider culture' (Laborde, 2002: 610) and simply by virtue of its artificiality (is 'wider culture' not artificial?), in the words of Bhikhu Parekh, is 'comparatively easy to elucidate'.[18]

This does not render it any less important to understand and confront its parameters. However, we should expect that some of them are also cultural in the sense of unacknowledged, structuring assumptions, far too obvious to be talked about. One final aspect of Danish political culture is particularly self-supporting in this regard. A prominent politician from the Socialist People's Party, as part of a wider public debate in 2000, took issue with what she considered to be typical immigrant conceptions of democracy and political practice. Echoing Hal Koch, Christine Antorini associated Danish democracy with a concern for the common good, compromises and consensus, as opposed to strategic, interest-driven issue politics (Kehlet Christoffersen, 2002: 31–32). Whether Danish politics conforms to such standards may of course be questioned. However, the controversy conspicuously lacked any questioning of the superiority, in every respect, of (the ideology of) Danish-style democracy. By contrast anthropologists have pointed to its downsides, for instance that the obsession with equality goes along with extreme discomfort with in-group diversity and overt conflict (Knudsen, 1992). It facilitates a culture of enforced consensus, where much is left unsaid, and where newcomers are never openly initiated to norms and rituals (this would show their 'unequalness'). But it also facilitates strong sanctions – as in the free speech controversy – against those who disagree and expose the one-sidedness of the consensus, or simply stick their heads out as conspicuously different. Democracy, from the smallest circles of civil society to national politics, is egalitarian in a Rousseauan way, where civic virtue means listening to your heart and sharing the comfort of knowing that others will hear the same.[19] To Fabienne Knudsen – a French–Danish scholar incidentally – Danish discourse has become confrontational now because immigrants have only recently made it from exotic aliens to would-be equal citizens. Only now has the threat of manifest diversity *inside* the community become real (Knudsen, 2001: 14). To immigrants it may be hard to understand this peculiar aspect of political culture – outbursts against 'misplaced tolerance' mixed with unwillingness to examine what tolerance and other values might reasonably mean. Whatever else happens when new voices enter the discourse, one may hope that some of the silence about the particularity of Danish universalism could be broken, and some deep assumptions of civic superiority could become unsettled.

Notes

1 But more than a third of those who associate minorities with 'problems' score positively on measures of tolerance and willingness to accept refugees (Goul Andersen, 2002: 14).

2 Analysis of this debate is a work in progress of the author. It is a species of argument-content analysis of public and party elite discussion over the last six years (1998–2004).

3 To The Danish People's Party, in its official programme (Dansk Folkeparti, 2004), 'the culture consists in the sum of the history, experiences, faith, language and ways of life of the Danish People'. The duty to preserve the 'Danish cultural heritage' is mentioned in the first line of the programme, immediately followed by a declaration of support for the Danish monarchy. What this culture consists of, however, cannot be explicated. It is 'undefinable', unavoidable because 'it is ourselves', 'all the thousand little things' and 'the air that we breath' (Party leader Pia Kjærsgaard's speech to party conference, 15 September 2001, cited in Karpantschof, 2002).

4 From a press release on Ramadan holidays in Danish high schools (MP Louise Frevert, 20 December 2003) (Dansk Folkeparti, 2004).

5 Christian fundamentalism, in the sense of scripture-based opposition to abortion, gay church marriage and female priests, exists in certain rural areas in Denmark but its political influence historically has been negligible.

6 Danish People's Party programme, sections on 'Christianity, the People and Ethics' (Dansk Folkeparti, 2004).

7 A church minister oversees organization of the church and is final arbiter of disciplinary disputes (for example, priests who change the wording of rituals or declare themselves to be non-believers). Clergy are state employees and churches are state owned. Members of the People's Church or *Folkekirke* pay a special tax, whereas other religious communities enjoy fiscal exemptions.

8 To Hanne Severinsen of the Liberal Party, 'Through many years Denmark has been a homogeneous society … Christianity, for more than a thousand years, has enjoyed a prominent position, which has influenced and penetrated Danish society. … Some have argued that [cultural] conflicts should be solved by our removing religious symbols from the public space. … We think that the Christian cultural heritage, which is characteristic of Denmark, must be preserved. It is not … free mindedness (*frisind*), but rather a sign of unhealthy relativism, when participants in public debates demand that Christian culture should be sent home behind closed doors so as not to offend other religions. Free mindedness is a question of respect for others, but also of holding some values and choices to be more valuable than others' (Severinsen, 2002). The argument against 'relativism' is a staple of the DPP (Party programme on 'Christianity, the People and Ethics' (Dansk Folkeparti, 2004)), as well as the Conservative Party (Bendtsen, 2004).

9 Party programme sections on 'Politik'; 'Dansk kultur skal bevares og styrkes'; 'Udlændinge-og asylpolitik'; Press release 'On Karen Jespersen and humanism' (Dansk Folkeparti, 2004).

10 Hanne Dahl of the Euro-sceptical *June Movement* notes that 'when I look into your eyes, I recognize myself as human, and this makes it easier to have solidarity with you. I am not speaking of the colour of your eyes or your hair, or about ethnicity. I simply mean that we live in this here secluded geographical area where we do so and so, and can recognize (genkende) each other' (Dahl, 2000).

11 'In our daily life we do not talk much about why our society functions as well as it does, and it is probably not clear to us why Denmark, like the other Nordic countries, is so distinct from most of the rest of the world. What is the foundation for democracy, for our high production rates, for the welfare society, and for the high level of peacefulness, which has characterized the Danish society so far? It is obvious that the qualities just mentioned are internally connected, but that behind them lie certain attitudes to life, which are inherent in the concept of Danish culture. … Protection and further development of this culture is a precondition for maintaining the country as a free and enlightened society' (Party programme, section 'Dansk kultur skal styrkes og bevares' (Dansk Folkeparti, 2004)).

12 The liberal church minister argued, against a socialist MP's wish to separate Church and state, that 'she wishes to have politics and religion completely separated as in the USA, but does not realize, that the boundary she wishes to mark, is itself religiously conditioned. … Christianity constitutes the distinction … the words of Christ make it possible for Pernille Rosenkrantz-Theil and me to cooperate in parliament, because through it politics is no longer a holy matter, but a practical issue' (Fergo, 2003: 3).

13 To the Prime Minister in a recent interview, 'We have a deeply rooted democracy, which is not merely based on certain formal institutions and laws, but exists as a culture in the Danish population. … Conversation (*samtalen*) is an important part, we are very consensus-orientated, and we prefer to take the views of minorities into account' (Rasmussen, 2003a: 16).

14 'By Danish culture we often think of small gardens, village churches, *smørebrød* [the Danish open sandwich], cosyness and *Dannebrog* [the flag]. Behind these wonderful Danish symbols however, lies something deeper and more important. There lies the story of a country, which through political struggles has become one of the best in the world. Popular involvement … has created a safe and rich society, where "few have too much, and fewer too little" [Grundtvig, PM]. There lies the story of a country which, through struggles over sexual politics (*sexualpolitisk kamp*), is characterized by equal opportunities and equal treatment of men and women. Here lies the story of a country which, through democratic conversation (*samtale*) and respect for minorities has built a solid democracy' (Social Democrats, 2004: 7).

15 Party programme section on 'Immigration and Asylum Policy' (Dansk Folkeparti, 2004).
16 Very similar arguments were constantly used by the former Minister of Culture from the small Social Liberal Centre Party (for instance, Gerner Nielsen, 1999).
17 To President De Gaulle, cited in Holm (1993: 22), 'our action is directed towards goals which ... because they are French, reflect the aspirations of all mankind'.
18 B. Parekh, 'The concept of national identity', *New Community*, 21: 260, cited in Laborde (2002: 611).
19 Rousseau, in his *First Discourse*, talks of 'a state in which all the individuals being well known to one another, neither the secret machinations of vice nor the modesty of virtue should be able to escape the notice and judgment of the public; and in which the pleasant custom of seeing and knowing one another should make the love of country rather a love of the citizens than of its soil' (Rousseau, 1973: 28).

References

Bauböck, R. (2001) 'Public culture in societies of immigration', Working Paper, Malmö: IMER.
Bendtsen, B. (2004) Constitution Day Speech, 5 June 2004. Online. Available: http://www.konservative.dk/ (accessed 16 December 2004).
Brubaker, R. (1999) 'The Manichean myth: rethinking the distinction between 'civic' and 'ethnic' nationalism', in H. Kriesi (ed.) *Nation and National Identity. The European Experience in Perspective*, Zürich: Rüegger.
Dahl, H. (2000) 'Småt er godt', Interview, *Weekendavisen*, 31 March–6 April.
Danish Government (2003) *Action Plan to Promote Equal Treatment and Diversity and Combat Racism*. Online. Available: http://www.inm.dk (accessed 6 December 2004).
Dansk Folkeparti (2004) Party programme and press releases. Online. Available: http://www.danskfolkeparti.dk (accessed 15 November 2004).
Demaine, J. (2004) *Citizenship and Political Education Today*, London: Palgrave Macmillan.
Eisenstadt, S. N. and Giesen, B. (1995) 'The construction of collective identity', *Archives Europeenes de Sociologie*, 36: 72–102.
Esping-Andersen, G. (1990) *Three Worlds of Welfare Capitalism*, London: Polity Press.
EUMC/SORA (2001) *Attitudes Towards Minority Groups in the European Union*, Vienna: SORA.
Favell, A. (2001) *Philosophies of Integration*, 2nd edn, London: Palgrave.
Fergo, T. (2003) 'At skelne i sammenhængen', *Folkevirke*, 58: 3–5.
—— (2004) 'En rummelig folkekirke', *Politiken*, 11/9.
Gerner Nielsen, E. (1999). Speech to the Nordic Council of Ministers, 10 November 1999. Online. Available: http://www.norden.org (accessed 16 December 2004).
Goul Andersen, J. (2002) 'Danskernes holdninger til indvandrere', Working Paper 17/2002, Aalborg University: AMID.
Habermas, J. (2001) *The Postnational Constellation*, Cambridge: Polity Press.
Hansen, L. (2002) 'Sustaining sovereignty: the Danish approach to Europe', in L. Hansen and O. Wæver (eds) *European Integration and National Identity*, London: Routledge.
Haarder, B. (2004) 'Frygten bliver det værste', *Weekendavisen*, 19–25 March.
Hedetoft, U. (1999) 'The nation-state meets the world. national identities in the context of transnationality and cultural globalisation', *European Journal of Social Theory*, 2: 71–94.

—— (2003) 'Cultural transformation: how Denmark faces immigration', *Open Democracy*, 30 October. Online. Available: http://www.opendemocracy.net (accessed 1 January 2005).

Hervik, P. (2004) 'The Danish world of unbridgeable differences', *Ethnos*, 69: 247–267.

Holm, U. (1993) *Det franske Europa*, Aarhus: Aarhus Universitetsforlag.

Hornbech, B. (2000) 'Må vi så være her', *Jyllandsposten*, 9 September.

—— (2001) *En lige venstre*, Copenhagen: Gyldendal.

Ingram, A. (1996) 'Constitutional patriotism', *Philosophy and Social Criticism*, 22: 1–18.

Jensen, B. (2001) *Foreigners in the Danish newspaper debates from the 1870s to the 1990s*, Copenhagen: The Rockwool Foundation Research Unit.

Jespersen, K. (2003a) 'Moderne dyder', Interview, *Weekendavisen*, 3–9 January.

—— (2003b) 'Et moderne socialdemokrati', in C. Jensen, J. Jensen and T. Jensen. (eds) *Nye vinde, nye veje*. Copenhagen: Samfundslitteratur.

Karpantschof, R. (2002) 'Populism and right wing extremism in Denmark 1980–2001', Sociological report series, No. 4, Department of Sociology, Copenhagen University.

Kehlet Christoffersen, C. (2002) 'Den demokratiske barriere', in J. Schwartz (ed.) *Medborgerskabets mange stemmer*, Aarhus: Aarhus Universitetsforlag.

Knudsen, A. (1992) 'Danske dyder', *Exil*, 1: 28–34.

Knudsen, F. (2001) 'Løven og barnet. Tolerance som skalkeskjul for ulighed', *Jordens folk*, 4: 5–14.

Koch, H. (1945) *Hvad er demokrati*, Copenhagen: Gyldendal.

Korsgaard, O. (2001) 'Hal Koch: En republikaner i grundtvigiansk klædedragt', in O. Korsgaard, O. (ed.) *Poetisk demokrati – Om personlig dannelse og samfundsdannelse*, Copenhagen: Gad.Â

—— (2004) *Kampen om Folket*, Copenhagen: Gyldendal.

Krarup. S. (2000) *Dansen om menneskerettighederne*, Copenhagen: Gyldendal.

—— (2002) 'Politik og religion i Danmark', *Jyllandsposten*, 5/7.

—— (2004a) 'Længe leve folkekirken', *Kristeligt Dagblad*, 6 July.

—— (2004b) 'Ideologisk hovmod', *Weekendavisen*, 29 October–4 November.

Krauel, T. (2000) 'Was ist "deutsche Leitkultur"?', *Die Welt*, 20 October.

Kymlicka, W. (2002) *Contemporary Political Philosophy*, 2nd edn, Oxford: Oxford University Press.

Krusell, J. (2004). 'Ytringsfrihedens flydende grænse', *Berlingske Tidende*, 5 December.

Laborde, C. (2002) 'From constitutional to civic patriotism', *British Journal of Political Science*, 32: 591–612.

Lacroix, J. (2002) 'For a European constitutional patriotism', *Political Studies*, 50: 944–958.

Markell, P. (2000) 'Making affect safe for democracy? On constitutional patriotism', *Political Theory*, 28: 38–63.

Miller, D. (1995). *On Nationality*, Oxford: Oxford University Press.

Modood, T. (1994) 'Establishment, multiculturalism and British citizenship', *Political Quarterly*, 65: 53–73.

Mortensen, H. (2004) 'Dialog i eneværelse', *Weekendavisen*, 26 November–2 December.

Mouritsen, P. (1995) 'Denmark: the agonies of innocence', in B. Baumgartl and A. Favell (eds) *New Xenophobia in Europe*, London: Kluwer Law.

Mouritsen, P. and Jørgensen K. E. (eds) (forthcoming, 2006) *Constituting Communities. Political Solutions to Cultural Conflict*, London: Palgrave.

Mørk, Y. (1998) *Bindestregsdanskere*, Copenhagen: Forlaget Sociologi.

Nannestad, P. (1999) *Solidaritetens pris*, Aarhus: Aarhus Universitetsforlag.

Necef, M. Ü. (2001) 'Indvandring, den nationale stat og velfærdsstaten', in P. Seeberg (ed.) *Ubekvemme udfordringer*, Odense: Odense Universitetsforlag.

Nielsen, H. J. (2002) 'De udenlandske rapporter om danskernes uvilje mod fremmede', *Nyt fra Rockwool Fondens Forskningsenhed*, June.

Østergaard, U. (1991) 'Peasants and Danes: the Danish national identity and political culture', *Comparative Studies in Society and History*, 34: 3–27.

Parekh, B. (2000) *Rethinking Multiculturalism. Cultural Diversity and Political Theory*, Basingstoke: Macmillan.

Pittelkow, R. (2004) *Forsvar for nationalstaten*, Copenhagen: Lindhardt & Ringhof.

Rasmussen, A. F. (2003a) 'Demokratiets pris', Interview, *Danmarksposten*, 84: 16–19.

———— (2003b) The Prime Minister's New Years' Speech 2003. Online. Available: http://www.dr.dk/pubs/nyheder/html/nyheder/baggrund/tema2002/taler/ (accessed 14 December 2004).

Rawls, J. (1993) *Political Liberalism*, New York: Columbia University Press.

Redder, G. (2004) 'S vil fastholde danske værdier', *Ugebrevet A-4*, 6 September. Online. Available: http://www.ugebreveta4.dk (accessed 1 January 2005).

Rousseau, J.-J. (1973) *The Social Contract and Discourses*, London: Dent, Dutton.

Rudolf, T. (2003) 'Debating headscarves in Europe', Paper presented to the Conference *What's the Culture in Multiculturalism? What's the Difference of Identities?*, University of Aarhus, 22–24 May.

Severinsen, H. (2002) 'Kristne værdier skal ikke relativeres'. Online. Available: http://www.hanneseverinsen.dk/Laeserbreve/kristne.htm (accessed 22 November 2004).

Social Democrats (2004) *Principprogram 2004: Hånden på hjertet*. Online. Available: http://www.socialdemokratiet.dk (accessed 22 November 2004).

Taylor, C. (1989) 'Cross-purposes: the Liberal-Communitarian debate', in N. Rosenblum (ed.) *Liberalism and the Moral Life*, Cambridge, MA: Harvard University Press.

Togeby, L. (1998a) 'Prejudice and tolerance in a period of increasing ethnic diversity and growing unemployment: Denmark since 1970', *Ethnic and Racial Studies*, 21: 1137–1154.

———— (1998b) 'Danskerne og det multikulturelle', *Politica* 30: 184–203.

———— (2004) *Man har et standpunkt*, Aarhus: Aarhus Universitetsforlag.

———— (2002) *Etniske minoriteters deltagelse i demokratiske processer, herunder politiske partier, valg og offentlig debat*, AMID Working Paper 20/2002, Aalborg University: AMID.

Tranæs, T. and Zimmermann, K. F. (2004) *Migrants, Work, and the Welfare State*, Odense: Syddansk Universitetsforlag.

6 Enemies within the gates

The debate about the citizenship of Muslims in Germany*

Werner Schiffauer

Introduction

A sense of moral panic underlies the current debate about Islam in Germany which is apparent in discussions concerning citizenship, religious minority rights and access to public funds. The hypothesis of this chapter is that this panic is only partly motivated by fear of Islamic terrorism since 11 September 2001 and Beslan,[1] but instead additionally reflects the change in Turkish migrants' civic status. The growing number of naturalizations turns '*Ausländer*' (foreigners) into citizens and threatens to change the balance of power between those who are 'established' and the 'outsiders' (Elias and Scotson, 1993). Immigrants who were hitherto considered different and unequal and who have been, in German politics, taken care of, rather than integrated into the political system, are increasingly becoming citizens who fight for their rights and seek to establish them by democratic means. This leads to fears of losing control of key issues of German society: The reaction to it is moral panic.

The term 'moral panic' was coined by Stanley Cohen when analysing the Clacton disturbances in 1964 (Cohen, 1972). It was taken up and systematized by Goode and Ben Yehuda (1994). The concept refers to states of collective hysteria which periodically appear in civil societies. They are characterized by (1) a strong concern 'over the behaviour of a certain group or category and the consequences that that behavior presumably causes for the rest of society' (Goode and Yehuda, 1994: 33); (2) an increased level of hostility towards that particular group implying a division between 'us' and 'them' (*ibid.*: 33); (3) a remarkable consensus between actors which usually hold widely divergent views, such as journalists, politicians, scientists and the security forces (*ibid.*: 34); (4) an exaggerated representation of the threats and a disproportionate reaction to them (*ibid.*: 36); and (5) a certain volatility. After a fairly sudden eruption of moral panic, it gradually subsides (*ibid.*: 38). The examples Goode and Ben Yehuda refer to are the prohibition movement, the crusade for anti-marijuana legislation in the 1930s, and the sexual psychopath laws of the 1930s to the 1950s. A much more powerful example, however, is provided by the McCarthy era which, incidentally, is not mentioned by the authors. The fear of communism during the 1950s and the fear of Islam today have strong similarities. In both cases a reflex reaction to an external threat is connected with fears concerning the loss of control over internal affairs.

In this chapter I shall attempt to illustrate how this moral panic functions. To this end, I shall analyse policies and public reactions with regard to three domains in which the change of civic status becomes apparent: (1) *Citizenship*: The refusal to grant citizenship to members of conservative Muslim organizations by some *Länder* (German federal states) reflects the attempt to limit the influence of unwanted immigrants and to maintain control over them. In the current atmosphere of moral panic, this endeavour follows the logic of a purification rite. (2) *Minority rights*: The success of Muslims in gaining legal recognition for minority rights[2] has stirred intense reaction in Germany. Migrants turning to the courts with regard to minority rights was widely considered to be an abuse of those courts. Widespread public irritation in Germany finally led to a witch-hunt. For example, Fereshta Ludin, who achieved partial success in the fight for her right to wear the headscarf as a public school teacher, was demonized in a smear campaign. (3) *Access to public funds*: The case of the organization Muslim Youth, the funding of which was suddenly cut off, shows how the logic of rumour operates in the general atmosphere of moral panic.

The public reaction to the Muslim quest for civil rights in Germany

German society has only recently abandoned the self-delusion that it is not an immigration country. Against all demographic and sociological evidence, German politics and society long maintained the illusion of guest-workers who would (or could) some day return to their home countries. Foreigners were associated with, rather than integrated into, German society. Although German society has meanwhile accepted the fact 'that they will stay', it is still extremely reluctant to face the consequences of having to become an immigration country. The relationship between majority society and immigrants continues to be structured by the 'us' and 'them' distinction.

This is particularly evident in the political field. Migrants were essentially long seen as objects of politics. A patronizing attitude continues to prevail to the present day. Migrants who have demands, for example with regard to the construction of a mosque, are well advised to find some German politician to take up their interests and represent them in the institutions. No less telling are public discussions in which German experts discuss migrant issues mostly among themselves, in some cases supplemented by a few hand-picked migrants. This patronage has been institutionalized in the Office of the Ausländerbeauftragten, an office which functions as an ombudsman for foreigners, taking up migrant issues and representing their demands to state institutions.

The challenge migrants posed by actively voicing their demands themselves is succinctly summed up in an interview given by Ahmet Iyidirly in April 2004:

At some point in time we said we want to be subjects. We did not say it explicitly but implicitly, by acting: We want to be subjects. We want to participate, to exert influence, or to decide. Like that. They have never liked that – not up to the present day. As long as we remain objects, we are the nice guys. But as soon as we try to become subjects or to operate as emancipated citizens, they do not like it, not even today.

(Iyidirli, 2004)

It is important to note that the speaker is a secular Social Democrat of Turkish origin. The irritation caused by migrants who speak up for themselves and begin to exert their citizenship rights actively by claiming rights and demanding access to funds is by no means restricted to Muslims. It is, however, particularly outspoken when it refers to Muslims, especially conservative ones who symbolize the quintessential 'Other' for a great part of the German public. Their fight for the right to difference as an integral part of their citizen status arouses suspicion and fear. Especially with regard to the Muslim population, worries exist that a growing number of naturalization processes – which turn foreigners into citizens – will change the power structure between the established inhabitants and the outsiders, perhaps not in the society as a whole, but certainly in regions or districts of massive immigration. As Klaus Böger put it with regard to attempts to introduce Islamic education in schools:

I think that the question Islam/Islamic teaching activates concern and fears in our population. Being a politician, I can feel that … [t]here is the fear that the presence of Islam, and of Muslims, might gradually change our culture, which is occidental through and through.

(Böger, 2000: 4)

The fear of terrorism adds to a widespread concern that the situation is getting out of control. As the term 'Islamism' refers both to internal challenges and to external threats, both tend to be merged.[3] It is the naturalization of the Muslim Others which confronts German society with the problem of the true stranger, with 'the man who comes today and stays tomorrow' (Simmel, 1971: 143). The Muslim Other confronts German society with the problem of ambivalence which Zygmunt Bauman (1991) has so brilliantly analysed. They are neither friend – as practising Muslims they represent a culture which has been and still is considered to be the quintessential Other to the 'Christian Occident' – nor enemy – because they live and work in Germany and intend to stay. They are strangers who challenge the 'master opposition between the *inside* and the *outside*' (Bauman, 1991: 53). They represent disorder and this causes the fear of loss of ability to act. 'The main symptom of disorder is the acute discomfort we feel when we are unable to read the situation properly and to choose between alternative actions' (*ibid.*: 1).

The majority of Muslims in Germany are Sunnis of Turkish origin. They are represented by several competing organizations. The divisions between the

Sunni organizations refer to different opinions about the role of Islam in Turkey. The focus on Turkey reflected the desire someday to 'return home' prevalent in the early years of migration. Only two of the communities accepted at that time the secular Turkish Republic: the DİTİB (Turkish–Islamic Union of the Office of Religion) represents official state Islam in Turkey and favours a position which restricts Islam to the private sphere, while the semi-fascist 'associations of idealists' (or Grey Wolves) work for a Turkish–Islamic synthesis. The four other major organizations rejected the secular Constitution of the Turkish Republic until the early 1990s: the Islamic Community Milli Görüş is the European branch of the Islamist party founded by Necmettin Erbakan in Turkey in 1968.[4] The latter favoured, and still favours, a parliamentary path towards the Islamization of Turkey. The Caliphate state, which broke off from Milli Görüş in 1983, saw in an Islamic revolution the only way to establish an Islamic Republic. After being outlawed in 2001, it has worked underground. Also critical of the secular state at that time were the Süleymanci and the Nurcu, both of which have their roots in mystical Islam. During the 1990s, two important developments took place: Milli Görüş, the Nurcu and the Süleymancl replaced the goal of overthrowing the regime in Turkey with newly developed visions of working within the system instead. Only the Caliphate state has maintained its revolutionary outlook to this day. More important still was a reorientation towards Europe related to the coming of age of a second generation. Milli Görüş, the Süleymancl, the Nurcu and factions of the 'associations of the idealists' took up the challenge and are currently in the process of developing perspectives of a diasporic Islam defining a role for Islam in a non-Muslim environment. The 1990s also saw the development of new groups. Particularly second-generation high school and university students were often dissatisfied with the sometimes extremely narrow confines of ethnically based communities and founded new organizations of Muslims of mixed ethnic background using German as a lingua franca. Muslim Youth mentioned below is one of these groups. A general characteristic of current developments is a stronger emphasis on religion and international Islam replacing the traditional focus on homeland politics. Remarkably enough, the one organization not taking up the challenge of developing a European outlook is the DİTİB, which, as an organization funded and organized by the Turkish state, retains the homeland-based approach.[5]

Muslim citizens

In the past, the question of membership of Muslim organizations played no role in the naturalization process.[6] This has changed considerably due to the impact of 9/11. Two of Germany's federal states, Bavaria and Baden-Württemberg, already check the database of the Verfassungsschutz (the Internal Intelligence Service)[7] in all naturalization processes; and there are demands, particularly by members of the conservative CDU, to extend this practice to other federal states as well. If the Verfassungsschutz has information about the applicant's active membership of a Muslim organization that is judged unconstitutional (again, by the Verfassungsschutz's own standards), the application for citizen-ship is usually turned down even if the organization is not forbidden by law. The Verfassungsschutz is thus, in practice, though not by the Constitution, given considerable definitional power. Statements by the Verfasssungsschutz are generally accepted as *Behördenzeugnis* (testimony of a state agency) by the courts and deemed authoritative. Integration and naturalization become a security matter, to be decided by the Verfassungsschutz.

The office of the Verfassungsschutz is thus endowed with the task of solving the problem of the ambivalence of the Muslim Other. It has to draw the lines between inside and outside. The intention to delineate categorically the 'real' versus the 'misguided' Muslims becomes quite apparent in the concept of an exhibition organized by the Federal Office of the Verfassungsschutz which neatly sums up the office's assessment:

> The exhibition's aim is to inform the population about the threats of Islamism in order to counter the 'hostility against Islam caused by the widespread fear of Islamic Terrorism and a general lack of information concerning the varieties of Islam'.
>
> (Bundesamt für Verfassungsschutz, 2004: 1)

According to the Office, drawing a clear line between Islam and Islamism can help to improve the situation of Muslims in Western society. Islamism itself is again to be differentiated in three subcategories. Subcategory A refers 'to Islamist groups which conduct a pan-Islamist jihad (holy war) and threaten worldwide stability through terrorist acts' (*ibid.*: 5). Subcategory B refers to

> Islamist organizations which want to change the state and society in the countries of origin by violent means [by terrorist acts or by guerrilla warfare]. Members of these organizations have come to Germany mostly as political refugees and support from armed actions in regions of crisis.

Examples given are HAMAS, GIA, Hizb Allah, etc. (*ibid.*: 6). Finally, subcate-gory C refers to organizations 'which fight for Islamist positions in the context of the social life of the Federal Republic or at least try to establish spaces for organized Islamist engagement'. Examples are the Islamic Community Milli Görüş or Muslim Brotherhood (*ibid.*: 6). Subcategory C, of course, poses a special classificatory problem. The groups belonging to category C declare their allegiance to the German Constitution and explicitly refrain from violence as a means of political action. This is also recognized by the Office of the Verfassungsschutz. According to Erhart Körting, Berlin Senator of the Interior, in a Verfassungschutz conference in Berlin on 30 October 2003, however, those groups resort to 'subtle means' in order to pursue their basic aim, that is to establish a state in which Islam is the dominant religion and where freedom of religion and freedom of expression are abolished. Members of organizations classified as 'category C' are thus also put into the Islamist camp. This has far-reaching implications such as the refusal to grant citizenship on the grounds that they belong to organizations working against the Constitution and are registered on an 'Islamist file' which has been set up in the fight against terrorism.

The distinction between real Islam ('religion') and Islamism ('ideology') is drawn primarily by German politics and the Verfassungsschutz. Muslim authorities are hardly referred to when making this distinction. In fact, only Muslims supporting this distinction are accepted as partners in the debate. *Ulema* (Muslim scholars) questioning it would immediately and by this very act qualify themselves as Islamists and be deemed partisan. The self-confidence with which German politicians and intellectuals judge what is or is not Islamic is one of the debate's most striking features.[8]

It is, of course, in 'category C' referring to 'law abiding Islamists working with subtle methods' that this endeavour becomes particularly problematic. A closer look at the developments taking place within Milli Görüş brings to the fore some of the difficulties connected with it. Members of Milli Görüş emphasize that the difference between Muslims and Islamists is not the distinction which is crucial to them. As believers, their key point of reference is the revelation and the consequences which are to be derived from it in present-day society. The first generation in the community dreamed of Islamizing Turkey in the 1980s and 1990s. These dreams referred to a rather vague vision of establishing a 'just society' on the basis of an Islamic moral order. Among the members living as labour migrants in Europe, this vision was related to the hope that an Islamized Turkey would allow them to return home. On that basis, they supported the welfare party of Necmettin Erbakan. A second generation, born, or at least raised, in Germany, took over the leadership positions in the community during the late 1990s. Whereas the first generation had been oriented towards Turkey, the second generation consists of Germans (in an existential, though not necessarily legal, sense) of Turkish descent and has a definite European outlook. This changes everything, as the essential task facing this generation is to draw consequences from the spiritual message for life in Germany and other immigration countries. According to the members of this generation who are in leadership positions, migration created a situation novel to Islam, as Islamic law did not foresee the case of Muslims staying permanently in non-Muslim territory. According to them, this is a challenge (and a chance) for the development of an Islamic law on minorities. They feel that this would be absolutely compatible with the European rule of law, as the latter guarantees freedom of religion. They also feel that the European welfare state is a solution for the problem of solidarity and could serve as a role model for the Islamic world. They are critical about positions which claim that a veritable Islamic life is only possible within the framework of an Islamic state (which would only allow either withdrawal or a revolutionary outlook for a Muslim living in Europe). They are also critical about Muslims who favour a hermeneutic and historicizing approach to Islam, because they feel that this would relativize the revelation. But all this does not mean that these points are expressed by other members of the community or banned from discussion. The only clear boundary drawn is to terrorist Islam, which is considered to be clearly against the spirit of the religion (Schiffauer, 2004).

Members of the Verfassungsschutz concede that they see some development within Milli Görüş.[9] There seem to be several reasons why they nevertheless insist on clear and absolute boundaries between Muslims and Islamists (including Milli Görüş). They are related to the organizational duty of a security service to avert all kinds of possible threats to democracy. This implies professional suspicion. If the leadership of an organization that has a record of radicalism claims that it has changed, the authorities quite naturally react with scepticism. Second, it is only rational for the Verfassungsschutz to be overly cautious since it runs a greater risk if it oversees a danger than if it treats someone unjustly. For these reasons, the Verfassungsschutz screens Milli Görüş for signs that it is still Islamist.

It is telling what kind of arguments are presented to strengthen the claim that Milli Görüş is Islamist. One group of arguments refers to the fact that Milli Görüş in Europe is still closely tied to the Saadet Partisi in Turkey which, after the reformist AKP under Erdoğan split off, indulges in straightforward Islamist rhetoric and thus provides ample material for the Verfassungsschutz.[10] A second group of arguments refers to the claims by Milli Görüş in Europe that it pursues a different agenda from Milli Görüş in Turkey. In order to counter this claim, the reports of the Verfassungsschutz provide an infiltration scenario. What is seen by Milli Görüş as a struggle for a space for Muslims is interpreted as an attempt thus to establish Muslim spaces. This is interpreted as the first step to creating a parallel society with the aim of establishing areas outside of the control of the German state and under the control of Milli Görüş. These would serve as a power base in the struggle for an Islamic state, both in the home country and in the country of immigration. In the short term, the Muslim organizations would establish themselves as gatekeepers. The Verfassungsschutz has ignored explicit and repeated statements that Milli Görüş has no intention of setting up a parallel society[11] and in some cases even resorts to distorting those statements.[12] Against this background, a campaign addressed to the believers to acquire German citizenship, which could be read as an attempt at integration, can be interpreted as a sign of infiltrating the German electorate.[13] The organization of social work, which could be interpreted as self-organization assisting integration, is interpreted as a sign of separation.[14]

There is, of course, no way objectively to settle which interpretation is correct, either Milli Görüş's own interpretation, which could be dictated by enlightened self-interest, or the scenario advanced by the Verfassungsschutz, which is dictated by institutional suspicion related to its duty to analyse developments which might pose a risk for German society. It can be safely argued, however, that an organization binds itself by public statements in an open society (Luhmann, 1968) with regard both to its members as well as to outsiders. It cannot abruptly change its course without risking friction or undermining co-operation. It can also be argued that any step into society – be it by acquiring citizenship or by frequenting institutions of higher education – develops its own dynamic, which can only partially be controlled by the organization.

The problem with Verfassungsschutz's professional distrust is that it leaves Milli Görüş without a chance. The more carefully the community moves, the more minute the details become which are taken as signs to show that the organization is unconstitutional after all. A highlight so far is an article on the website of the Verfassungsschutz in Baden-Württemberg in which specific bathing trunks were considered to be against the spirit of the Constitution. Under the heading: 'Activities of the IGMG (Islamic Community Milli Görüş) question their willingness to integrate' it said:

> The youth organization of the IGMG Düsseldorf region announced an event in the Düsseldorf Unterrath public bath on March 31. The appeal was directed to male youngsters older than eleven years. It was requested that they should be dressed according to Islamic rules (in this case meaning bathing trunks covering the body between knee and navel. The IGMG evidently considers it to be appropriate to distance itself from the majority society by ostentatious emphasis on religious rules.
>
> (http://www.verfassungsschutz-bw.de, accessed 10 December 2004)

It can be only explained by the strength of the infiltration scenario that the passage quoted above passed the control mechanisms of the organization without anybody taking offence. The suspicious reading of Milli Görüş's activities culminates in the fact that practically everything can be used against it. It is here that the quest for clear classifications turns into an obsession with boundary lines which suspects dangerous transgressions everywhere.[15]

As Zygmunt Bauman has shown, the categorical enterprise which aims at dissolving the ambivalence of the stranger is within the logic of all modern nation-states. A specificity of German civil culture[16] adds to its salience (Schiffauer, 1997a). In Germany, unlike, for example, the Netherlands, it is often stated that granting citizenship is the conclusive act of the integration process (and not its beginning). This is related to a widespread conviction that societal exchange can only function properly if every participant identifies with the common good or the political community as a whole. This identification is usually formulated in a manner indicating that freedom should be exercised in a responsible way. This type of identification with the common good differs from the identification with rules which is demanded in France and in Britain. I have the impression that in both countries there is a feeling of trust that the common good will prevail only if the social preliminaries are correct: in France, if equality is established and the individuals keep to the rules; in Britain, if the rules of liberty remain inviolate and the rules of combat are observed. In both cases (1) affirmation of the rules is demanded, which then permits (2) ordered social competition, which finally (3) results in the formation of the common good. This trust in rules working is missing in Germany's political culture. There is the feeling that rules can easily be bent or manipulated in order to favour one's own strategic interest. The identification with the whole aims at avoiding these pitfalls of pure rule orientation. Commitment only to the rules of the game appears unsatisfactory, as 'merely external': before and in addition to the affirmation of the rule, an inner identification with the general well-being is demanded.[17] One cannot and may not participate in the free exchange until the *bien commun* has been internalized. This scepticism is often justified by the Nazi takeover of power in 1933 through perfectly legal means, which demonstrated that undemocratic movements can turn to democratic means in order to gain power.[18] The frequently heard statement that the 'acquisition of citizenship is the conclusion and not the beginning of the integration process' is related to this understanding of rules. Also related is an extremely frequent reference to the 'spirit of the Constitution' rather than to 'the letter of the Constitution'.

In a civil culture where identification with the whole is deemed a condition for social participation, the problem of ambiguity poses itself more radically than in others. Can one accept this inner (and hence invisible) affirmation from someone who has grown up in a different culture? After all, perhaps 'the outsider' only identifies her/himself externally with the common good; does such a person really consider *her/himself* committed? The obsession with the inner affirmation together with the attempt to resolve ambivalence by creating classificatory clarity result in a paranoid discourse: Nothing is so trivial that it cannot serve as a sign of a problematic attitude.

An analysis of immigration authority hearings is telling. They are organized when somebody who is suspected of belonging to an organization, in this case Milli Görüş, which pursues aims against the Constitution, applies for citizenship. A reading of the protocols shows that the hearings are a farce. In a hearing conducted in the Aschaffenburg Landratsamt (District Council Office) on 3 June 2003, the person interviewed distanced himself from all kinds of terrorist acts and Islamist statements, swore his allegiance to the Constitution, and declared that he sees no contradiction between Islam and democracy. Such efforts, however, did not help. The fact that he had been on the executive committee of a Milli Görüş mosque weighed heavier than any declaration. In the end, the person presiding over the hearing suggested that he should withdraw his application. It would cost more if he maintained it and were turned down (Landratsamt Aschaffenburg, 2003).

Claiming rights

Muslim communities have been quite successful in turning to the courts in their fight for rights such as dispensation from co-ed swimming lessons or school trips. Two cases in which Muslims managed to get favourable decisions from the Supreme Court received particular public attention. In 2002, Muslims won the right to perform ritual slaughter; in 2003, Muslims had a partial victory in a decision relating to the wearing of the headscarf by teachers. In essence, it was ruled that a teacher's headscarf does not per se violate the Constitution and cannot be forbidden on the basis of existing laws (see below). These court verdicts have led to considerable irritation. It is noteworthy that there is a widespread feeling of foul play among the German population. It is as if the Constitution, which was set up after the experience of the Nazi era and which is generally hailed as supreme, was not made for *this kind* of people or as a colleague of mine put it: 'The fathers of the constitution did not think about Muslims when they were drafting it.' One of the gatekeepers of the Christian–Muslim dialogue, Johannes Kandel from the Friedrich-Ebert Stiftung, clearly articulated his irritation about what he considers to be an abuse of the courts:

> Muslim representatives should ask themselves what kind of practices could be considered offensive in a non-Muslim environment (e.g. the call to prayer or ritual slaughter) and how a balance based on mutual respect could be achieved between Islamic cultural practices and the culture of the majority society. However, they try to push through *their* interpretation of Islam by means of the German courts.
>
> (Kandel, n.d.: 6)

This quotation is remarkable for several reasons. On the one hand, it is clear that it is dictated by an 'us–them' distinction. It is clearly not the case that one group belonging 'to us' is fighting for a right, but rather that the 'Muslim representatives' are clearly marked as newcomers. They should secondly not claim legal rights as a group but consider what is offensive to the majority of society (it seems to be taken as self-evident what the majority feels or thinks). This follows closely the rhetoric of the guest-worker who should simply adapt or leave. Finally, it is claimed that the organization abuses German courts and laws in order to pursue its particular aims. This argument consists of two sub-arguments: (1) the organizations do not represent Islam as such but only *their* version of Islam (implying that their version is a minority one); and (2) they use their version not out of conviction, but strategically, in order to mobilize for their cause and to install themselves as gatekeepers.

> What motivates the organizations to take the headscarf as an index for the acceptance of their religious community and as a yardstick of tolerance and religious freedom? What is taking place here is a struggle for maintaining one's position and dominance.
>
> (*ibid.*: 7).[19]

The courts are often reprimanded for deciding the way they do, which is interpreted as giving in to the will of the Muslims. In an article in *Der Spiegel*, to which we will return below, the argument is as follows:

> In court proceedings about the issue whether a mosque of alien character would fit into a neighbourhood, the courts almost always decide in favour

of the Muslims. Already in 1992, the Federal Court decided that non-Muslim neighbours generally have to accept being woken up before sunrise when believers come by car to morning prayer.

(*Der Spiegel*, No. 40, 29 September 2003: 94)

How carelessly German courts ignore the suppression of girls in favour of the parents' religious freedom is reflected by a decision by the Bundesverwaltungsgericht (Federal Administrative Court): a Muslim girl can be exempted from swimming lessons if these are not sexually segregated (*ibid*.: 86).[20]

Not infrequently, a court decision is followed by a debate as to whether the laws should be changed. A widespread reaction to these court verdicts is an unwillingness by the administration to put the decisions into practice, sometimes reasoning that the courts 'unfortunately' could not deliver other verdicts on the basis of existing laws. After a verdict was handed down that the Islamische Föderation (Islamic Federation) may offer religious education in school, the administration resorted to delaying tactics until it was forced by another court order to execute the judgment.[21] After a verdict was delivered that ritual slaughter is generally legal, ritual slaughter actually became more difficult than ever. What had previously been arranged on an informal, and often ad hoc, basis now had to be achieved by legal proceedings.

Most court decisions have been grudgingly accepted by the German public, without causing much reaction. However, this changed with the headscarf decision by the Bundesverfassungsgericht (Federal Constitutional Court) in September 2003. The case was brought to the court by Fereshta Ludin with the support of Muslim organizations hoping for a favourable precedent. The court (ending five years of litigation) decided that, on the basis of existing laws, Ms Ludin cannot be denied the right to teach in school. The judgment weighed freedom of religion against neutrality in the schools, demanding that the Parliaments of the *Länder* (responsible for the school system) should pass additional laws either generally forbidding or generally allowing teachers to wear religious garb.

Although it was a decision not to decide, it triggered an intensive and extremely emotional debate. The key reasons for it seem to be that a teacher is a *Beamter* according to German law. The term *Beamter* can only loosely be translated as 'public servant', as its role is quite specific to German political culture. The *Beamter*, as representative of the state, supposedly stands above and beyond social conflicts. The *Beamter* can be said to be charged with the task of representing the common good, which, as I argued above, is so crucial for German civil culture. One of the key aspects of this role is its neutrality: a *Beamter* may not strike and in her/his duties may not show any allegiance to political parties. Religious symbols, such as the habit, did not seem to infringe the neutrality of the school. This changed with the Ludin case. By winning her case, Muslims appeared to have conquered a citadel of German civil culture. In the public debate that followed, the headscarf was identified as a symbol of totalitarian politics and associated with the swastika (for example, see Amir-Moazami, 2004: 139); it was seen as a symbol of intolerance (*ibid.*: 136) and of inequality (*ibid.*: 139). The headscarf stood for the very opposite of the democratic, tolerant and egalitarian society the Bundesrepublik likes to consider itself to be.

The reaction was a smear campaign against Ludin which extremely personalized and emotionalized the issue. The campaign was started by Alice Schwarzer in the feminist magazine *EMMA*. It culminated in a leader in *Der Spiegel* (No. 40, 29 September 2003: 82–97)[22]. The article is worth analysing, not only because *Der Spiegel* is an extremely influential political weekly, but also because the article develops a widely supported line of argument. After an introduction to the case, *Der Spiegel* turns to Ludin with the following statement:

> She wants to be treated better than her fellow citizens. ... Freedom of religion has a limit when it aims (in the very name of freedom of religion) at undermining or abolishing that freedom. This is basically the aim of Islamic Fundamentalists whose flag is among other things the headscarf.
>
> (*ibid.*: 83)

The article then quotes Alice Schwarzer, who had claimed that Ludin had refused to shake hands with men and had allegedly declared that German women were impure, without mentioning that Ludin had denied having made the latter statement. Then the text goes on:

> Ms Ludin demands tolerance for intolerance. The severe headscarf-fetishists from the Islamic Council and the 'Central Council of Muslims in Germany' who supported her case distinguish themselves from most Islamic associations active in Germany by their strange understanding of the democratic rule of law. ... It is respected only until one is in a position to abolish it wherever possible in order to install a theocracy without separation of the powers of the state and the church. The self-appointed 'Caliph' Metin Kaplan, whose deportation to Turkey was stopped by the courts, once confessed: 'Islam and democracy can never be reconciled. When we take power we will destroy and burn down the parliament and distribute the ashes in the sea.' ... The Iranian supreme Shiite Ayatollah Khomeini has referred to human rights as a 'collection of rules thought up by Zionists' who wish to destroy all true religion. ... Certainly one should not identify Ms Ludin with Kaplan or Khomeini. There are enough Muslims who fight for modernization of their religion. The Egyptian author Farag Ali Foda demanded modernization of Islam by saying: 'We Muslims lack a Martin Luther.' And the Iranian professor of history Hashem Agadshari criticized the Mullah state by saying: 'Men are not apes who have to imitate a cleric. ... What kind of religion is one that justifies torture?' Foda, however, was murdered because of his heresies in 1992, and the Iranian historian was arrested and condemned to 74 whiplashes, 10 years prohibition of exercising his profession, 8 years prison, and in the end,

unless pardoned, death by hanging. ... Has the teacher Ludin ever explicitly distanced herself from this variant of Islamic purity? It is not known yet.

(*ibid.*: 84)

The eleven-page article passes on to the Rushdie affair, suicide bombers, honour disputes, violence against women, parallel societies, migrant quarters. The most striking feature of the article is that the arguments are almost never put into context. People, places and times are constantly conflated. In the passage quoted, the two Muslim umbrella organizations that supported the case are associated with Metin Kaplan, the head of the Islamist Caliphate state, without mentioning that the sectarian Caliphate state never was a member of either of the general organizations. Also, it is not mentioned that both umbrella organizations (unlike the Caliphate state) never declared an Islamic Republic to be their aim. The article then turns to the 'Supreme Shiite' although all protagonists so far mentioned are Sunnites. The concession that one should not identify Ludin with Kaplan or Metin is immediately withdrawn, as it is followed by the statement that the German Muslim Ludin did not distance herself from atrocities that happened in Egypt and in Iran, the Foda case having taken place eleven years before the trial while Ludin was still in high school.

The first aspect of this article is its strong emotive drive. The arguments follow the logic of displacement and not that of rational discussion. They are not presented in a way which would allow the reader to distance her/himself, to weigh up the arguments, or to reflect on the exact nature of the relations postulated (for example, between the umbrella organizations and the Caliphate state, or the relationship of the local and the global in Islam). Instead, the reader is drawn into an argumentation which constantly shifts in space and time. The emotive message conveyed is fury about Muslim presumptuousness and fear which evidently allows the reader and the author to pass over the logical flaws in the argument.

The article is secondly a remarkable testimony both to the personalization of a social demand and to its complete depersonalization. Although Ludin figures prominently in the article, there is no attempt to portray her point of view or, for that matter, that of the organizations that supported the case either. The case of a practising Muslim trying to become a teacher in German schools is not interpreted as an attempt somehow to reconcile the necessities of professional life with religious convictions. Nothing is written about the complex reasons leading an increasing number of young Muslim women in Germany to decide to wear the headscarf. Ludin thus is reduced to a mask. The technique used here is prosopopoeia (Menke, 1998). *Prosopon* is the mask which gives an abstract entity a voice (and a face). In this case, it is the abstract Muslim threat that appears in the person of Fereshta Ludin.[23] She was made into a condensed symbol[24] of a public enemy.[25] After all, she was the teacher who had dared to 'carry her headscarf up to the constitutional courts' (Vera Gaserow, *Tagesspiegel*, 7 November 2003).

The result of this article was the demonization of Ludin. After it appeared, her reputation was ruined. All the fury and fear which set the tone of the article was directed against her person. In public discussions, her name became synonymous with Islamism. In the Ludin case, an example was made. It was demonstrated what happens if a Muslim dares to go 'up to the Verfassungs-gericht [Constitutional Court]'. After having received threats, Fereshta Ludin is today living anonymously in Berlin. She has the feeling that it makes no sense to continue to fight. Any school which would employ her would run the risk of a parents' initiative protesting against a 'fundamentalist' teaching their children.

How intensely young Muslim women perceive the latent threat to Muslims who fight for their rights is reflected by the statement of a young Turkish Muslim woman quoted in Amir-Moazami. She said that she would not fight for her rights:

> because then everyone would say, 'Go back to Turkey', and then they would not necessarily be a Nazi, or something like that. But it would just mean, 'Listen up, if you don't like it here, then you can leave.' And I would be satisfied with that in the first place, because what right do I have to reshape everything here as I would like to have it? ... This is why I would first of all do everything right in my country, and then I might continue here.
>
> (J., 19 years old, Berlin, quoted in Amir-Moazami, 2004: 232)

This quotation brings to the fore the consequences of the hostile attitude of German society towards new citizens claiming their rights. Whereas Fereshta Ludin had fought for the right to wear the headscarf because she considered herself German, the young Muslim woman quoted above quite clearly has the perception that German society is withholding this right, and she consequently defines herself as an outsider without full rights and orients herself towards her home country.

Access to public funds: the case of Muslim Youth

Muslim Youth was founded by young Muslims in 1994. A group of German-speaking second-generation Muslim high school students and students who had met in summer camps decided to set up their own organization. Engagement in Muslim Youth was attractive because it promised a Muslim engagement beyond the narrow confines of the ethnically homogeneous Islamic Communities set up by the first generation. In Muslim Youth they would meet other young Muslims from different ethnic backgrounds. They emphasized spirituality and a transna-tional outlook. There was a decided attempt to remain independent from the other organizations. According to its self-description, the aim of the organiza-tion was 'to help Muslim youngsters to integrate into society as self-confident young Muslims and to consider themselves members of this society. At the same time, the aim is to uphold and maintain Muslim identity.' During its existence, Muslim Youth organized several projects. The project 'Trialog – Together in Difference' was organized in co-operation with the Katholische junge

Gemeinde (Catholic Young Community) and the Bundesverband der jüdischen Studenten in Deutschland (Federal Association of Jewish Students in Germany). The three organizations presented their project on inter-religious dialogue at the ecumenical Kirchentag (Church Convention) in Berlin in May 2003. The project in question, *Ta'ruf*, was conceived to address Muslim young-sters growing up in immigration regions. The intention was to develop strategies to counter racism, prejudice and violence. The idea was also to dispel preconceived and traditional ideas about religion and to counteract the instru-mentalization of Islam for the justification of aggressive behaviour. The teams organized workshops in youth centres, vocational schools and mosques. Teams were composed of immigrants from different cultural backgrounds and were mostly, but not exclusively, Muslims. To my knowledge, this was the only project run by a Muslim organization ever funded by a state agency in Germany (in this case, the Ministry of the Interior). On 6 November 2003, newspaper articles appeared in the *Tagesspiegel* (a leading Berlin newspaper) and the *Frankfurter Rundschau* (an important liberal/left-wing newspaper) which started to question Muslim Youth in general and threw the funding of the project into doubt. In particular three arguments were raised.

The first argument was that Muslim Youth would use public funds in order 'to proselytize in a subtle way': 'One cannot discuss forbidding the headscarf for teachers and bring groups into school which preach that Islam should be lived in a visible way. … The leadership of Muslim Youth has as its most prominent aim to achieve the pleasure of God' (Vera Gaserow, *Tagesspiegel*).

The second argument was related to the accusation of anti-Semitism. In an article in the *Tagesspiegel* (11 November 2003), Susanne Vieth-Enthus refers to a Friday sermon, which had appeared half a year earlier during the early days of the Iraq War, during which Qur'ān 5:67 was quoted:

> The Jews say: 'God's hand is tied up.' Be *their* hands tied up and be they accursed for the [blasphemy] they utter. Nay, both His hands are widely outstretched: He giveth and spendeth [of his bounty] as He leaseth. But the revelation that cometh to thee from God increaseth in most of them their obstinate rebellion and blasphemy. Amongst them we have placed enmity and hatred till the day of Judgement. Every time they kindle the fire of war, God doth extinguish it; but they [ever] strive to do mischief on earth. And God loveth not those who do mischief.

The verse was interpreted in the following way.

> You can read in the introductory verse that Allah also sends us things which we do not like and lets things happen which appear to us to be unjust. But he will always be on our side and he will extinguish any fire which is set by the infidels.

The sermon went on with the appeal that Muslims should pray for the Iraqi population and made no further references to Jews. This was the only *hutba* published by Muslim Youth in which Qur'ān *surahs* referring to Jews in a possibly anti-Semitic manner were quoted. This was enough, however, to charge Muslim Youth with anti-Semitic tendencies. 'During the Iraq war there were open hostilities against Jews in the *hutbas* published in the Internet' (Vera Gaserow, *Tagesspiegel*).

The third argument which was brought up related to Muslim Youth's alleged connections to Muslim Brotherhood:

> The extremely well organized group has close relationships, both on a personal and an ideological level, to Muslim Brotherhood and the Islamic Community, which preach an Islamic Republic and are now looking for fields of recruitment in schools and youth centres.
>
> (Vera Gaserow, *ibid.*)

The *Tagesspiegel* specified these close relationships:

> The *Verfassungsschutz* sees it as proven that there are close connections. The association was founded in the 'House of Islam', which is a member of the Central Council of Muslims. The Central Council is in turn an umbrella organization, one member of which is the Islamic Community, which is in turn influenced by Muslim Brotherhood. Guggenberg also reports that a member in the executive council of the MJ is the brother of the head of the Islamic Community.
>
> (Susanne Vieth-Enthus, *Tagesspiegel*, 11 November 2003)

These statements were sufficient for the Ministry of the Interior to cut support for the project overnight. There were protests against the decision, particularly by the Catholic Young Community, which had co-operated with Muslim Youth in the Trialog project. In a letter of 13 November 2003 the Catholic Young Community states that it had come to know Muslim Youth as an 'open association which is interested in inter-religious dialogue' and had never seen any signs indicating 'fundamentalist tendencies' or 'proselytizing activities'. The protest also quotes a press release by the Catholic Young Community, the Federal Association of Jewish Students in Germany and Muslim Youth stating that the three associations desire a peaceful cohabitation and reject all tendencies making the coexistence of religions dangerous or difficult. The protest fell on deaf ears.

This affair shows different aspects of how rumours operate. The first aspect is the operation of the logic of contagion. It becomes particularly apparent in the *Tagesspiegel* article quoting the 'close' connections the Verfassungsschutz sees between Muslim Youth and Muslim Brotherhood. In fact, the connections claimed could hardly be any looser. Muslim Youth was founded in one institution, namely the House of Islam, which itself does not appear in any report by the Verfassungsschutz, being part of an umbrella organization to which another organization (that is, the Islamic Community) belongs, which in turn is said to be influenced by Muslim Brotherhood. In this way, Muslim Youth is said to be influenced by Muslim Brotherhood. It is as if mere contact (albeit only indirect) is already enough to get infected.

This logic of contagion is related to the construction of condensed symbols mentioned above. Using a condensed symbol relieves one of the necessity of putting forth an argument. This becomes particularly evident in a circular argument linking Fereshta Ludin and Muslim Youth. Heide Oestreich argues in her comment that Fereshta Ludin herself was 'not quite without fault' as she was a member of Muslim Youth, which is suspected of 'operating in the vicinity of fundamentalists' (Oestreich, 2004: 118) Whereas Oestreich uses engagement in Muslim Youth as an argument for raising doubt about Fereshta Ludin's orientation, the *Tagesspiegel* argues exactly the other way around:

> It is somewhat dubious why the Ministry spends money for motivating youngsters to a Muslim way of life and for inviting them 'to live according to the guidance of Allah.' It is less amazing to meet old acquaintances there. The teacher Fereshta Ludin who carried her headscarf to the Constitutional Court was in this organization's executive committee for two years, an organization which cooperates with radical fundamentalists, according to Green Party MP Özcan Mutlu.
>
> (*Tagesspiegel*, commentary, 7 November 2003)

Evidently the argument works both ways. Doubts about Fereshta Ludin can be based on the fact that she had worked for Muslim Youth and Muslim Youth is questionable because Fereshta Ludin had worked there.

A second aspect of the logic of rumour which becomes apparent is the readiness to believe negative rumours. This becomes evident in the eagerness with which newspapers accepted the rather far-fetched argumentation of the Verfassungsschutz quoted above; it is also evident in the newspapers' willingness to believe statements that Muslim Youth supposedly proselytizes. In fact, any attempt to verify the statement would have shown its extreme unlikelihood. Islam was just one of five topics discussed with students in the workshops. Moreover, the institution where the workshop took place decided which topics were to be discussed. Religion certainly played a role in the workshops, but that was the basic idea of the project, which was 'to tell misguided Muslim high school students who feel that they should beat up a Jew that this is completely against our religion' (Chaban Salih, personal communication in an informal conversation). In fact, the journalists behind the inaccurate reporting did not ask Chaban Salih, who was responsible for the project, for a comment before publishing their article. Finally, some teams were multi-religious in composition, which in itself could have been taken as a clear sign that the charge should have been more intensively checked.

But also the readiness to accept the charge of anti-Semitism is telling. It cannot be ruled out that the Qur'ān *surah* could serve as a subtle (and seemingly innocent) way of conveying an anti-Semitic statement all too well understood by the readers. In fact, the organizers of Muslim Youth admit it was a mistake and Chaban Salih distanced himself publicly from the *hutba* quoted. The important point is that, given the background of an otherwise remarkable record of inter-religious dialogue – which included the Jewish community – the importance attached to that single *hutba* (which was published at the height of the excitement about the Iraq War) seems overstated. The relativizing comments were not quoted. None of the articles mentioned the co-operation with Jewish students, nor the anti-racist intention of the project as whole.

After the newspaper articles appeared, the charge of abuse of public funds arose, and financial support for the project was immediately cut off. In the Office of the Ausländerbeauftragten (Commissioner for Foreigners), where the funds were administered, voices were heard expressing regret about the decision (especially after several organizations protested against it). But it was stated that the political pressure was just too great to allow further funding of the project.

Moral panic?

The growing number of applicants for citizenship, immigrants' battles in courts for their rights, and the application for public funding confront German society today with the realities of being an immigration country. This is a challenge which is historically new for a society which had long considered itself ethnically homogeneous. This has never excluded immigration, but has implied turning one's back on its consequences. The return of the repressed creates anxieties which refer to the (grossly overstated) fear of losing control over one's own affairs and of becoming a minority in one's own realm, perhaps not yet in society as a whole, but definitely in neighbourhoods and regions of high immigration. These anxieties crystallize where Islam is concerned, because society fears the capacity of religion to articulate, to organize and to sustain difference in the migration process. It makes apparent that the immigrant is '*physically close* while remaining *spiritually remote*' (Bauman, 1991: 60). Islam, especially in its orthodox version, epitomizes the challenge German society faces today. While this would hold true for any religion, it is accentuated with regard to Islam for two reasons. The first one concerns a long-standing tradition of orientalism, that is of perceiving of Islam as the quintessential Other. This is taken up today by the feeling that Islam in many way contradicts the ideal German society has of itself according to the collective perception that Islam pits patriarchalism against gender equality, ideals of collectivity against individual autonomy, intolerance against tolerance, authoritarianism against liberalism. The second reason is, of course, Islamic terrorism. Although relations between the German majority and the Muslim minority had been characterized for over forty years by rather peaceful mutual indifference, 9/11 and Beslan are taken as a sign that Muslims are not only different, but also dangerous. These recent events underlie the moral panic analysed in this chapter which is characterized by the construction of a public enemy and the reinforcement of the boundaries between 'us' and 'them'. A striking feature of this panic is the amazing degree of consensus between actors who usually belong to different social and political factions. The leftist feminist Alice Schwarzer suddenly finds herself in happy cohabitation with the right-wing politician Günther Beckstein, and left-wing journalists embrace and affirmatively quote the Verfassungsschutz. The most characteristic feature of the moral panic that I have analysed in this chapter is the apparent irrationality of the arguments brought forth. Purification rites, witch-hunts and rumour follow the logic of association characterized by condensation and displacement operating in fantasies and dreams (Freud, 1972). They also follow the logic of contagion and similarity which are characteristic of acts of magic (Mauss, 1974). They are characterized by the strong emotional drive underlying them.[26]

To respond to the very real challenge that German society faces by falling into moral panic is extremely counter-productive. For one thing, it is regressive. It implies a return to an assimilationist immigration policy related to a vision of the nation-state which had already become obsolete during the last quarter of the twentieth century. This precludes tackling the real challenge of developing visions of citizenship that do justice to an increasingly transnational and multicultural reality. Rather than opening up to multicultural citizenship, the perspective is an increasing emphasis on a mono-cultural *Leitkultur* ('leading culture').

To neglect (or to reject) the challenge of developing a vision of organizing diversity and recognizing difference can be dangerous. It can function as a self-fulfilling prophecy since it can polarize Muslim immigrants and German society. It also can be destructive of all the syntheses and combinations German Muslims have successfully developed in recent years. Thus, it can give rise to the very conservative and hostile minority it fantasizes about and fears.

Notes

* I owe thanks to Julia Eckert, Urmila Goel and Anna Triandafyllidou for their constructive and helpful criticism. I also want to thank all participants in the anthropological research colloquium at European University, Frankfurt/Oder, for their comments. Last, but not least, I want to thank Richard Gardner for correcting my English.
1 After the hostage drama in Beslan in September, 2004, the Allensbach Institute registered a clear increase in Islamophobia in Germany. According to the survey, Islam is conceived as alien and menacing. A clear majority opts for increased measures of security, 46 per cent favouring arrests of potential terrorists without court authorization (Noelle, 2004).
2 In the sense of individual rights of members of a specific community (e.g., exemption from swimming lessons).
3 This is reflected in the Allensbach poll. Islam is considered to be alien and threatening. In fact, the feeling of constant threat prevails: 46 per cent of the population agree with the statement: 'There are so many Muslims living among us in Germany. Sometimes I am afraid that there are many terrorists among them' (Noelle, 2004).
4 The party has been banned and re-founded several times. This is reflected in the different names the party has had: Party of National Order (1968–1969); National Salvation Party (1971–1980); Welfare Party (1983–1996); Virtue Party (1997–2001). The party split into the Justice and Development Party under Erdogan and the 'Well-being Party' under Erbakan.

5 For a more extensive discussion, see Schiffauer (1997b).
6 Up to the late 1990s, Muslims were in fact more hesitant to apply for citizenship than other groups of the population as they were more prone to foster the illusion of returning to their country of birth.
7 There are offices of the Verfassungsschutz at the state and federal levels. Although they work independently they exchange information. In the case of naturalization usually the state offices are appealed to.
8 Quite telling in this aspect is the interplay of administration and hand-picked intellectuals in the headscarf debate. 'Cultural minister Schavan (press note 119/98) similarly pointed out that the "wearing of the headscarf is not part of the religious duties of a Muslim woman. This is recognizable, for example, in that a majority of Muslim women do not wear the headscarf." With her statement, Schavan repeated the advice she had received from the political scientist Bassam Tibi, who acted as a political adviser on the case' (Amir-Moazami, 2004: 137). Amir-Moazami correctly points out that this self-confident exertion of the power of definition is 'characteristic of Western approaches to Islam, which, since colonial times, have contributed to determining which forms of Islam were legitimate and authentic' (*ibid.*).
9 For example, the President of the Verfassungsschutz, Heinz Fromm, has said as much in a hearing in the Bundestag (Deutscher Bundestag Innenausschuss, 2004).
10 The leaders of Milli Görüş in Europe claim that they pursue a different agenda than the Milli Görüş movement in Turkey without, however, seeking to separate from it, because that would only lead to frictions in the community.
11 For example, by Mehmet Sabri Erbakan, who was president of the community until 2003, in an interview with the newspaper ZAMAN, 5 June 2002. It is telling for the strength of this preconceived idea that the journalist Claudia Dantschke, in a publication of the Ministry of the Interior, completely reversed this statement declaring that Erbakan had opted for the introduction of a parallel society.
12 The Verfassungsschutz in Lower Saxony writes about a speech delivered by Mehmet Sabri Erbakan (the then president of IGMG) in Arnheim in 2002 in which he 'suggested a threat from outside in order to motivate the Muslims to withdraw into a parallel society' (Verfassungsschutzbericht Niedersachsen, 2002: 131). In fact, there is nothing in this speech which allows this conclusion to be drawn.
13 'The recommendations to apply for German Citizenship aim at the acquisition of rights and not at the recognition of the democratic constitutional state and its value-system or its rule of law. According to the IGMG, integration should have its limits where religion, culture, and national identity are concerned' (Verfassungs-schutzbericht Bremen, 2002: 65).
14 'In so called summer-schools ... general and Islamic knowledge are taught by trained hodjas. ... The IGMG offers a broad range of leisure-time activities and qualification courses. This is motivated by the aim to keep children and youngsters away from the "influence of western society" ("the non-believers", the "god-less", "immorality"). The IGMG thus acts against integration' (Verfassungsschutzbericht Bremen, 2002: 65).
15 For the logic of classifications see Douglas's analysis of pollution and purification (Douglas, 1966).
16 We coined the term civil culture in our project on civil enculturation in European schools as a missing link between civil society and civic culture (Schiffauer et al., 2004). 'Civil culture combines three elements: competence in the workings of a country's civil society; competence with regard to its nationally specific conventions of civic culture and norms of civility; and some familiarity, conformist or hopefully critical, with its dominant national self-representation, what Taylor calls its "social imaginary"' (Castoriadis, 1984; Taylor, 2002: Baumann, 2004: 4).
17 An example of this demand for identification can be taken from Kandel (2004). After mentioning that the Muslim communities organized themselves as

associations, Kandel continues: 'They adapted quite pragmatically to this legal form. It is open however whether this fact can be interpreted as an act of "integration" or whether it is just a factual adjustment to the existing juridical order. Integration here means evidently identification which is opposed to mere adjustment' (2004: 2).

18 The parallel drawn with legalist Islamic movements, however, does not hold. The Nazis never concealed their contempt for parliamentary democracy.

19 The same charge is made by Klaus Lefringhausen, Integrationsbeauftragter (Integration Commissioner) of North Rhine Westphalia. By insisting on the right to wear the headscarf, the Muslim associations would 'threaten a favorable climate for integration in order to legitimate their role as advocates of Islam'. With regard to religious education, he stated: 'For the associations that had sued, the defeat before the Oberverwaltungsgericht [Upper Administrative Court] Münster counted as a success. Not to recognize the associations as religious communities shows the anti-Islamism of society and demonstrates the necessity for strong Muslim associations' (Lefringhausen, 2003).

20 Commenting on demands for segregation of the sexes in swimming lessons, Kandel complained that 'unfortunately German appeal courts upheld this' (Kandel, 2004: 6).

21 In a discussion with the Friedrich-Ebert Stiftung, however, Peter von Feldmann, Presiding Judge of the Upper Administrative Court, expressed sympathy with the very hesitant policy of school authorities: 'One hesitates to put this decision into practice because one is afraid that a political religious fundamentalism is spread by this group, something which would be inappropriate for Berlin schools (von Feldmann, 2000: 9).' It is almost as if the courts regret that their hands were bound by the legal situation and that they had no alternative to issuing the decision.

22 Descriptions of the Ludin case are found in Oestreich (2004) and Amir-Moazami (2004).

23 This was quite evident in the iconographic representation. Her photo was on the cover of *Der Spiegel* and another one inside (p. 83). Although I had seen the photos the same day I met Fereshta Ludin for the first time, I did not recognize her because both photos were taken at an angle and from below, thus giving a distorted impression of her.

24 The term is taken from Mary Douglas, who took it from Basil Bernstein and integrated it into her theory of natural symbols (Douglas, 1970).

25 This symbolization is apparent in rhetorical expressions, such as: 'Will there be a second Fereshta Ludin?'

26 This becomes most apparent in the emotional outburst scientists (mostly anthropologists) are confronted with when articulating doubts concerning the construction of the public enemy or only trying to represent the emic point of view. They are suspected of being naive or driven by selfish motives if they do not partake in public condemnation.

References

Amir-Moazami, S. (2004) 'Discourses and counterdiscourses: the Islamic headscarf in the French and German public spheres', PhD thesis, European University Institute, Florence.

Bauman, Z. (1991) *Modernity and Ambivalence*, Cambridge: Polity Press.

Baumann, G. (2004) 'Introduction: nation-state, schools and civil enculturation', in W. Schiffauer, G. Baumann, R. Kastoryano and S. Vertovec. (eds) *Civil Enculturation: Nation-state, Schools and Ethnic Difference in the Netherlands, Britain, Germany and France*, New York and Oxford: Berghahn Books.

Böger, K. (2000) 'Contribution to a discussion, in Friedrich-Ebert Stiftung, *Islamischer Religionsunterricht an deutschen Schulen. Probleme, Fragen, Antworten*', Berlin: Friedrich-Ebert Stiftung.

Bundesamt für Verfassungsschutz (2004) 'Vorüberlegungen zu einer Ausstellung des Verfassungsschutz zum Thema "Islamismus in Deutschland" ', Working Paper, Berlin.

Castoriadis, C. (1984) *Gesellschaft als imaginäre Institution. Entwurf einer politischen Philosophie*, Frankfurt am Main: Suhrkamp.

Cohen, S. (1972) *Folk Devils and Moral Panics: The Creation of the Mods and Rockers*, London: MacGibbon & Kee.

Deutscher Bundestag Innenausschuss (2004) 'Protokoll 42.Sitzung. Öffentliche Anhörung von Sachverständigen zum Thema: "Islamistische Einflüsse auf die Gesellschaft und ihre Auswirkungen auf Integration" ', Protokoll Nr. 15/42, Berlin.

Douglas, M. (1966) *Purity and Danger: An Analysis of the Concepts of Pollution and Taboo*, London: Routledge.

—— (1970) *Natural Symbols: Explorations in Cosmology*, Harmondsworth: Penguin Books.

Elias, N. and Scotson, J. L. (1993) *Etablierte und Außenseiter*, Frankfurt am Main: Suhrkamp.

Freud, S. (1972) *Die Traumdeutung*, Studienausgabe Band II, Frankfurt am Main: Fischer.

Goode, E. and Ben Yehuda, N. (1994) *Moral Panics: The Social Construction of Violence*, Oxford: Blackwell.

Iyidirli, A. (2004) Unpublished interview conducted by Alke Wierth, Berlin.

Jonker, G. (2004) *Distant Communications: Europe and the Muslim Other. The case of Germany*, Manuscript.

Kandel, J. (no date) 'Lieber blauäugig als blind? Anmerkungen zum "Dialog" mit dem Islam', in Friedrich-Ebert Stiftung (ed.) *Islam und Gesellschaft Nr. 2*, Berlin: Friedrich-Ebert Stiftung.

Kandel, J. (2004) '*Organisierter Islam in Deutschland und gesellschaftliche Integration*', Berlin: Friedrich-Ebert Stiftung.

Landratsamt Aschaffenburg (2003) 'Niederschrift der Anhörung von Murat Gökbulut', Internal document.

Lefringhausen, K. (2003) 'Der Politik fehlt es an einer Islampolitik – Es geht gar nicht um das Kopftuch – ein kritischer Ansatz von Klaus Lefringhausen'. Online. Available: www.politikforum.de/forum/archive/1/2004 (accessed 9 December 2004).

Luhmann, N. (1968/1989) *Vertrauen. Ein Mechanismus der Reduktion sozialer Komplexität*, Stuttgart, Enke.

Mauss, M. (1974) 'Entwurf einer allgemeinen Theorie der Magie', in M. Mauss, *Soziologie und Anthropologie*, München: Hanser: 43–182.

Menke, B. (1998) 'Allegorie, Personifikation, Prosopopoie', in B. Menke (ed.) *Allegorie – zwischen Bedeutung und Materialität*, Wiesbaden: Westdeutscher Verlag: S.59–S.73.

Noelle, E. (2004) 'Allensbach Studie. Der Kampf der Kulturenat'. Online. Available: www. faz.net (accessed 8 October 2004).

Oestreich, H. (2004) *Der Kopftuchstreit*, Frankfurt am Main: Brandes & Apsel.

Schiffauer, W. (1997a) 'Die civil society und der Fremde. Grenzmarkierungen in vier politischen Kulturen', in W. Schiffauer (ed.) *Fremde in der Stadt*, Frankfurt am Main: Suhrkamp Verlag: 35–49. (English translation, 'The civil society and the outsider. Drawing the boundaries in four political cultures'. Online. Available:

http://viadrina.euv-frankfurt-o.de/~anthro/veronli-s.html (accessed 10 December 2004).)

———— (1997b) 'Islamic vision and social reality – the political culture of Sunni Turk Muslims in Germany', in S. Vertovec, *Islam in Europe – The Politics of Religion and Community*, London: Macmillan.

———— (2004) 'Die Islamische Gemeinschaft Milli Görüş – ein Lehrstück zum verwickelten Zusammenhang von Migration, Religion und sozialer Integration', in K. J. Bade, M. Bommes and R. Münz *Migrationsreport 2004. Fakten – Analysen – Perspektiven*, hrsg., Frankfurt and New York: Campus Verlag: 67–96.

Schiffauer, W., Baumann, G., Kastoryano, G. and Vertovec, S. (eds) (2004) *Civil Enculturation: Nation-state, Schools and Ethnic Difference in the Netherlands, Britain, Germany and France*, New York and Oxford: Berghahn Books.

Simmel, G. (1971) 'The Stranger' (1908), in *On Individuality and Social Forms*, Chicago. University of Chicago Press.

Taylor, C. (2002) 'Modern social imaginaries', *Public Culture*, 14: 91–124.

Von Feldmann, P. (2000) Einführung, in *Integrative Konzepte wertbezogener Bildung. Anregungen und Vorschläge für die Berliner Schule. Podiumsdiskussion am 22.Juni 2000 in der Friedrich-Ebert Stiftung in Berlin*, Berlin: Friedrich-Ebert Stiftung.

7 Religious diversity and multiculturalism in Southern Europe

The Italian mosque debate*

Anna Triandafyllidou

Introduction

Italy is a 'new' immigration country, having experienced migration as a host only since the early 1990s. Regional diversity and centrifugal tendencies both at the cultural and political levels have characterized the Italian nation-state ever since its creation in 1860. The bases of national unity have been judged by many scholars and politicians (see, for instance, Galli della Loggia, 1998) to be weak and problematic. Regional, cultural and economic diversities have at times been seen as endangering or defying national unity and as providing an insufficient basis for identification and political organization. However, there has been little doubt that this diversity can be accommodated in a common national whole and that there are important elements of commonality that permit Italian citizens to constitute a nation (Diamanti, 1999; Nevola, 1999; Rusconi, 1993). The new immigration to Italy, however, adds a further challenge to this debate and to the very conception of the Italian nation and nation-state as an internally diverse community.

The immigrants who reached the Italian shores or crossed the Italian borders in the 1980s and 1990s came predominantly from Central and Eastern European countries (that is, until 1 May 2004, mainly non-EU 30 per cent, Asia 18.5 per cent and Africa 26.5 per cent) (Caritas, 2003: 118). Although approximately one-third of them are Catholics and another 20 per cent of other Christian denominations (Protestant and Orthodox mainly), Muslims represent the single largest religious community among the immigrant population with an estimated share of 36.5 per cent by the end of 1999 (Pittau, 2000: 177). Moreover, the immigrant community is highly multinational and multicultural in itself: it includes people from over thirty different countries (Caritas, 2003), who bring with them a large variety of cultural and religious practices and customs (Pace and Perocco, 2000). Thus, this new recent immigration brings with it an important challenge at the normative and the policy levels. As the contribution of economic migrants to the Italian economy starts being recognized (Carillo et al., 1999; Gavosto et al., 1999; Reyneri, 1998; Reyneri et al., 1999), the question arises as to how to integrate immigrants into Italian society. The comprehensive Immigration Law No. 40 of 1998[1] puts the emphasis on integration mechanisms, including a whole network of consultative bodies and a set of instruments (Zincone, 2000a; 2000b).

The policy question is posed at the level of policy design and implementation and in this respect the Reports on Integration (*ibid.*) – which, unfortunately, were discontinued – provide for a first assessment of the situation. However, the question of immigrant membership in the Italian nation and, more specifically, of whether and to what extent immigrant religious and cultural needs can and should be accommodated in the host society, raises a challenge at the normative level and thus implicitly at the identity level as well. Should it be assumed that a relatively homogeneous national culture exists or should Italy be seen as a multicultural society even without non-EU immigrants? What kind of multiculturalism is desirable and/or plausible in the Italian context? Is a civic, liberal form of nationalism (Kymlicka, 1998: 147) prevalent in Italy or should the nation be defined as a closed ethno-religious community? And if a common civic culture provides the basis of identification among Italian citizens, to what extent can immigrants become members of this civic nation and under what terms?

The question that I want to address in this chapter involves a double – policy and normative – concern. Using as a nodal point for the immigration debate a specific event that received wide attention by the media and party leaders in the last months of 2000, I want to explore the kind of multiculturalism that is debated in Italy. In line with Modood's argument (2001) that institutions and contexts embody values, I use the issue of new mosque construction in Lodi and in Milan, over the month of October 2000, as a specific example of 'multicultural crisis' that reveals the values that structure the Italian debate. I also explore how the issue of immigrant integration and the overall debate on multiculturalism relate to, and indeed may be instrumentalized by, the Italian political and party system.

In order fully to contextualize multiculturalism debates and practices it is necessary to consider not only dominant discourses on nationhood but also a set of more specific cultural and political features that characterize a given society (see also Jacobs, 1998; 1999). In the Italian case, these features include the contested link between Italian national identity, the Italian Republic and the Catholic Church, and the ways in which this link has structured the political party spectrum in the post-war period.

Italian debates on multiculturalism are related to the issue of regional diversity that characterizes Italy and the secessionist claims of the Northern League Party (as well as their more recent abandonment of such claims in favour of an advanced version of federalism). The shifting Othering discourse of the Lega Nord between Italy, Europe and Muslims/immigrants provides important insights as to the context within which multiculturalism and immigrant integration are to be implemented.

Another important feature that interferes with multiculturalism debates is the somewhat paradoxical positive link between Italian national identity and integration into the EU (Triandafyllidou, 2002; 2005). The EU provides a basis for civic identification and positive in-group evaluation for Italian media and elites which consider national identity and civic virtues to be rather weak.

The gradual 'normalization' of immigration in the late 1990s and the increasing emphasis on immigrant integration coexist with a diffuse use of terms such as '*intercultura*', or multicultural education, the precise policy or normative content of which remains vague (Chaloff, 1999). Moreover, the present government (in office since May 2001) has given priority to migration control rather than integration, thus undermining further the weak efforts of the previous government to create a multicultural society (Chaloff, 2003).

Eventually, the question that we need to ask further to this case study is whether Italy will follow a multicultural path towards immigrant integration in conjunction with deeper integration into the EU, or whether these two processes will take opposite directions and a boundary will be built between Europeans/non-Europeans to replace the Italians/non-Italians distinction of the national state order.

Recent political developments in the country are not promising in this respect. The neo-liberal government elected in May 2001, led by Silvio Berlusconi, a media magnate and businessman, is supported by Berlusconi's party Forza Italia, the Alleanza Nazionale, a right-wing party with links to the former Italian Fascist Party, and the regionalist and populist Lega Nord. The new government – or at least some leading members of it – holds very conservative views in cultural and migration issues. Berlusconi's government is one of the few European governments to have so wholeheartedly supported American President Bush's 'fight against evil' and 'global war' against 'Islamic terrorism'. In the aftermath of the events of 9/11, Italian television channels broadcasted visits to local mosques in Southern and Northern Italy with implied suggestions that these mosques harboured presumed fanatic Muslims and potential terrorists. Obviously, neighbours appeared alarmed and argued before the journalist that mosques should be closed down or transferred elsewhere because they feared for their security.

The statements by the would-be Italian Commissioner to the European Commission, Rocco Buttiglione, in October 2004 regarding, on the one hand, his predictions of a massive exodus of 1 million immigrants from the recently opened borders of Libya into Italy and, on the other hand, the extreme, conservative views he expressed in his speech before the European Parliament regarding the position of women and homosexuals in society, are also telling of the government's overall positions and policies.

Despite having enacted the largest 'amnesty' of undocumented immigrant workers in 2002 and thereby regularizing 350,000 factory workers and another 350,000 maids and care providers, this government emphasizes a purely economic understanding of migration. Residence permits (*permessi di soggiorno*) were replaced in 2002 by resident contracts (*contratti di soggiorno*). The government thus emphasizes that immigrants are accepted onto Italian territory only if they have a work contract and that if and when the work relationship is ended, they are expected to leave at once. Such a view is obviously detached from an in-depth understanding of contemporary international migration. Moreover, such rigid laws are largely inapplicable, as past experience in Italy and in neighbouring countries (for example, Greece) has shown, and are most likely to lead to further exploitation and marginalization of immigrant workers. Moreover, 'doom prophecies' like those of Mr Buttiglione foster a general feeling of insecurity. They tend to equate all Muslim migrants with terrorists and present immigration as a liability for European economies – an image that is very far from the truth (see, among others, Baldwin Edwards, 2001). Eventually such accounts tend to reinforce both internal and external boundaries between Europeans and 'others' where the category of 'others' includes migrants, and in particular Muslim migrants.

This chapter is divided into two parts. In the section that follows I will briefly outline the main features of the immigrant population in Italy and its level of integration in the host society. The aim of this section is thus to discuss critically the social, economic and policy background against which multiculturalism debates or practices should be seen. The second part of the chapter will concentrate on the 'multicultural crisis' of the mosque construction issue that unfolded in October 2000 in the cities of Lodi and Milan. Through the analysis of the public and political debates on that issue, I will highlight how Muslim immigrants' claims for appropriate places of worship put to the test the liberal character of Italian democracy and led to the emergence of different versions of multiculturalism supported by political parties and other social or political actors. In the final part, I will assess how the debate has evolved since and whether there can be hopes that an Italian form of multiculturalism will emerge in policy or in practice.

The immigrant presence in Italy

According to the Caritas data and estimates (2003: 100), there were 2,469,324 legal immigrants present in Italy in 2002 (Pittau, 2000: 176), who account for just over 4 per cent of the total 57,844,017 resident population (as of 2000). This percentage is lower than that of most 'old' immigration countries in Europe, such as France, Britain and Germany. Although present throughout the country, foreigners concentrate in the urban areas of the centre and north of Italy where work opportunities are greater, especially in the tertiary sector and mostly in the informal labour market. Immigration was until recently dealt with through temporary administrative measures and special legal provisions – so-called 'amnesties' – aiming at regularizing undocumented immigrants, who had already settled in the country (SOPEMI, 2000; Vasta, 1993; Veugelers, 1994; Woods, 1992). After more than a decade of 'emergencies', a comprehensive law was passed by the Italian Parliament in 1998 (Law 40/06.3.1998, entered into force in October 1999) creating a unitary corpus of norms that regulate the rights and obligations of foreigners in Italy, their stay and work conditions, and other matters regarding family reunion, social integration and cultural and political life in the host country.[2] In recent years, the Italian government has been providing for a limited number (several tens of thousands) of legal entries per year as a means of controlling and regulating immigration into the country. Law 189/2002 (known as the Bossi Fini Law) – the full implications of which are not yet discernible – introduced some amendments to immigration channels and flows as well as to the rights of legal immigrants making it overall more difficult for them to settle down in Italy (Chaloff, 2003: 11; OECD LEED, 2004: 12).

The ethnic and cultural heterogeneity of the immigrant population is reflected in the ways in which immigrant workers are inserted into the Italian economy. Some analysts assert that ethnic specialization in the labour market is particularly strong (Campani, 1993: 515). Indeed, some sectors may be identified with specific national groups. For instance, migrants from the Maghreb and Eastern Europe find jobs in the construction sector. Seasonal jobs in agriculture rely heavily on male workers from Latin America, India and Sri Lanka. Trading is largely characterized by self-employment in informal activities such as street vending and involves immigrants from Morocco, Senegal and China. Domestic services employ women from the Philippines, Albania, Poland and Eritrea. Chinese communities are mainly engaged in handicraft activities. The occupational distribution is accompanied by the regional distribution of migration chains, that is the concentration of certain nationalities in specific regions within the country: Moroccans in the industrial North, Chinese in the area around Florence and Prato, Senegalese in the small cities of the North East (Veikou and Triandafyllidou, 2001). A large proportion of immigrants (about two-thirds) who hold a residence permit for work purposes are employed in the informal economy (Reyneri, 1998; Zincone, 2000a; 2000b).

Despite their weak economic position, immigrants' networking has flourished during the past decade giving birth to informal networks (Knights, 1996) and a number of immigrant associations (Kosic and Triandafyllidou, 2004). Furthermore, representatives from immigrant communities have been incorporated into the major Italian trade unions such as CGIL and CISL. The integration of the newcomers into trade unions was seen by the latter's leadership as the best way to protect the rights of both domestic and foreign workers and preserve their bargaining power with employers and the policy authorities. Religious (Catholic) non-profit organizations, Caritas in particular, have played an active role in immigrant integration, regardless of the immigrants' religious faith. The activities of Caritas, for example, have benefited from its extended network of local associations and voluntary networks that exist nationwide. The Italian state has promoted and, to a certain extent, funded these activities, which often substitute for public services.

Thus, although independent immigrant institutions such as national associations, political parties, minority media, educational bodies and religious hierarchies have not yet developed, immigrants are partly integrated into Italian structures of representation. Their political participation, however, remains in the sphere of denizenship. The Italian Constitution limits the right to vote in national elections to Italian citizens only. Experiments in the realm of civic citizenship, for example the 'additional city councillor' elected by foreign nationals, have varied among cities and regions and no national standard or guaranteed rights exist. Although legal immigrants enjoy, at least in theory, equal access to work, public housing, education and health services, as do citizens, they have neither passive nor active political rights.

Immigrant naturalization has hardly been an issue of concern in Italy. In a symbolic move the Social Affairs Ministry declared 1999 to be the 'Year of the New Citizens'. Nonetheless, 1999 was not really the year of the new *citizens*, since the naturalization process remained arduous and, not unlike any other year, a majority of the thousand applicants made per annum were rejected in 1999. According to the SOPEMI Report issued in January 2000: '[t]he "citizenship" promised by the government is one in which the immigrant can hope to receive a permanent residence card after five years, eliminating the need to meet the criteria for biannual renewal.' (SOPEMI, 2000: 34).

Italian citizenship is predominantly ethnic in character because it is related to kinship by blood or through marriage (Pastore, 2001; Triandafyllidou and Veikou, 2001). The law allows for foreign permanent residents to apply for naturalization and does not require cultural assimilation (knowledge of the Italian language, for instance, is not required). However, the bureaucratic procedure established for naturalization is so complex and time and effort consuming that it effectively acts as a deterrent to potential applicants. Thus, while the law adheres to a conception of the nation as a civic community and not just an ethno-cultural one, it does so only in form and not in substance. In reality, the principal means for acquiring Italian citizenship is through marriage.[3]

Even though much lip service has been paid to multiculturalism and the social integration of immigrants, the content of such terms remains highly vague and acceptance of cultural and religious diversity is a contested matter. Although the Constitution and Law 40/1998 protect immigrant rights, their acceptance in practice is much less straightforward. In some policy areas, efforts have been noticeable. The increasing number of immigrant children in Italian schools has prompted attempts to change the school curriculum to make it more inclusive, although an overall policy for educational integration has not yet emerged. The definition of who or what is 'Italian' in school texts has remained unaltered. Nevertheless, a large number of 'intercultural' initiatives have been launched, aimed at promoting a better understanding of foreigners and their cultures (SOPEMI, 2000: table 62; Melchionda, 1996).

The situation in education policy mirrors the overall approach of the Italian state to immigration. As of Law 40/1998, the long-term character of immigration has been recognized and immigrant integration has been established as a policy goal. However, this integration is limited in character and does not include a fuller political participation, or the integration of foreign cultures and traditions into the national identity. As the interviewees in a different study (Triandafyllidou and Veikou, 2001) pointed out: 'they have to realize that they are in Italy and they are foreigners'.

The quest for new mosques in Northern Italy

Although cultural and religious diversity is in theory recognized by the Italian state, when it comes to conceding actual religious rights to Muslim immigrants, local conflicts and national debates arise. One case that received much publicity in the year 2000, and that reopened the debate on cultural diversity and immigrant integration among parties and in the press, was the opening of two mosques on the periphery of Milan. The issue was raised after the Mayor of Lodi, a small city on the southern outskirts of Milan, conceded a piece of land that belonged to the municipality to an Islamic organization, upon its request for such a plot in order to build, at its own expense, a mosque. The issue attracted the hostility and xenophobic reactions of the local branch of Lega Nord, which on 14 October 2000 organized a public rally to protest against the mayor's decision and declare their will to oppose the establishment of the new mosque.

The issue was followed closely by the national media for a short period and triggered a larger debate concerning the rights of legal immigrants in Italy and also Italian culture and identity and their compatibility with religious and cultural diversity. Issues of preserving 'our traditions' and 'our identity', 'Islamic fundamentalism' and the quest for 'reciprocity between Islamic and Christian countries' were contrasted with notions of 'religious freedom', 'solidarity', 'integration', 'civic values' and their protection by the Italian Constitution as well as the EU Charter of Fundamental Rights. Nearly a fortnight later, on 25 October 2000, the opening of a new mosque in Milan gave new impetus to the debate and to the symbolic 'fight' between the various political and social actors that took part in it.

The initial events in Lodi and their follow-up in Milan offer two eloquent examples of the tensions arising from the slow integration of the immigrant population in Italy and the challenges this brings to a regionally diversified but nationally monocultural and largely mono-religious society. In the following sections, my aim will be to analyse the public and political debates triggered by the events at Lodi and Milan so as to highlight how 'multiculturalism' and cultural or religious diversity are defined in the Italian context. I will explore how the different actors define the relationship between the host country and Muslim immigrants.[4] I will also highlight the guiding principles which, according to the different 'voices' represented in the debate, should guide the relationship between 'hosts' and 'guests'. Naturally, the analysis will also discuss which social and political actors are given 'voice' in the media and which are silenced. Ultimately, my aim will be to check if there is a specifically Italian discourse on multiculturalism emerging and, if so, what its main tenets are.

Methodology and data

The material used to study the political and public debate on the Lodi events comes mainly from the national and regional daily press in Italy. The press is seen here as the discursive arena in which public and political debates develop. In line with the agenda-setting approach, I am concerned with how the media describe social reality and present a list of issues on which people need to have an opinion and/or talk about (Shaw, 1979). Thus the focus is on the role of the press as a mediator of social reality which defines the issues that should be seen as public problems (Gusfield, 1981), sets the terms on which these issues should be understood and debated, and gives public 'voice' to some actors rather than others. The media, and here the press in particular, also reflect, therefore, the power relations in a given society.

At the same time, the media play a role in constructing 'moral panics', and in particular in this case 'multicultural crises' (see also Schiffauer, this volume). Although immigrants have been present in consistent numbers in Italy for over a decade and a relatively large number of mosques operate across the Italian territory, it was the Lega Nord's rather small and marginal public rally in Lodi, against the construction of the new mosque, that attracted media attention and gave rise to a larger debate on religious freedom and diversity. The role of the press (and of other mass media of course) was crucial in giving visibility to the Lega's protest, which had some news value as a dramatic event. The visibility that this event acquired, attracted a debate between the competing party coalitions which tried to increase their electoral support in view of the forthcoming national elections (May 2001). The coverage was extended to include a new event: the request by some Italian Muslims in the city of Milan, some ten days after the Lodi events, for permission to construct a mosque. In either case, the press played the role of mediator by giving voice to the political parties, the state authorities (national, regional and local), the Catholic Church, intellectuals, and more rarely to Muslim organizations and hardly ever indeed to Muslim immigrants themselves (see Table 7.3).

The material analysed has been collected from four leading Italian newspapers, *Corriere della Sera*, *La Repubblica*, *il Giornale* and *Il Messaggero*, which have a high national and regional circulation.[5] Although a clear distinction between tabloid and broadsheet press in the sense understood, for instance, in Britain, does not apply to the Italian newspaper market, it is worth noting that *La Repubblica* and *Il Giornale* generally use dramatic and sensationalist language while news reporting in the *Corriere della Sera* tends to be more sober. *Il Messaggero* lies somewhere in between the two categories.

The material collected includes all articles published in the four newspapers in the period between 10 October and 10 November 2000 which referred either to the mosque controversies in Lodi and Milan and/or generally to issues of cultural and religious diversity and freedom in Italy. News reports on immigration and on racial diversity published in this period were also included in the database because they reveal the wider context within which the mosque issue was debated.

A total of 209 articles (see Table 7.1) were collected and stored in a Microsoft Access database. The indexing scheme (see Appendix I) systematized what has turned out to be a rather large corpus of data. It enabled me to perform

Table 7.1 Distribution of the articles analysed per newspaper

Newspaper	Abbreviation	N
Corriere della Sera	CdS	57
Corriere della Sera Inserto Lavoro	CdSLA	3
Corriere della Sera Cronaca di Milano	CdSMI	2
Il Giornale	G	32
Il Giornale Cronaca di Milano	GMI	22
La Repubblica	LaR	68
La Repubblica Cronaca di Firenze	LaRFI	9
La Repubblica Cronaca di Roma	LaRRO	3
Il Messaggero	M	13
Total		209

a simple quantitative analysis of the data with the aim of mapping the discursive universe created by the press. I have thus identified how often the different social and political actors are given a 'voice' through the daily press. Both passive/implicit and active/explicit involvement of a given actor in the discourse were counted as a 'voice' instance and within each article several 'voices' could be indexed.

After a preliminary reading of the material, five thematic dimensions have been identified. First, the citizenship dimension, which includes references to citizenship, civic values or human rights and hence indicates that the issue of religious diversity is debated along civic, liberal lines. Second, the cultural traditions dimension, which is distinguished from national or regional identity that is indexed separately, covers references to 'our traditions' and 'our values' that define Italy as a monocultural society, based on a common past, common traditions and an apparently homogeneous and coherent value system. The third and fourth categories relate to the national and regional identity dimensions and refer to feelings of belonging to the Italian nation or to a specific region or locality. Finally, the thematic dimension of Europe includes references to the EU, the European Charter of Fundamental Rights, and Italy's position in relation to them. Often more than one thematic dimension was included in a single article. These dimensions refer to the main line of argumentation employed to define the relevant 'problem' and propose 'solutions'. Their scope has been to provide for a basis for indexing and quantitatively analysing the press discourse. They are complemented by an in-depth qualitative analysis of the data.

Voices and thematic dimensions: mapping the discursive universe

The quantitative analysis of the press coverage shows that citizenship was the dominant theme that organized the public and political discourse, followed closely by the issue of cultural traditions (see Table 7.2). The relative importance

Table 7.2 Thematic dimensions

Thematic dimensions	N	%
Citizenship	77	34
Cultural traditions	59	26
National identity	40	17.6
Regional identity	18	7.9
Europe	33	14.5
Total	227	100

Note N = number of articles in which a thematic dimension was indexed

of each theme, however, varied in relation to the different voices cited in the press. Thus, the Catholic Church and the Lega Nord voices coincided more often with references to the Italian cultural traditions than with civic values, in contrast to all other actors whose discourse was predominantly framed in terms of citizenship (see Table 7.3).

There is a clear imbalance in the representation of the various social and political actors in the debate: the political parties tend to monopolize the discourse having their 'voice' heard in nearly half of the articles analysed. Local and regional authorities and the Catholic Church account also for a large part of the arguments and positions expressed, being 'heard' in nearly one quarter of all the texts analysed (see Table 7.3). Muslim 'voices' in contrast are under-represented, with a total of 11 per cent (8 per cent for Muslim organizations and 3 per cent for Muslim or immigrant individuals). Given that the main events of the coverage, namely the building of new mosques in Lodi and in Milan, arose from requests by Muslims for permission to build a mosque, it is interesting that the press ignores the very 'voices' of the claimants. On the other hand, this is hardly a surprising finding given the structurally marginal position of immigrants and Muslims in Italian society. Italian citizens' 'voices' are also hardly ever heard (in only 13 per cent of the articles) while the Lega Nord activists and local leaders are present in 9 per cent of the coverage (see Table 7.3).

Concerning Muslim organizations, little information is given by the press about their activities or role in the Muslim community in Italy. The role of Italian Muslims in such organizations and, in particular, the fact that the creation of the mosque in Milan was requested by COREIS (Association of Italian Converts to Islam) are downplayed. Tellingly, La Repubblica entitles the relevant news report: 'The Islamic community wants it [the new mosque], the municipality is leaning towards a positive answer' (#53),[6] leaving undefined the composition of the members of the Islamic community.

As regards Muslim immigrants as individuals, the few references to their views or actions refer to protest marches in Milan (#92) and Genoa (#194) requesting new mosque buildings. In a third article (#91) where immigrant participation in the 'Rights Fair' (Carovana dei Diritti) and staged protest against the Catholic Church was reported, the emphasis was put on the response of the Cardinal of Milan's response: '[Cardinal] Martini to the immigrants: you will receive help if you abide by the law. The cardinal met the representatives of the 'Rights Fair': the Church listens to your requests' (title and subtitle of #91). These were the only instances in which Muslim immigrants

Table 7.3 Voices and thematic dimensions

Voices	N^a	%	Thematic dimensions	N^b
Political parties	96	35.3	Citizenship	45
			Cultural traditions	28
			National identity	23
			Regional identity	12
			Europe	26
Catholic Church	51	18.7	Citizenship	19
			Cultural traditions	20
			National identity	10
			Regional identity	7
			Europe	8
Lega Nord local leaders and activists	18	6.6	Citizenship	6
			Cultural traditions	7
			National identity	4
			Regional identity	3
			Europe	2
Local and regional authorities	56	20.6	Citizenship	20
			Cultural traditions	10
			National identity	5
			Regional identity	8
			Europe	2
Local citizens	28	10.3	Citizenship	12
			Cultural traditions	8
			National identity	1
			Regional identity	4
			Europe	0
Immigrants/Muslims	7	2.6	Citizenship	4
			Cultural traditions	1
			National identity	1
			Regional identity	0
			Europe	0
Muslim organisations	16	5.9	Citizenship	7
			Cultural traditions	2
			National identity	2
			Regional identity	0
			Europe	0
Total	272	100		

Notes
a N = number of articles in which a 'voice' was present.
b N = number of articles in which a given thematic dimension and a given 'voice' were simultaneously present.

were conveyed as somehow the protagonists of the mosque debate. These findings confirm that ethnic minority and immigrant community 'voices' are under-represented, usually subordinate to or patronized by the native political actors when decisions over issues of their immediate concern are taken (see also Jacobs, 1998; 1999).

In the section that follows, the press discourse will be analysed qualitatively with the aim of answering two main questions. First, who is the in-group and who is/are the out-group(s). My focus here is on the symbolic identity politics activated by the various actors in the cultural and religious diversity debate. Second, I will identify the principles that guide the Italian approach to integration of diversity. My aim is thus to demarcate the contours of an emerging Italian approach to multiculturalism.

The politicization of the mosque issue

Even though it may seem obvious, defining the in-group and the Other(s) is not such a straightforward issue. Discursive constructions of 'us' and 'them' shift to support varying identity claims and, in the case of party 'voices', to mobilize electoral support. In multiculturalism debates, defining who is 'us' and who is labelled as the Other is particularly important because the extent to which a minority is defined as part of the in-group conditions the success of its claims.

In the coverage of the Lodi and Milan events, two sets of in-group/out-group contrasts emerge. First, the in-group and out-group are constituted along national lines: on one side stands the host society, the Italians, and on the other side stand the 'guests', the immigrants and, in particular, Muslim immigrants. The two groups are qualified in cultural and religious terms. The in-group, Italians, are assumed to be 'Catholics' or 'Christians' – the two terms are used interchangeably – they are 'Westerners', 'Europeans', 'liberals', people with 'open minds', who uphold a 'civic' conception of society. The out-group is the negative mirror image of the in-group: its members are 'non-Westerners', they tend not to distinguish between religion and civic values, they are 'fundamentalists'. In this in-group/out-group contrast, the wider 'West and the rest' dichotomy is used so that Italy is represented as part of Europe, Christianity and the West (three groups that largely coincide in this discourse) and differentiated from 'oriental' and 'Islamic' Others.

A second distinction between the in-group and the out-group is internal to the host society and reflects the politicization of the mosque issue in an effort to gain electoral support by the competing party coalitions. In the period studied, two major party coalitions dominated Italian politics: the *Ulivo* (Olive Tree) centre-left coalition that was in government from spring 1996 until May 2001, and the *Polo delle Libertà* (Pole of Liberties) centre–right coalition, at the time the main opposition force and currently (since May 2001) in government. The mosque controversies at the end of 2000 were embedded in a pre-election campaign climate and the mutual efforts of the two party coalitions to discredit each other's platform. The competition was further complicated by the Lega

Nord factor. The Northern League started as a regional protest movement in the late 1980s but later developed into a party with secessionist tendencies. Through its political action and populist discourse – notably the proclamation of a Padanian Republic on 15 September 1996 and the mobilization of its supporters against the government in Rome – the Lega Nord has brought much upheaval to the Italian political scene. However, it abandoned its secessionist tendencies in 2000 to enter a wider centre–right coalition with the Forza Italia Party led by the media tycoon Silvio Berlusconi and the right-wing party Alleanza Nazionale headed by Gianfranco Fini.

In the press discourse, each party coalition defines its opponents as the out-group. The division is ideological in character. The incumbent centre–left coalition parties represent themselves as the democratic, Europeanist, progressive in-group that represents Italy as a whole and promotes social justice and solidarity. 'We need to regulate things such as a true democracy and realize democracy where one lives' argues the President of the government's Commission for Immigrant Integration (#169). From this perspective the centre–right coalition and the Lega Nord in particular are the out-group because they are xenophobic, authoritarian, racist, anti-European, they violate the Constitution and endanger Italian democracy:

> In the European Right, movements whose message is based on the re-discovery of the territory, on national regionalism and the 'little homelands', have increased their strength. What they have to offer is politically efficient because it does not only promise reduced taxation or jobs but also offers an identity to populations that are alarmed by social insecurity.
>
> (#27)

In the text above, the similarities between the *Lega Nord* and Jörg Haider in Austria are implicitly emphasized. Moreover, the two are framed as part of the 'European Right' so that right-wing forces are discredited as a whole. At the same time, the governing coalition asserts itself as the political force that will guide Italy into Europe, an issue that plays an important role in defining Italian civic national identity (Galli della Loggia, 1998):

> After the attack at gay couples, [the *Lega* attacks] the European Union Charter of Fundamental Rights, and then the last incident, [the attack] at the Islamic communities in Italy.
>
> (#29)

The Lega Nord discourse reverses the in-group/out-group division and represents itself as the truly democratic party that listens to the people but is vigilant (hence, contrasted with those moderate Catholics that are indifferent and passive) against the 'Nazi-communists' (#72) and protects the traditions of the nation:

Azzurri [Forza Italia supporters] and *Lumbard* [Lega supporters] united against the construction of a mosque: Muslims get out of Lodi. ... One thousand protesters at the march, insults to passers-by [inhabitants of Lodi]: cowards, rabbits.

(#129)

In the Lega's discourse, the preservation of the popular, cultural traditions and the 'purity' of the nation are more important than civic values. The centre–left coalition is in the Lega's view authoritarian, because it is, in its opinion, communist, and a threat to the survival and security of the nation. The Lega reinforces its image as the true representative of 'the people' by proposing a 'local referendum'[7] in the Milan neighbourhood where the new mosque would be built (#161).

The two major components of the centre–right coalition, Forza Italia and Alleanza Nazionale, partly subscribe to the Lega's discourse that defines the centre–left and the Muslims/immigrants as the out-group. Forza Italia is, however, against 'any kind of exaggeration'. The 'right of religious freedom remains inalienable' but there is a problem in balancing the situation because if people participate in public rallies which are 'almost xenophobic', 'there must be a reason' (#140).

However, the extreme views of the Lega and its public rallies against the mosques at Lodi and in Milan internally divide the centre–right wing forces. Thus, Alleanza Nazionale and the Christian Democrat Party (CCD) argue that they are the civic-minded conservative forces who will protect national traditions, while the Lega Nord is demagogic and violates the civic values of Italian democracy by its anti-Islamic campaigns. Their positions are not in favour of religious freedom; their aim is to 'respect balance' and 'reciprocity' (#23). A leading member of the Alleanza Nazionale Party and granddaughter of Mussolini, Alessandra Mussolini – in agreement with the party leader Gianfranco Fini (#86) – argues that they have to 'be alert towards the danger of islamization of society' and defend 'the natural predominance of the Catholic and Christian religion and culture' (#23). Indeed, the distancing of political parties from the Lega anti-Islam campaign seems to be motivated more by the fear of losing votes, as overt racism tends to be censored in Italian politics (ter Wal, 2000: 348), rather than by a genuine concern for democracy and civic values. Berlusconi, the leader of the Forza Italia Party and the centre–right coalition, is reported to criticize Umberto Bossi in private: 'on Islam you make us lose votes' (#34). However, another member of the Forza Italia rank and file adds: 'Muslims endanger our purity. Their true scope is to marry our women' (#34). When the new mosque issue was presented in the Milan context at the end of October 2000, Forza Italia rank and file engaged in a civic discourse:

[T]he mosque [construction] is alright, because in Italy there is religious freedom, ... it is a matter of decency and civility. Muslims in Milan are numerous and there is a need for a mosque.

(#161)

Nonetheless, when the Municipal Council voted for the concession of land to COREIS (the Community of Italian Converts to Islam), Alleanza Nazionale and Lega Nord abstained from the vote. A Lega Nord councillor argues:

> If the Municipality is going to give tomorrow a terrain to the mosque, will it not do the same the day after tomorrow with a synagogue, and the day after with an Orthodox church?

(#162)

In this climate of discord within the centre–right coalition, the municipal and regional authorities seek to mobilize electoral support by striking a localist chord. They represent themselves and the city as efficient and democratic Italians contrasted to both the extremist Padanians of the Lega and the communist, inefficient, corrupt left-wing forces of the government.

The Church's 'voice'[8] in the mosque debate tries to strike a fragile balance between supporting the civic values embodied in the Italian Constitution without negating the presumed superiority of Catholicism. Thus, although the Church's representatives were in favour of the construction of the mosques and the Cardinal of Lodi condemned the priest that celebrated a mass in the Lega protest march on 14 October 2000, they at the same time defined popular 'fears' towards Muslim immigrants as normal because hosting immigrants, rather than being emigrants themselves, is a new experience for Italians (#102). This discourse is wrought with internal contradictions because on one hand it recognizes that the Muslim community in Italy is rather small but, on the other hand, alludes to an 'immigrant invasion'. It favours civic integration of immigrants and religious freedom but defines 'multiculturalism as a dangerous concept that means the end of the European nation' (#90). The Church's discourse appears both confusing and confused in front of the quest for multiculturalism.

The mosque debate includes two levels of discourse that are inextricably intertwined. First, a more general debate on the recognition and accommodation of cultural and religious diversity in Italian society, which includes a distinction between Us–hosts–Italians–Catholics and Them–guests–immigrants–Muslims. Second, an intense party campaigning for mobilizing electoral support in which each side promotes a positive view of itself along a common set of values. The most striking feature of the discourse is that either coalition tries to represent itself as democratic, civic minded and defending the national interest. They both agree that it is in the national interest to preserve and/or strengthen the Italian identity and cultural traditions. But they disagree on how best to achieve this: through rejecting religious diversity and halting immigration or through a politics of integration into the dominant cultural frame.

Guests and hosts: multiculturalism *all'Italiana?*

Although the different parties supposedly propose different answers to the quest for recognizing and accommodating religious diversity, a careful look at their discourses reveals a significant degree of convergence. It is my aim in this section to outline the common set of values and views that underlie the different party positions and thus highlight a specific version of multiculturalism emerging in Italy.

The mosque debate is characterized by a given set of values, identity and interest claims that determine the relationship and coexistence of 'hosts' and 'guests'. The values on which this discourse is based are predominantly civic. The main argument is that Italy is a democratic society where civic values are guaranteed for all, citizens and non-citizens alike. Religious freedom is protected by the Constitution (Article 8) and the European Charter of Fundamental Rights. To these principles subscribe both political and religious elites.

In this perspective, solidarity towards immigrants and a desire to integrate them in the host society are also seen as important civic values. Integration, however, has to be framed in a secular, civic framework, which dictates reciprocity of duties and rights for all. In this context of civic integration, the Catholic Church assumes an active role in collaboration with local and regional authorities (#21, #28, #83, #202). The leading role of the Church is neither contested nor seen as a threat to the civic character of Italian society by any of the leading social and political actors quoted in the press.

Integration has to take place under a set of principles and preconditions. First, different groups have to live together under the rule of law, 'respecting the rules' that are set by the host society. These rules and laws emanate from the cultural traditions and values of the host society, which should prevail, as, so the argument goes, Italy 'belongs' to Italians. Muslim immigrants are welcome to the extent that they abide by the law and customs of their 'hosts'. This law and order discourse is often complemented by implicit or explicit references to immigrant criminality (for example, #77) and the risks of clandestine immigrant invasion of Italian territory (for example, #93). Moreover, the acceptance or exclusion of Muslim diversity in Italian society is seen as an issue similar to that of acceptance of gay people. The argument is put forward both by left-wing local authorities (#87) and the Lega Nord leadership (#29, #82), as if Muslims and gay people belong to a single category of socially and/or morally 'deviant' communities.

In a more reactionary version of this discourse, the centre–right parties and some representatives of the Vatican argue that integration should be made conditional upon reciprocity at a universal level. Mosques should not be allowed in Italy as long as there are Islamic countries that do not permit the existence of Christian churches on their soil (#76, #77). This argument is used further to emphasize the distinction between the hosts that are liberal and democratic and the guests who raise claims for religious freedom while in their own countries they are illiberal and oppressive. This 'reciprocity' argument is, however, rejected by the centre–left parties and intellectuals (for example, #19).

Second, both government and opposition representatives emphasize that Italian identity is fragile (#7, #31, #19, #124): Italians should therefore act to safeguard their national identity and cultural traditions. The traditions of their

Muslim 'guests' are seen as inferior and in any case undesirable (#73, #40). All parties confirm the intrinsic value of preserving the 'purity' and 'authenticity' of the national traditions and identity.

The discourse is complemented by a third line of arguments that relate to the interests of the host society. The main quest here is to find the ways in which immigration can best serve the 'hosts'. Immigrants are 'welcome' because they respond to the economic and demographic needs of Italian society. They are seen as a 'resource' for Italian society: they contribute labour that is necessary for domestic businesses and money that is valuable for the national welfare system. A table published in *Il Giornale* (#95) concerning demographic growth in Italy is entitled: 'in risk of extinction' (#93, #94). Immigrant cultures, religions and traditions are not seen as resources but rather as problems because they have to be galvanized to fit the host society's civic and cultural framework. For this reason, Christian immigrants are preferable (#95) to Muslims.

Even though the media discourses analysed refer to events that took place in late 2000, their relevance is still salient today. The two main party coalitions have remained in place, though exchanging their government–opposition roles. Both sides have maintained their views largely unchanged. For the right-wing coalition migration is at best a necessary evil and should be confined to the economic realm, limiting thus the social and cultural rights of immigrants to the bare minimum. Thus, Law 189/2002 is more restrictive than the law of 1998 in its provisions for permit renewal, welfare rights (such as public housing) and the eventual acquisition of a residence card (now given after six instead of five years of continuous residence). Moreover, it ties the stay and work permit to a specific contract with the specific employer, depriving the migrant worker from the basic right to change job or employer if s/he wishes.

The centre–left wing political forces remain more open to issues of immigrant integration and cultural diversity. However, their moral and political power has been reduced not only because they no longer hold office but also because of the general post-9/11 security agenda. The Berlusconi government has made its views on cultural and religious diversity explicit also on the occasion of the intervention in Afghanistan. While the left-wing forces engaged in a critical discourse concerning the causes and consequences of international terrorism and the feasibility of a military solution in Afghanistan, Prime Minister Berlusconi made public statements about the 'superiority' of Western values and lifestyle that should be 'taught' to other peoples.[9] Even though this statement caused widespread embarrassment among European governments and was later 'explained' and rectified by Berlusconi himself, it has marked Italy's political profile in the early twenty-first century.

Conclusions

The main aim of this chapter has been to analyse the emergence of multiculturalism debates and practices in Italy in relation to their specific social and political context. I have thus briefly assessed the size of the immigrant population in Italy, its religious and national composition, the structural position of immigrants in Italian society, with particular reference to their access to the labour market, but also to citizenship and multicultural education and also the development of immigrant networks.

The second part of the chapter has concentrated on a specific instance in the multiculturalism debate: I have analysed the public and political discourse developed after a protest demonstration of the Northern League, in October 2000, against the building of a new mosque in Lodi in the periphery of Milan. The analysis of the debate has revealed the marginality of immigrant 'voices' as well as the predominance of civic views concerning the recognition and acceptance of religious diversity. A close look at the different party positions and their discursive construction of alliances and in-group/out-group oppositions shows that there is a large degree of convergence in their views. Italian multiculturalism is based on a civic conception of the nation and the host society. While rights appear to be conceded not only to individuals but also to communities – in this case the Muslim communities in Milan and Lodi requesting land for a new mosque – their integration in the host society has to take place under the conditions determined one-sidedly by this last. In other words, the core cultural values of the 'hosts' cannot become a matter of negotiation with the 'new arrivals'. They have to accept the rules and laws of Italy. The issue of citizenship is not raised with regard to immigrants. And it is clear that if any disagreement arises, this has to be settled in line with the views of the majority

The Italian multiculturalism debate may appear at first glance to follow the lines of 'constitutional patriotism' (Habermas, 1992). The main line of argument is that immigrants should abide by the host country's laws while their rights are guaranteed by the Italian Constitution. Moreover, the self-conception of Italian society as a democracy imbued by civic values such as religious freedom and equality is emphasized.

However, between the lines of this civic, liberal approach, a nationalist line of argumentation can be read, which asserts the intrinsic value of national identity and traditions, including a strong Catholic Church which also plays a role as a political actor in this debate. The internal diversity of Italian identity and culture and the strong regionalist centrifugal tendencies are to a large extent silenced. It is assumed that

> for each group there is a single culture, that it is homogeneous, that it has always been the same ... so that one can talk about a group and its culture without any reference to context, to contact or interaction with other groups, to economic circumstances, political power and so on.
>
> (Modood, 1997: 10)

It is also assumed that the host group's culture is better than that of immigrants. Both the national in-group and the Muslim/immigrant out-group are constructed as cohesive, homogeneous blocks. Italy's internal division related to the Southern question (Schneider, 1998) or the plurality of Islamic communities present in the country (Pace and Perocco, 2000) is ignored.

After more than twenty years of mass migration, Italian society still finds it hard to recognize and accommodate cultural and religious diversity. Debates and practices favouring multiculturalism have been in decline since 2001, when the Berlusconi government came to power. In the mid-to late 1990s, hesitant steps had been taken by the *Ulivo* centre–left government coalition to promote immigrant integration and to recognize that immigrants 'are here to stay'. The *Ulivo* coalition instituted provincial migration councils with a consultative character, issued multicultural education programmes in schools (limited in number, though) and overall encouraged immigrant participation in public life. It did not, however, contest the dominant role of the Catholic Church and of Catholic associations in assisting immigrants, both legal and undocumented, to find shelter, employment and be reunited with their families. As government agencies were not able to provide for the extended associational network and voluntary work provided by the Catholic sector, most immigrant integration activities – especially those regarding primary socio-economic integration – took place under the auspices of Caritas. Even though Caritas provides assistance and support to Christians and non-Christians alike, this government policy of outsourcing migrant integration has unavoidably confirmed the dominant role of the Church in matters of migration and multiculturalism. Such dominance is reflected in the discourse analysed and is, to my mind, a factor preventing the empowerment and full political and civic integration of migrants from non-Christian faiths.

The Italian debate does not subscribe to the French tradition of republicanism. Although it has some commonalities with it, to the extent that immigrants are expected to assimilate to a dominant national civic culture. The Italian approach, though, goes beyond the level of civic values to include cultural traditions in the dominant national framework to which immigrants should adapt. It borrows some elements from the British discourse as it recognizes the existence not only of Muslim individuals but also of Muslim communities whose requests need to be taken into account. However, the Italian understanding of national civic culture is much 'thicker' than that predicated by the British liberal communitarian multiculturalism (Delanty, 2001).

In conclusion, the current Italian debate is at best ambivalent, at worse outright nationalist. Even left-wing political and intellectual elites find it hard to separate the civic values of Italian democracy from their national cultural framework. The fact that both 'host' and 'guest' cultures may change through coexistence and interaction is also largely ignored. It is safe to say that more advanced scenarios on transnational citizenship (see for instance Bauboeck, 2003) are out of touch with the Italian political debate and public understandings of citizenship, even though they might provide a satisfying answer to the immigrant communities' claims. The bottom line of the Italian debate is that cultural and religious diversities have to be assimilated. Contrary to the argument of more radical multiculturalism theories (Parekh, 2000), cultural diversity is framed as a 'problem' rather than as a 'good thing'.

Appendix I: Indexing scheme

I *Identifiers*

Newspaper (Text)
Date (Date)
Page number (Num)

Title (Text)
Subtitle (Text)
Lead (Text)
Author (Text)

II *Voices (all yes/no variables)*

1   Parties and their leaders or other party rank and file (this tag includes the governing parties and the President of the Republic)
2   The Catholic Church
3   Lega Nord Party rank and file and/or activists
4   Local authorities and/or local party representatives at Lodi
5   Local citizens
6   Immigrants/Muslims
7   Muslim organizations/associations

III *Thematic dimensions (all yes/no variables)*

1   Italian citizenship
2   Italian cultural identity/traditions
3   Italian national identity
4   Europe and/or Italy as part of Europe

IV *The relationship between Us/the country/the nation and Them/immigrants/Muslims/foreigners/third-country nationals (extracomunitari)*

1   What is the relationship? (Text)
2   By what principles or rules should it be guided or on which principles or rules should it be based? (Text)

Appendix II: List of articles cited

Rec. no.	Newspaper	Date	Page	Title
7	M	17.10	14	Fazio: Porte aperte a chi rispetta le regole (Fazio) [Governor of Bank of Italy]: open doors to those who respect the rules)
19	LaR	15.10	17	L'identita degli italiani e la paura degli immigrati (The identity of Italians and the fear of immigrants)
21	LaR	15.10	13	Ma il vescovo non ci sta Ce liberta religiosa (But the bishop disagrees there is religious freedom)
23	LaR	16.10	14	Il Polo spaccato sull'Islam (The Pole divided on Islam)
24	LaR	16.10	14	Berlusconi richiami il Senatur (Berlusconi recalls the [leader of Lega Nord])
27	LaR	17.10	17	Lo spettro della paura s'aggira per l'Europa (The threat of fear is wandering in Europe)
28	LaR	17.10	18	Condanniamo chi discrimina. Intoccabili i diritti religiosi (We condemn anybody who discriminates. Religious rights [are] untouchable)
29	LaR	17.10	19	Il Senatur: liberta di culto? Non e un diritto garantito (The [leader of the Lega Nord]: religious freedom? It is not a right that is guaranteed)
31	LaR	17.10	20	Fazio. No alla xenofobia ma salviamo le identita (Fazio [Governor of Bank of Italy]: No to xenophobia but let's save [our] identity)
34	LaR	18.10	25	Caro Bossi, cosi non va (Dear Bossi [leader of Lega Nord], we cannot continue this way)
40	LaR	19.10	23	Solo 560 mila immigrati ecco l'Islam italiano (Only 560,000 immigrants. Here is the Italian Islam)
53	LaR	25.10	22	E ora anche a Milano si discute di una moschea (Now also in Milan [the opening of] a mosque is debated)
65	LaR	04.11	16	Imparate a essere tedeschi. Die Welt pubblica la bozza della proposta di legge della Merkel sull'immigrazione. La Cdu: corsi di linguae cultura per stranieri (Learn to be Germans. Die Welt publishes the draft Merkel bill on immigration. The CDU: language and culture courses for foreigners)
72	LaR	05.11	4	Bossi: Ma il Papa fa il suo mestiere (Bossi: But the Pope does his own job)

(continued on next page)

Appendix II: (cont.)

Rec. no.	Newspaper	Date	Page	Title
73	G	11.10	8	Martini: Gli immigrati islamici devono accettare le nostre leggi (Martini [Cardinal of Milan]: The Muslim immigrants must accept our laws)
76	GMI	13.10	41	Milano sempre piu straniera (Milan [becoming] ever more foreign)
77	GMI	13.10	44	Sull'Islam sono piu vicino a Martini (On Islam I am closer to Martini)
82	G	15.10	14	Faremo a pezzi la moschea di Lodi (We will cut down into pieces the mosque of Lodi)
92	GMI	22.10	35	Stranieri e Leonka sgomberati da piazza Duomo (Foreigners and Leonka [Leoncavallo] swept away from the Cathedral square)
93	G	25.10	1	Gli immigrati divisi reato per reato (Immigrants classified by type of criminal act)
94	G	25.10	16	In Italia aumentano gli immigrati ma anche i reati (In Italy immigrant [numbers] increase but so do criminal acts)
95	G	25.10	16	Troppi extracomunitari? Il rimedio e fare piu figli (Too many third-country nationals? The remedy is to have more children)
102	GMI	29.10	37	La liberta di culto non e in discussione (Religious freedom is not under question)
123	G	05.11	6	La Cdu: gli stranieri dovranno frequentare corsi d'integrazione (CDU: foreigners will have to attend integration courses)
124	G	05.11	6	La giustizia virtuale (Virtual justice)
129	CdS	15.10	9	Marcia anti-Islam, Forza Italia con la Lega (March against Islam, Forza Italia [Party] with the Lega [Party])
140	CdS	16.10	13	Urbani: Bisogna respingere ogni tipo di eccesso (Urbani: We have to reject all kinds of exaggeration)
159	CdS	25.10	1	Gli islamici e noi italiani (Muslims and us Italians)
161	CdS	25.10	10	Milano, la Lega contro la nuova moschea (Milan, the Lega against the new mosque)
162	CdS	25.10	10	Lodi media sull'Islam, anche i lumbard ora frenano (Lodi mediates on Islam, the [Lega supporters] also pull over)

(continued on next page)

Appendix II: (*cont.*)

Rec. no.	Newspaper	Date	Page	Title
169	CdS	30.10	9	Ma non e vero che le loro richieste sono inaccettabili (But it is not true that their requests are unacceptable)
194	LaR	16.12	27	Allah nel tempio dei portuali (Allah, in the temple of the port workers)
202	LaRFI	11.10	2	Insieme, nel rispetto dei ruoli (Together, respecting our roles)

Notes

* A slightly different version of some sections of this chapter have been published in Triandafyllidou, A. (2002) 'Religious diversity and multiculturalism in Southern Europe: the Italian mosque debate', *Sociological Research Online*, 7(1): www.socresonline.org.uk/ 7/1/ triandafyllidou.html and are reprinted here with the kind permission of the publisher.

1 Revised partly by Law 189/2002 (*legge Bossi Fini*).

2 Law 40/1998 showed for the first time the political will of the Italian government to deal with immigration as a long-term phenomenon providing for ordinary, rather than extraordinary or temporary, measures. The law reiterates and reinforces the equality of treatment and rights between Italians and immigrants and aims at a long-term planning of migratory flows with the co-operation of the governments of the immigrants' countries of origin, acknowledging that there is space in the Italian labour market for foreign workers, provided flows and stays are regulated (see also Guida al Diritto, Inserto speciale, 12 September 1998).

3 In 1998, 3,937 applicants acquired Italian citizenship, 88 per cent of whom did so through marriage to an Italian citizen (SOPEMI, 2000: table 12).

4 Throughout the debate the terms 'Muslims' and 'immigrants' are used as nearly synonymous. For the purposes of the chapter, unless otherwise specified (that is, when specifically referring to Christian immigrants or to Italian Muslims), all Muslims are considered as immigrants and all immigrants as Muslims.

5 *La Repubblica* is a leading daily published in tabloid format, of centre–left political orientation. The newspaper is organized into two sections: the first is related to international and national news and the second is devoted to news of local and regional relevance. The newspaper is published in Bologna, Florence, Genoa, Milan, Naples, Rome and Turin. It belongs to the De Benedetti-L'Espresso group of media enterprises. The *Corriere della Sera* daily is the Milan newspaper *par excellence*. It is published in Milan (a Rome edition also exists) in broadsheet format and has a large circulation at a national level. It is of centre–right political orientation and belongs to the Fiat-Rizzoli group. *Il Giornale* is also based in Milan and belongs to the Berlusconi-Mediaset group. The newspaper was founded by a famous Italian journalist, Indro Montanelli, who sold it to the Berlusconi-Mediaset group in the early 1990s because of financial problems. Following Silvio Berlusconi's involvement in Italian politics, the newspaper has become the unofficial voice of Forza Italia, his political party. The language used in the newspaper is dramatic, and the coverage clearly partisan. *Il Messaggero* is the main local newspaper in Rome and is of centre–left orientation. A large section of the newspaper is devoted to local and

regional news of Rome and the Lazio region. In terms of format it resembles very much *La Repubblica* but the language it uses is less dramatic. *Il Messaggero* was included in the newspaper selection because of its large circulation in the capital city but also as a good case for testing how issues of local relevance, such as the Lodi or Milan controversies, were constructed into national ones, attracting coverage by *Il Messaggero* too, despite its regional bias.

6 All quotes originally in Italian have been translated by the author. A list of the newspaper articles cited is given in Appendix II.

7 *Corriere della Sera* reports the Lega initiative to collect signatures against the building of the new mosque in a Milanese neighbourhood using interchangeably the terms 'referendum' and 'collection of signatures', thus implicitly legitimizing the initiative as a democratic action (#168).

8 The Catholic Church has played an important role in Italian politics in the post-war period, securing overwhelming support for the former Christian Democrat Party (Democrazia Cristiana) in rural areas. When the DC collapsed from a series of corruption scandals in the early 1990s, the Catholic Church lost its powerful ally in domestic politics but continued to exert important influence over part of the electorate. Moreover, the Church's voluntary sector has played an important and active role in assisting both documented and undocumented immigrants, regardless of their religious faith, in the past decade.

9 Berlusconi, at a briefing to journalists in Berlin, praised Western civilization as 'superior' to Islam and urged Europe to 'reconstitute itself on the basis of its Christian roots' (Steven Erlanger, *International Herald Tribune*, 27 September 2001 (article published also in electronic form in: http://www.globalpolicy.org/wtc/analysis/0927berlu.htm (accessed 30 November 2004))).

References

Baldwin Edwards, M. (2001) 'Southern European labour markets and immigration. a structural and functional analysis', MMO Working Paper No. 5. Also available at: http://www.mmo.gr/pdf/publications/mmo_working_papers/MMO_WP5.pdf (accessed 23 September 2004).

Bauboeck, R. (2003) 'Towards a political theory of migrant transnationalism', *International Migration Review*, 37(3).

Campani, G. (1993) 'Immigration and racism in Southern Europe: the Italian case', *Ethnic and Racial Studies*, 16(3): 507–535.

Carillo, M. R., Quintieri, B. and Vinci, P. C. (1999) 'Causes and economic effects of migration flows: an overview', *Labour*, 13(3): 587–602.

Caritas (2003) *Immigrazione. Dossier Statistico*, Roma: Anterem.

Chaloff, J. (1999) 'Current research into education for immigrants in Italy', Paper presented at the 4th International Metropolis Conference, Washington, DC, December.

—— (2003) 'Italy', in J. Niessen, Y. Schibel and R. Magoni (eds) *EU and US approaches to the management of immigration*, Brussels: MPG. Also available at: http://www.migpolgroup.com (accessed 15 September 2004).

Delanty, G. (2001) 'Ideas for multicultural citizenship in Europe', Discussion paper presented at the Workshop on Racism and Xenophobia. Key Issues, Mechanisms and Policy Opportunities, Brussels, 5–6 April.

Diamanti, I. (1999) 'Ha senso ancora discutere della nazione?', *Rassegna Italiana di Sociologia*, XL (2): 293–321.

Galli della Loggia, E. (1998) *L'identità italiana*, Bologna: Il Mulino.

Gavosto, A., Venturini, A. and Villosio, C. (1999) 'Do immigrants compete with natives?', *Labour*, 13(3): 603–622.

Gusfield, J. R. (1981) *The Culture of Public Problems: Drinking-driving and the Symbolic Order*, Chicago: University of Chicago Press.

Habermas, J. (1992) 'Staatsbürgerschaft und nationale Identität', in M. Suhrkamp, *Faktizität und Geltung*, Frankfurt am Mainz: Suhrkamp.

Jacobs, D. (1998) 'Discourse, politics and policy: the Dutch Parliamentary debate about voting rights for foreign residents', *International Migration Review*, xxxii(2): 350–374.

——— (1999) 'The debate over enfranchisement of foreign residents in Belgium', *Journal of Ethnic and Migration Studies*, 25(4): 649–663.

Knights, M. (1996) 'Bangladeshi immigrants in Italy – from geopolitics to micropolitics', *Transactions of the Institute of British Geographers*, 21(1): 105–123.

Kosic, A. and Triandafyllidou, A. (2004) 'Understanding the conditions for immigrant active civic participation: the case of Italy', Project Report prepared for the POLITIS project, Florence: EUI.

Kymlicka, W. (1998) 'Introduction: an emerging consensus?', *Ethical Theory and Moral Practice*, Special Issue on Nationalism, Multiculturalism and Liberal Democracy, 1(2): 143–157.

Melchionda, U. (ed.) (1996) 'Intercultura e discriminazione culturale nella scuola: una ricerca-azione nella scuola', *Quaderni di ERIS*, No.1.

Modood, T. (1997) 'Introduction: the politics of multiculturalism in the New Europe', in T. Modood and P. Werbner (eds) *The Politics of Multiculturalims in the New Europe*, London and NY: Zed books: 1–25.

——— (2001) 'Multicultural integration: identifying the normative challenges in European contexts OR: North American political theory, British multiculturalism and Europe', Paper presented at Workshop 24, Immigration, Integration and European Union. Institutional Practices and Normative Challenges, ECPR Joint Sessions, Grenoble, 6–11.

Nevola, G. (1999) 'Nazione-Italia', *Rassegna Italiana di Sociologia*, XL(3), luglio–settembre: 435–460.

OECD LEED (2004) 'Italy. The case-study report. Local integration of immigrants in the labour market', September.

Pace, E. and Perocco, F. (2000) 'L'Islam plurale degli immigrati in Italia', *Studi Emigrazione/Migration Studies*, xxxvii(137): 2–20.

Parekh, B. (2000) *Rethinking Multiculturalism: Cultural Diversity and Political Theory*, Basingstoke: Macmillan.

Pastore, F. (2001) 'Nationality law and international migration: the Italian case', in R. Hansen and P. Weil (eds) *Towards a European Nationality*, New York: Palgrave.

Pittau, F. (2000) 'Distribuzione religiosa degli immigrati in Italia', *Studi Emigrazione/Migration Studies*, xxxvii: 176–183.

Reyneri, E. (1998) 'The mass legalization of migrants in Italy: permanent or temporary emergence from the underground economy?', *South European Society and Politics*, 3(3): 82–102.

Reyneri, E., Baganha, M., Dal Lago, A., Laacher, S., Palidda, S., Papantoniou, A., Papantoniou, M., Solé, C. and Wilpert, C. (1999) 'Migrants' insertion in the informal economy: deviant behaviour and the impact on receiving societies (MIGRINF). The comparative reports', January, Final Report, TSER programme (Contract No. SOE2-CT95–3005).

Rusconi, G. E. (1993) *Se cessiamo di essere una nazione*, Bologna: Il Mulino.

Schneider, J. (ed.) (1998) Italy's 'Southern Question': Orientalism in One Country, Oxford: Berg.

Shaw, E. (1979) 'Agenda-setting and mass communication theory', International Journal for Mass Communication Studies, xxv(2): 96–105.

SOPEMI (2000) Immigration and Foreign Presence in Italy, 1998–1999, Rome: Fondazione CENSIS, January.

ter Wal, J. (2000) 'Italy: Sicurezza e Solidarietà', in R. Wodak and T. van Dijk (eds) Racism at the Top. Parliamentary Discourse on Ethnic Issues in Six European States, Vienna: Austrian Federal Ministry of Education, Science and Culture: 311–353.

Triandafyllidou, A. (2002) Negotiating Nationhood in a Changing Europe. Views from the Press, Ceredigion, Wales and Washington, DC: Edwin Mellen.

——— (2005) 'Italy and Europe: internal others and external challenges to national identity', in A. Ichijo and W. Spohn (eds) Entangled Identities: Nations and Europe, Aldershot: Ashgate.

Triandafyllidou, A. and Veikou, M. (2001) Organisational Culture and Identity Processes in the Implementation of Immigration Policy in Italy', 2nd project report, Florence and New York, April. See also: http://www.iue.it/RSC/IAPASIS (accessed 12 January 2004).

Vasta, E. (1993) 'Rights and racism in a new country of immigration: the Italian case', in J. Wrench, J. and J. Solomos (eds) Racism and Migration in Western Europe, Oxford: Berg.

Veikou, M. and Triandafyllidou, A. (2001) 'Immigration policy and its implementation in Italy: the state of the art', in A. Triandafyllidou (ed.) Migration Pathways. A historic, demographic and policy review of four countries of the European Union, Brussels: European Commission Research Directorate: 63–85.

Veugelers, J. W. P. (1994) 'Recent immigration politics in Italy: a short story', in M. Baldwin-Edwards and M. Schain (eds) The politics of immigration in Western Europe, West European Politics, Special Issue, 17(2): 33–49.

Woods, D. (1992) 'The immigration question in Italy', in S. Hellman and G. Pasquino G. (eds) Italian Politics: A Review, Volume 7, London: Pinter.

Zincone, G. (ed.) (2000a) Primo rapporto sull'integrazione degli immigrati in Italia, Bologna: Il Mulino.

——— (ed.) (2000b) Secondo rapporto sull'integrazione degli immigrati in Italia, Bologna: Il Mulino.

8 The Muslim community and Spanish tradition

Maurophobia as a fact, and impartiality as a desideratum

Ricard Zapata-Barrero

Introduction

In Spain, whenever the members of a Muslim community want to construct a mosque in a city, a deep-seated and immediate reaction of neighbourhood protest begins, generally supported, or at least not hindered and/or not contradicted, by local authorities. The attitude of local authorities towards the issue of Muslim residents can be summed up by their recognition of the existence of a place of worship on private premises (private homes, community centres, etc.) and their reluctance to recognize the need to give Muslims the public visibility enjoyed by the Catholic Church (Moreras, 1999; 2003). The management of this issue of recognition almost always constitutes a landmark for political authorities and citizens in any account dealing with the way Spain is handling the (latter-day) Muslim presence in its territory. Invariably, public opinion polls on these topics reveal that the majority of Spanish citizens link their opposition to immigrants in general and to the Muslim community in particular, especially the most numerous one, the Moroccan community (Pérez-Diaz *et al.*, 2004). It is a fact that in Spain Muslim and Islamic issues have appeared in the public sphere with rather rigid images attached to them. Almost all the negative immigration news is related to the Muslim community.

It is also a reality that the Spanish identity, like the European one but with many more historical points of reference, has been built in opposition to the picture of the Muslim in general and the Moroccan in particular, considered in pejorative terms as 'the Moor' ('*el moro*'). Yet nobody can deny that Spanish tradition cannot be understood without the Islamic legacy and cultural heritage. How is Spain managing the fact that a historical stereotypic picture of the Moor is governing public opinion and political arguments? How can Spain fight against this deep-rooted negative perception of the Moors without threatening its national identity as expressed through its citizens? How should Muslims express their self-identity in a Spanish society and polity which has a public discourse that refuses to recognize its own Islamic tradition, that assumes that Islam belongs to 'a historical anomaly'? In accordance with the general framework of this book, I contend that these questions and their potential answers will give us the main distinctive elements to contribute to the debate on multi-cultural citizenship in Europe.

Let me begin with the premise that these questions have as a common point of analysis the link between the Muslim community and Spanish tradition. I argue that there are actually two ways of answering these questions: one that says that Islam is an anomaly to the Spanish historical process (something abnormal that remained for eight centuries!), something alien to our cultural tradition and identity; and the other which establishes that Islam belongs to our cultural tradition and identity. Depending on which focus we follow, we will have different sources of production of political arguments. The first focus tends to see two separate traditions that have been historically at odds. It will tend to follow a political discourse that stresses what is different between the Muslim and Spanish traditions, what separates the two traditions. The second focus will defend the theory that there is one tradition (rather than two) that has historically converged. It demonstrates that Spain is the only Western European context in which the Islamic tradition developed a cultural society and a political system that lasted centuries. Spain is the only country in Western Europe to have been Islamized for so long (we know that the Balkans and Sicily were also Islamized). This focus thus gives rise to a political discourse emphasizing what is common (Roque, 2003).

My argument in this chapter is that Spanish public discourse tends to follow the first 'route' as a heuristic framework for political arguments, whereas I will defend the second 'route' as a desirable interpretative frame of reference for producing political arguments. Islam in Spain is not a new reality that citizens are discovering, but a historical fact that people tend to repress, in almost Freudian terms. In this light, it is possible to incorporate the Muslim legacy into the tradition of Spanish citizenship without threatening Spanish identity.

The chapter is divided into five sections. In the first section I present my focus, contending that there is a *Maurophobia* in Spain that has been constructed throughout history and that this picture is not a contingent fact but a substantive element of the process of Spanish identity building, without which Spanish citizenship cannot be understood. Historically, there is a parallel process between the construction of a negative perception of the 'Moor' and the process of building the Spanish identity. In the second section I describe the main social events that transform what I will call 'contact zones' between the Muslim community/institutions and Spanish citizens into 'conflict zones'. In the third section I will summarize the main legal framework regulating the relationship between Muslims and the state, established in Spain in 1992. In the fourth section I discuss the main elements that characterize the Spanish discourse on the Muslim presence, concentrating mainly on evidence from the media, tradition and politics. Finally, in the fifth section, and as a concluding argument, I will argue for the need to think of impartiality as a criterion of justice and as the main approach to treating Muslims from our European perspective. Spain could provide an example to follow.

The focus: Maurophobia as an aspect of the Spanish identity and the revival of 'Hispanidad'

Maurophobia is not a contingent fact characterizing Spain in the face of Muslim immigrants, but a substantive feature of Spanish tradition. The question is, then, how to deal with this Maurophobia without threatening Spanish iden- tity? I believe that this matter also has a European dimension, but I will limit my argumentation to the Spanish context. We cannot understand the citizens' perception of – and attitude against – the Moroccan community in Spain only in terms of sociological and political variables and without historical arguments. Indeed, the latter is the most appropriate focus to construct explanatory argu- ments relating to citizenship, the Muslim question and multiculturalism in Spain. Tradition matters in Spain, and it is at the forefront of most policies concerning the Muslim community.

In this section I will argue that it is not exactly Islamophobia or religious/cultural racism that exists in Spain, but *Maurophobia* (phobia of the Moors). From this viewpoint, the questions heading the chapter can be speci- fied: why this Maurophobia if public spaces are historically packed with the Muslim presence – even our language is replete with words coming from Arabic, most of our family names have an Arabic origin, and our regional division of Spain into seventeen communities has its historical source in the Muslim division of Spain?[1] Still today, the traditional picture is perpetuated in schools through history textbooks that consolidate the idea of Muslims versus Christians and the negation of the '*moro*' (Navarro, 1997). One of the reasons for this Maurophobia is surely that Spain is the only Western European country to have belonged to the Islamic area of influence. The negation of any Muslim signifi- cance can thus be explained as some sort of historical revenge (Bernal, 2002).

This historical iconography of the Moors belongs to Spanish tradition since the period of the *Reconquista* or Reconquest, when the Spanish Queen Isabel and King Ferdinand, known as the Catholic Kings, using mainly Christian argu- ments, expelled the Muslims (together with the Jews and the gypsies) from Spain in 1492. The presence of the kingdom of Al Andalus over eight centuries (from 711 to 1492) finished in fact in 1609 with the expulsion of the *moriscos* (that is, Muslims who converted to Christianity and stayed in Spain after the *Reconquista*; today we would call them 'Spaniards of Muslim origin'). If this is the beginning, other phases of Spanish history contribute to this negative picture of the Moors. E. Martín Corrales (2002a), in an excellent work tracing this historical construction of the Moors, reminds us that the propaganda of the *Reconquista* worked to disqualify and satanize the Islamic religion. As well as emphasizing some ethnic and physical characteristics of these believers, it allowed for the formation of a corpus of stereotypes and clearly degrading clichés (depicting them as impure, treasonous, false, evil, perfidious, cruel, cowardly, lewd etc.). The process of negative construction of the image of the Muslims intensified from the sixteenth to eighteenth centuries, when Muslim corsairs filled the ports of the southern Mediterranean with Christian slaves (Martín Corrales, 2001).

The unsolved problems of Hispano-Moroccan relations (piracy from the region of the Rif, attacks on Ceuta and Melilla – still today Spanish enclaves in Morocco, let me say, the equivalent of British Gibraltar – and on the fishing boats that operated along the Saharan coast, among others) were the pretext for liberal Spain to embark on the African War of 1860, in which the Moroccans were described as vile, lewd monkeys, dogs, gangsters, etc. By then, the European powers had decided the distribution of the African continent (Ferro, 1994). The Conference of Algeciras in 1906 marked the beginning of the phase of the Franco-Spanish Protectorate of 1912. The illusion of a 'civilizing peaceful penetration' (Martín Corrales, 2002b) was very ephemeral, as the Spanish defeat showed. Again, we see the most degrading descriptions of enemies considered as the 'new barbarian', as simple savages. As the Spanish troops were imposing their dominion in Morocco, direct contact between colonized and colonizer put the latter in a better position as regards know-how. The submissive Moroccan, who apparently ceased to be a threat, became the object of mockery: the savage of an earlier period gave way to the peasant frightened and astonished by the technology and the fashions introduced by the Spaniards. However, the resounding Spanish defeat in Annual supposed the resurgence of the most horrifying images of Moroccans. In this regard, Martín Corrales (2002a) brings together about 800 pictures that exemplify the Spanish mental universe regarding the Moors.

After this period, the outbreak of the Civil War caused the bipolarization of the image of the Moroccans. The republicans, socialists, communists, anarchists and peripheral nationalists depicted the Moroccans enlisted on the pro-Franco side in the most terrible way: treasonous, cruel, cowardly, drunken, godless, mercenary, greedy, sodomites and rapists. In contrast, the triumphant Francoists made official the respectful and paternalistic image of the Moroccan. However, once the Protectorate was back in place, a new image was born: that of the 'morito bueno' (the 'good little Moor'), primitive, ingenuous, likeable, who cried: 'Paisa, I am your amigó (friend)' (Valenzuela, 2002). But this picturesque Oriental wave did not last long.

The participation of Moorish troops on the pro-Franco side against the Republic revived, then, the stereotypes of brutality, but this time from the Left. The Right had to invent myths, such as the community of belief in God of Moroccans and Franco supporters, to justify the resort of seeking military aid from the Saracens.[2] The still vivid memory of the war in the Rif and the part played by Moorish regular soldiers in the Civil War reinforced a very negative perception of the Moroccans in the minds of the losers.

Symbolically, then, it is meaningful that the Spanish identity has been codified as a negation of this historical debt, since the Sephardic Jews were expelled from Spain at the same time as the Muslims and gypsies, in the symbolic year of 1492, the official date of the beginning of the conquest of America and the global expansion of Spanish Catholicism and messianism (indeed the first global politics even conducted). The politics of the so-called Catholic Kings has many elements of what today we would refer to as *ethnic cleansing*. Behind this, there is also the politically constructed idea of *Hispanidad*, developed at the beginning of the twentieth century, precisely to counterweigh the loss of the last colonies in America (particularly Cuba in 1898). This idea of *Hispanidad* was also used under the Franco regime (1940–1975) to refer to a community of people linked together by linguistic and religious criteria. Within this framework, *Hispanidad* was clearly used politically to build a culturally homogeneous society and the discourse of exclusion.

Why this historical debt with Jews and not with Muslims? If we consider the criterion of colonial debt, there is no reason why Filipinos are included and not Moroccans as a nationality of preference in Spanish immigration law and the citizenship code (Zapata-Barrero, 2003b), as Morocco was one of the last Spanish protectorates (1912–1956, but until 1975 for the Spanish Sahara). Neither does geographical proximity work, if we compare the distance between Spain and Morocco with that of Spain and South America. Language affinity may work as a criterion if we consider the nationality preferences in the Spanish citizenship code, but it does not justify why Poles, with whom Spain has no historical ties, language affinities or geographic proximity, are favoured over Moroccans in the process of recruitment of workers. The only factor explaining this Spanish protectionism against Morocco is the bilateral conflict arising from the colonial period, since historically there has been permanent conflict between Morocco and Spain for the control of the Sahara, and the historical collective construction of the stereotype 'Moor' as somebody suspicious, physically dirty and pestilential, ugly and potentially criminal.[3] If we accept that in any selection process there is always an evaluation and a social model, the current management of immigration contributes to building a Spanish historical memory for selecting those 'good' and 'bad' immigrants following one or both of the following criteria: language and/or religion. These are the two basic pillars of the Spanish discourse of exclusion. We can therefore conclude that language and religion are the most tangible elements of Spanish tradition.

Since El Ejido in February 2000, but surely also as a consequence of 11 September 2001 in New York and even 11 March in Madrid, and more recently, the bombings in London (7 and 21 July) there has been an explicit and intentional policy favouring Central and Eastern European immigrants and South Americans over Moroccans. Moroccans were until recently the most numerous foreign nationality in Spain (about 21.8 per cent of the foreign population), followed by Ecuadorians, who accounted for 7.6 per cent (Zapata-Barrero, 2003a), although the latest statistics (2004) show that Ecuadorians have surpassed Moroccans. It is also apparent that the first bilateral agreements for sending immigrant workers were made with Ecuador and Poland. The only logical explanation for this policy is origin and Christian identity; that is, the protection of the Spanish identity (De Lucas, 2002a; 2002b) against those viewed as potential 'cultural invaders', even as a new Arab invasion (Mateo Dieste, 2002), a re-Islamization of Spain (Martín-Muñoz, 1996; Balta, 1996: 94–105) and Europe (among others, Vertovec and Peach, 1997; Alsayyad and Castells, 2003). It is revealing that the 2002 report by SOS Racism gave, for the first time, ample coverage to 'Islamophobia' as one of the increasing typologies of structural racism in the near future in Spain.

To conclude, we can say that there is a historical Spanish tradition of Maurophobia that is present in social and political discourse, and is used to legitimate citizens' attitudes against Muslim immigration in Spain. This Spanish identity building is also nourished by media which constantly remind us that the most negative news is related to Muslim presence and practice. Islam has historically been excluded from the formation of the Judaeo-Christian Spanish identity in which the formation of a Christian 'us' has been opposed to an Islamic 'other' (Martín-Muñoz, 1996: 14). The process of Islamization of Spain through the presence of Muslim immigrants is also driven by the Spanish authorities which draw on these historical stereotypes to restrict the public space available to the Muslim community, forcing its members to close in on themselves and search for their own identity, since the identity of Spanish citizenship is not open to them.[4] In this situation, the construction of Muslim facilities acquires vital importance, as does the Muslim presence in schools and the redesigning of cemeteries to allow for Muslim funeral rites. We will discuss these issues in the next section.

Social events: 'contact zones' between the Muslim community and Spanish institutions and citizens as 'conflict zones'

The case of oratories and mosques for the Islamic population is familiar to everyone, and many will take it as the only aspect under consideration in the process of multiculturalism we are witnessing in Europe (Zapata-Barrero, 2004b). However, there are also cases of confrontation ('conflict zones') that arise as a result of failure to allow religious identities to be manifested in public space. I am referring to the issue of the headscarf, France being the illustrative case (see contributions in this volume, especially chaps. 4 and 9). Recently, new issues have arisen in France that come under the same category, such as the establishment of schedules in municipal swimming pools for Muslim children. Each of these situations is very different to the other, but they all share the feature that there are 'contact zones' between the two religious traditions (the Catholic and the Islamic) that tend to turn into 'conflict zones'.[5] The reasons for this process of change from contact to conflict zones are different in different European countries, but there are many similar issues that deserve attention, since they constitute the 'European approach' to multicultural citizenship.[6] Spain is a context in which these categories of conflict zones are entering the social agenda and have been politicized since 2000.

It is true that we cannot say that a conflict arises every time there is contact between a Spanish citizen and an immigrant of Moroccan origin, but taken collectively it is on the whole frequent for the Muslim community to have serious problems to practise its culture and religion within a public space originally created and occupied by non-Muslim citizens (Zapata-Barrero, 2002). In short, we are faced with what B. Parekh (2000) would qualify as a structural problem of multiculturalism.[7] As G. Martín-Muñoz argues (2003: 38) there is a tendency to identify Muslims for what they are (their religious affiliation) rather than by what they do (that is, work like any other citizen). If we consider the main social events to have occurred over the last three years (2002–2004) we can say that Maurophobia really exists in a society that always transforms any contact zone into a conflict zone.

Indeed, one of the channels where this picture is produced and given feedback is in the media which, consciously or unconsciously, convey at least three negative pictures of Muslims that serve to legitimate racist and xenophobic attitudes: the Moroccans are linked to Bin Laden and are potentially criminal and inspire immediate distrust; Arabic people are opposed to democracy by nature because their Muslim practice violates the most elementary human rights; and finally, as a corollary, Islam is identified with barbarism (Valenzuela, 2003: 224).

In 2002, the annual report of SOS Racism drew attention for the first time to a new and growing type of racism in Spain: Islamophobia. This process is due to an expansion of the visibility of Muslims in public spheres (Moreras, 1999). The majority of conflict zones are related to Islamic community facilities, such as mosques or oratories. Generally, local authorities, instead of managing conflicts impartially, directly adopt an 'understanding' position towards the local inhabitants, no doubt because of the electoral cost of defending the Muslims' claims. One type of administrative action to contribute to these limits to Muslim public expression is to extend planning permits excessively. Other problems are related to refusals to grant trading permits for Muslims' shops or even, as was the case in Alicante, sending administrative inspectors only to Moroccan stores and then closing them, with the support of the local people.

Over the period 2002–2004 there have been at least four kinds of conflict zone: mosques, Muslim shops, cemeteries and racist attacks. In 2003, for instance, if only three xenophobic attacks (one is one too many, of course, but in comparison with other actions, it is few) against Muslim facilities (mosques) were reported by SOS Racism (two in Catalonia and one in Madrid), twelve cases of opposition to the opening of a mosque have been identified. The most important one, because it acquired social and political notoriety beyond the local context, was in a small seaside town near Barcelona called Premià de Mar, where an organized neighbourhood community pressurized local authorities through social protest and forced them to rescind the planning permit they had granted. The mosque was eventually moved from the original site in the town centre to one in the outskirts. The resolution of the conflict zone really has a symbolic dimension: religious practice is publicly recognized through the concession of planning permission to build a mosque, but in the outskirts; that is, far away from the citizens' gaze. Premià de Mar has been used, and it is still used, as evidence and a symbol in social and political arguments. Other structural conflict zones include cemeteries and halal food, but they give rise to a less intensive reaction from citizens than mosques.

Relationship between the Muslim community and the state: legal framework

Spain is one of the few European countries which has reached an agreement with religious communities regulating their activities and their visibility within society (the three religious communities concerned are the Islamic, the Evangelist and Protestant, and the Jewish). The agreement with the Muslim community is one of the most liberal in Europe. This legal framework was drawn up in 1992, coinciding with the 500th anniversary of the culmination of the *Reconquista* (another example of how tradition orientates current immigrant policies). For Spain this *Acuerdo de Cooperación entre el Estado Español y la Comissión islámica de España* (signed in Madrid on 28 April 1992, and promulgated as Law 26/92 on 10 November) represents a normalization of the situation with Muslims, a political will to right the wrong whereby they were categorically expelled from Spain and Spanish history. It is the first legal norm since 1492 which gives the Islamic religion a legal status (Borràs and Mernissi, 1997).

Before describing its main contents, we should stress that one of the first difficulties encountered by the state was the lack of an interlocutor representing the whole Muslim community. In order to present a single legitimate representative, the two main federations of associations, the FEERI (Federación Española de Entidades Religiosas Islámicas, 1989) and the UCIDE (Unión de Comunidades Islámicas de España, 1991) were obliged to join forces. In spite of discrepancies between them (Motilla, 2003), they created the Islamic Commission of Spain (Comisión Islámica de España or CIE) with the aim of negotiating with the state. There were many disagreements during the negotiations and several situations of deadlock, especially due to the undifferentiated treatment they were given and the state's refusal to give special treatment to one religious community with regard to the others (Motilla, 2003: 323). The agreements with the other religious communities are practically the same, in spite of their having different religious needs.[8]

Beyond these initial difficulties, the agreement has been viewed as the basis of a twofold primary recognition. First, that religion is a vital component for integration. It is, then, important to focus on the agreement as a first step towards a politics of religion and community (Vertovec and Peach, 1997), and as a politics of integration. Second, the agreement with the Muslim community is the first official recognition in Spain that Islam has a 'firm foundation' ('*notorio arraigo*'), on equal terms with other confessions, in what can be regarded as the beginning of a recognition of the religious plurality of Spain, usually seen as exclusively Catholic. In both cases, and following the focus of the chapter, the agreement has an impact on the Spanish tradition, which is beginning to be more permeable to other religious traditions.

The contents of the agreement deal largely with the recognition of traditions, such as: provision of religious needs in public buildings and legal protection of mosques; status for Islamic religious leaders and imams, with the determination of specific rights derived from the exercise of their religious function, personnel in key areas such as social security; authority to perform civil marriages in accordance with Islamic ritual; tax relief for religious activities; regulation of religious festivities in the workplace; prescription of halal food; the right to create an area within existing cemeteries for Muslims, and even to create their own cemeteries; the possibility of setting up Muslim schools at all educational levels and the possibility of Muslim students receiving religious education in public schools; and collaboration with the state for the conservation and promotion of the historical and artistic heritage of Islam.

These highly advanced and liberal-minded measures have received much comment and criticism. The most pertinent evaluation is that the agreement rests on a virtual framework without funding or any real possibility of implementation. It is a sort of architectural plan that lacks the materials it needs to become a building. Today there is a large gap between reality and the contents of the agreement, which is used in practice as the main justification for claims in the relationship between the Muslim community and the state. If, at the beginning, there was a high level of expectations, we are now in a phase of some uncertainty. Between the two federations that make up the Islamic Commission of Spain, there are no longer mere discrepancies, but rather there is an outright hostility in the form of competition to control the whole community. This situation of lack of co-operation has blocked any possibility of implementing some articles of the Agreement (Moreras, 2003). There is a serious fragmentation of the Muslim community, and competition between its factions to get projects financed and to extend their control beyond the local and regional scale. Naturally, this slows down any initiative aimed at a greater presence in the public sphere.

The state tends to see the agreement as something marginal, and may be much more concerned with the link between the Muslim community and the rise of Islamic fundamentalism, since many of the Islamic terrorists who have been identified live in, or have some link with, Spanish territory. We may now be experiencing the beginning of a new phase after the eight years of right-wing Popular Party government and the victory of the Socialist Party in March 2004. What we can say is that some government measures that are currently under way indicate a certain amount of gradual implementation of the 1992 agreement. We can quote two new initiatives that are, at the time of writing, at the ministerial office and undergoing public discussion. The first is the inclusion within the Spanish tax system of the possibility of choosing the religious confession for which a percentage of income tax is to be earmarked (Bastante, 2004a). Up to now, the two options available to taxpayers were the Catholic Church and social work. Other religious communities had no possibility of public recognition in the tax system. This is a real move forward towards equal treatment of religious communities in Spain and impartiality as a guiding criterion for managing religious pluralism (see the last section of the chapter).

The other new governmental initiative is aimed at regulating the figure of the imam, since after the terrorist attacks in Madrid on 11 March 2004 there is serious suspicion and evidence of the existence of uncontrolled imams with a fundamentalist discourse towards the Muslim immigrant community and a solid and clandestine Islamic network. The present government is aware that this 'mosque circuit' ('*circuito de las mezquitas*') requires urgent management by state institutions and political instruments. Two ways of regulating this 'circuit' and the figure of the imam are currently under discussion in Spain. One originates from the Muslim community, and proposes Islamic schools and universities as a way to manage the Islamic educational curriculum and even to control the training of imams in Spain, thus incorporating Spanish contextual elements within the curriculum (at the moment the majority of imams are 'imported'). The other proposal is to reach some sort of formula for financing the Muslim community through associations and supporting their mobilization, since financing communities is a very effective way to supervise them.[9]

If, at the beginning, just after the signing of the Co-operation Agreement, the Islamic Commission of Spain was the only body recognized by the state to regulate and manage the various aspects of Muslim practices in public and private life, such as the control of holy places, the training and selection of imams, negotiations with entrepreneurs about work timetables, the main Muslim festivities, even the control of the production of halal food, this fact is nowadays considered as a problem since most Muslim practices are performed outside the Islamic Commission, the only interlocutor with the Spanish state. One wonders in what ways this Commission is representative of the interests of poorer, newer (and often undocumented) Muslim immigrants from North Africa. In a recent article in the newspaper *La Vanguardia*, I. Ramos (2004c) gives a very instructive description of the current situation, synthesized in one of its headings: 'Lack of political will and confrontation between the two Islamic federations leave the Agreement void' ('*La falta de voluntad política y el enfrentamiento entre las dos federaciones islámicas dejan el acuerdo vacío*'). It is also a fact that the difficulties in reaching partial agreements between the state and the Muslim community foster a political and social discourse that tends to engender further deadlock.

The Spanish discourse on the Muslim community: media, tradition and political discourse, the interpretative framework

When there is a social fear of an unknown community, citizens tend to search for arguments to explain their feelings. These arguments help them to rationalize their emotions. The arguments citizens currently find in the public arena principally come from the media, tradition and political discourse. The argument to be defended is not that Islam is a source of social and political instability, but rather that it is the perception that citizens have of Islam and the interpretation politicians tacitly follow that are the main source of instability. For instance, it is not the presence of a mosque in a city that provokes instability, but the perception that citizens have of a mosque which transforms this previous contact zone into a conflict zone. When dealing with immigrants in general, and with Muslim workers in particular, we have to deal with interpretative situations. Objectivity becomes an empty word (see last part of Zapata-Barrero, 2004b).

We have already seen that the media tend to consolidate the perception of the Moroccan not only as somebody who is extremely different to us, that is as a non-citizen, but even as a person whose practices can endanger our values and our current quality of life, that is, as an anti-citizen. When the media try to correct this tendency, they are inclined to go to the other extreme and build an exotic icon of the Moroccan, close to the Rousseauesque universe, as an uncivilized but kind-natured human being, who reminds us of the philosophical discourses after the conquest of America in the sixteenth and seventeenth centuries (Todorov, 1991). In reality, the public perception of Muslim immigrants is much more based on media discourse than direct contact (Martín-Muñoz, 2003: 15).

When we speak of tradition we are confronted with two opposing approaches: one establishing that Spanish tradition has only a Graeco-Roman and Judaeo-Christian heritage, and the other that includes also a third cultural heritage: the Arab and Islamic legacy. The Spanish discourse, as we have already seen in the first section, has constructed a tradition drawing a negative (and even dangerous) picture of the Moroccan, synthesized in the figure of the Moor. The main line of this argument is that current Spanish tradition is the result of the Christian victory against Muslim invasion. Muslim people are by nature unable to be integrated into a society and a public sphere that is replete with Catholic customs. The Spanish public sphere is structurally Catholic.

Many do not realize that when an immigrant comes to Spain the first concern s/he has is not about religion, but work, health, school and home (Abu-Tarbush, 2002: 57). We can even say that if citizens' values are post-material, Muslims' values are material rather than spiritual. Muslim people are religious in their everyday life, like Spanish citizens. Religion belongs more to the realm of custom and habit than to the conscious (and, I would say, militant) realm of belief. When an immigrant publicly affirms her/his faith it may be a real concern, but there are also ingredients of social protest and a process of 'reactive identity', that is an identity that is being constructed as a reaction against an 'other' who has created walls of separation. This is, we could say, the basic danger of an unsound management of the Muslim presence, and the main effects are to force Muslims to practise their religious identity within an 'invisible' and 'clandestine' sphere, with the consequence of a lack of public control of mosques and the process of re-Islamization of Muslims living abroad (Fundació Jaume Bofill, 2004).

Within this framework, political discourse in Spain, but surely also in Europe as a whole, instead of having a socializing and pedagogic effect, reproduces this social imagery in a twofold course of action. Politicians not only avoid talking about immigration,[10] but when they do so, their discursive behaviour is alarmist and even contains populist components linking the Muslim community to insecurity, conflict and social instability. The reality is that in Spain there is an apparent absence of integrationist politics, a lack of political will to include Muslims in the public sphere. As Martín-Muñoz underlines, in an integrationist framework that favours the sentiment of social belonging, Islam could develop in Spain, and in general in Europe, without conflict. In the opposite case, it tends to turn into a closed and hostile space where Muslims search for their identity and their community (2003: 228).

It is important to stress that, following the social agenda, immigration has been incorporated into the political discourse of immigration at the expense of one specific ethnic group: Moroccans. The case of El Ejido has been symbolically constructed as the extreme case of the dangers of multiculturalism (Zapata-Barrero, 2003d) and of a lack of socialization (Zapata-Barrero, 2003c). It is multiculturalism seen in its most essentialist form (Modood, 2000), as an example of cultural and religious incompatibility (see for further discussion, Spinner-Halev, 2000). Two years on, the situation is almost the same, but with one very important difference: that is, the majority of workers are no longer Moroccan, but come from Central and Eastern Europe. If it was just a legal problem (the majority of workers were undocumented), why replace the Moroccans with a different ethnic group? The government's reading of events is straightforward: religion and culture matter. It is supposed, notwithstanding the Arab legacy in the Spanish identity and disregarding no less than eight centuries of coexistence, that the culture of Morocco is much more distant than that of Central and Eastern Europe. These cultural and religious criteria are not new, and have already been used for the formal selection of immigrants. It is even said that it is not immigrant selection that is taking place in Spain, but really an 'ethnic filter' and even a 'Darwinist politics of immigration' (López García, 2003). These criteria are present not only in the Aliens Law but also in the Spanish citizenship acquisition code, where there are seven nationality preferences: South Americans, Portuguese, Filipinos, Andorrans, Equatorial Guineans, Gibraltarians and Sephardic Jews.[11]

As we have already discussed in previous sections, language and religion are the only criteria to explain this shift in immigration management. In general terms, we would say that in Spain the labour market attracts immigrants, but politics selects them using colonial and national identity criteria. In the management of its new multicultural society, Spain is currently at the beginning of some sort of *Hispanidad* revival.

As we have discussed above, this *Hispanidad* is a political term that was created precisely to comprise the whole Spanish area of influence, designating a linguistic (Spanish) and religious (Catholic) community and creating a sense of belonging, to the exclusion of non-Spanish speakers, atheists, Masons, Jews and Muslims. The Franco regime (1940–1975) reconstructed this term as a symbol of homogeneity and unity, as a cohesive society with the slogan *Una, Grande y Libre* (One, Great and Free) (González Antón, 1997: 613). This *Hispanidad* was a political construction separating people in a Manichaean fashion (Vila Selma, 1966). Those following the regime were good citizens, those having some (republican) doubts about it were bad citizens. This political construction of *Hispanidad* aimed to create the notion of the Hispanic race in order to obtain a sentiment of loyalty and patriotism. Patriotism, race and religion were an explosive mixture that dominated the conservative political discourse (and academic arena) for the first half of the twentieth century (García Morente, 1938), and this is the idea that was selected to frame the legitimate basis of the Francoist regime (Carbayo Abengózar, 1998).

This binary logic still exists today, although with a rather different dimension. The bad citizens are those who do not speak Spanish and hold beliefs other than Catholic ones: Moroccans are the first candidates and are constantly used in a political discourse that reminds us of this imagery of *Hispanidad*. Society's perception of immigration is usually that of Muslims as a religious minority. Taking this link as a premise, there are conservative discourses on European identity and European civilization that call on Christian traditions and politically construct Islam as the new *barbarian people*, as anti-European.

Recuperating the notion of impartiality: an epistemological excursus to contribute to the European approach

If we accept that a conflict in society should be seen as an element of socialization (Simmel, 2003), we can say that in Spain we are engaged in a process of socialization between Spanish citizens and the Muslim community. But there is a great deal of work to do. Indeed, as those of any European country, Spanish citizens tend to consider Islam as a whole that is immutable in time and static in space (Balta, 1996: 17). Spanish identity is the most flagrant example of the fact that the European identity has been built in opposition to Islam. We cannot understand the 'European mental universe', as a political and social entity, without its historical hostility against any Muslim form of expression (Alsayyad, 2003). In Spain, the Muslim issue has an imaginary dimension that goes far beyond the quantitative reality (Martín-Muñoz, 2003: 219). Today two main stereotypes contribute to nourishing this sort of historical snowball: the demographic invasion and the spectre of the Holy War. The Muslim presence in Europe is related to one side of the politically constructed Clash of Civilizations, and multiculturalism in Spain is seen as a conflict between models of society (one Western and the other Muslim) which are incompatible, since these two main pillars which contribute to the Moorish stereotype are also at the origin of a constructed picture of the Muslim as somebody who is simply incapable of being integrated (López García, 2003).

It is not that some of our values are threatened by the Muslim presence, as in the 1989 Rushdie affair, which raised the issues of freedom of expression and liberal thought, or in the classical affair of the headscarf, a symbol of repression (Balta, 1996: 180), but rather the contrary: we are constantly threatening our values when dealing with the Muslim community, especially where the presence of Muslims in the European public sphere is concerned (Vertovec and Peach, 1997).

We have also to accept that the practice of a religion is a factor of integration for immigrants coming from Muslim societies. Islam cannot be kept apart from the public sphere if all religions deserve equal treatment. Perhaps the notion of justice we can use as a criterion for evaluating the treatment of minority groups is that of even-handedness (Carens, 2000) or, as I have argued (Zapata-Barrero, 2004b), we should recover T. Nagel's notion of 'impartiality' (1991).

The central idea is that an argument is impartial when it can be applied in different contexts to solve similar conflicts. It is the only possible resource for difficult cases admitting more than one legitimate interpretation.

On a theoretical level, it essentially means that the argument I employ to legitimize a discourse or a policy related to the management of multicultural situations (contact zones converted into conflict zones, we could say) must be the same for all the resident cultures and religions in a given territory. For example, if the basic structure of our society favours one particular religious practice over another, then an *impartiality problem* exists in that structure.

Impartiality is the form that an argument acquires to deny or defend a particular action, discourse or policy. I am talking specifically about the notion of impartiality defended by Nagel (1991) in an excellent work on the ethical bases of political theory. Starting with the premise that two or more points of view exist which must be reconciled, that of the individual and that of the collectivity, the impersonal demands are those that must govern the collectivity in order for it to have a public life. This impersonal approach is that which does not favour the point of view of any individual in particular, but of all. The clash between the personal and the impersonal positions is one of the acute problems of our society. If, due to the design of the institutional structures, the two positions cannot be reconciled because the goal of harmonious cohabitation of the collective and the personal points of view is pursued without impartiality, then there is no hope of being able to accept any political order. Impartiality requires, then, the reconciliation of personal and impersonal thinking.

The way forward to reach this reconciliation is to recognize that all people have a personal point of view that can be different from our point of view. This recognition requires us to cultivate empathy, that is to say, to know how to separate our point of view and knowledge from the point of view of others; to know how to leave aside our system of prejudices and to understand other views and knowledge. This is the process of abstraction that Nagel calls the 'impersonal point of view'. My argument is that this impersonal position should play a leading role in orienting policies for the accommodation of Muslim communities in Spain and Europe generally. From this perspective most of the controversies that take place on the level of interpretation are due to the difficulty we have, being as we are prisoners of our personal points of view, in being impartial in issues that directly or indirectly affect our daily life and limit our initial expectations of life or, simply, the difficulty we experience when confronted with situations that contradict the values that articulate subjective points of view.

Impartiality has an undeniably humanist dimension (Nagel, 1991: 25). It implies not only that we give the same value to all attitudes (and cultural/religious practices) that respect life, but also that the impersonal point of view agrees with the point of view of humanity. To deny impartiality is to suppress the human dimension in political decisions. We must, therefore, ask whether our political institutions and structures, understood as prime distributors of values, can justify their treatment of the process of multiculturalism in general, and that resulting from the Muslim presence in particular, through impersonal values.

Since the political management of the process of multiculturalism on numerous occasions not only involves managing 'conflict zones', but also can itself generate conflicts, the 'impartiality rule' says that the principles that legitimize a policy must be capable of being accepted by all, Muslim immigrants and citizens alike. An 'impartial policy' thus becomes a policy that includes all the possible points of view, a policy that is able to be justified from the impersonal point of view. It is important to stress that what we are asking here is not whether the treatment our institutions are giving the Muslim community is right or wrong, but whether our institutions and political structures are at the root of this unequal treatment. The analysis of the Spanish context teaches us that tradition matters in orientating the public discourse linking Muslims, citizens and multiculturalism, and that tradition is one of the main explanations of the partial treatment of different expressions of religious faith, since Spain demonstrates that it gives more advantages to Catholic 'points of view' that to others when resolving conflict zones.

Thus, the notion of impartiality applied to the management of the Muslim community and multiculturalism has three meanings: first, it means that all cultures and religions must have the same opportunities, in the sense that political action must not benefit one culture/religion more than another; second, that it does not favour any culture/religion in particular; and finally, applying the Rawlsian approach to justice to these matters, that it does not worsen the situation of those who are already at a disadvantage, where the disadvantage is very close to the notion of 'difference' (Wieviorka, 2001), that is skin colour, origin, religion and so on.

This impartiality principle has to be considered as the result of a process. In the Spanish context, we would say that although before the (latter-day) arrival of Muslims in Spain there was a certain congruence between the personal points of view and the impersonal points of view in the democratic form justifying our structures, principles and values, now that the Muslim presence has been publicly recognized, this original impartiality becomes partial, as it favours the positions of the citizens over the Muslim community with arguments that have much more to do with emotion and history than rationality and common sense. From this point of view, the main argument receives a new meaning: the process of socialization between Spanish citizens and the Muslim community which explains the existence of conflict zones demands a process of social and political change to recover the 'loss of impartiality'. That is, our institutional structures as such, the way we solve conflicts in particular, must return to the principle of legitimacy independently of particular cultural/religious points of view. This may be one of the principles to be incorporated within the debate on laicism that currently occupies the political forum.

Notes

1 For this historical legacy and the Muslim origin of the Spanish identity in everyday life, see, among others, Vernet (1993).
2 After the rise of Islam in the Middle Ages, and especially at the time of the Crusades, the word 'Saracen' was extended to all Muslims. It was the current designation among

the Christians in the Middle Ages for their Arab enemies, especially for the Muslims in Europe.

3 In addition to the illustrative work of Martín Corrales (2001; 2002a; 2002b), already mentioned, see also López García (1996; 2003), FIMAM (2002). For suggestive comments, see also Valenzuela (2003). The successive works of Martín-Muñoz (for instance, 1994 and 2003) are also devoted to this topic. See also the useful website belonging to the FEERI (Federación Española de Entidades Religiosas Islámicas, one of the two competing Islamic federations in Spain) called Webislam (http://www.webislam.com, accessed 14 September 2004), which has as its main objective to promote (or restore) the Muslim presence in Spain (Osuna, 2002).

4 This is not to say the private sphere is without conflict. There are some studies precisely concerned with how the culture of Islamic law can be integrated into a host society which has different legal channels for managing civil conflicts (Borràs and Mernissi, 1998).

5 An extended discussion of this general process in Spain can be found in Zapata-Barrero (2004b).

6 See different contributions sharing the premise that immigration is one of the explanatory factor of social and political change in Aubarell and Zapata-Barrero (2003).

7 See also the structural focus of an analysis of the process of multiculturality applied to Spain in Zapata-Barrero (2004b).

8 See various articles in http://www.webislam.com and http.//www.verdeislam.com (accessed 14 September 2004), especially the interview with M. Abdussalam Escudero (1995) making a provisional appraisal after the signing of the agreement in 1992. See also, among others, Coca (1995), Luna Romero (2003), Moreras (1994; 1999: 85–97), Motilla (2003).

9 See, for example, these newspaper articles: Ramos (2004a, 9 May; 2004b, 18 April; 2004c, 18 April), Sen (2004, 8 May), Bastante (2004b), Granda and Bárbulo (2004), Webislam (2004, 13 May).

10 See the report by R. Zapata-Barrero and C. Adamuz under the aegis of the Grup de Recerca sobre Immigració i Innovació Política (GRIIP) entitled *La polititizació de la immigració durant la campanya de les eleccions municipals del 25 de maig del 2003*, Fundació Jaume Bofill, October 2003 (see http://www.upf.edu/cpis/griip (accessed 14 September 2004), and the report by R. Zapata-Barrero and the Plataforma per la Ciutadania i la Convivència, entitled *Partits polítics, eleccions i immigració: El comportament discursiu dels partits polítics sobre immigració durant la campanya de les eleccions autonòmiques de Catalunya del 16 de novembre de 2003* (December 2003). See newspaper reports on 24 December 2003 in *El Punt*, *Avui* and *El Mundo*, among others.

11 According to the current legislation on nationality (Articles 17–26 of Spanish Common Law (*Código Civil*), most foreigners have to be resident for ten years to be able to request Spanish nationality. However, this is reduced to only two years for those with a preferential nationality and, if they can claim some historical link with Spanish nationality, just one year. The eight-year gap in residence requirement is a glaring example of selection following national identity. On these matters, see the analysis of the Spanish legal framework in Zapata-Barrero (2003b). See also the special issue of the *Anales de la Cátedra Francisco Suárez* (2003).

References

Abdussalam Escudero, M. (1995) 'Entrevista: Tras la firma del Convenio', *Revista Verde Islam*, No. 3. Online. Available:
http://www.verdeislam.com (accessed 14 September 2004).

Abu-Tarbush, J. (2002) *Islam y comunidad islámica en Canarias*, La Laguna: Universidad de la Laguna.

Alsayyad, N. (2003) 'Europa musulmana o Euro-islam: a propósito de los discursos de la identidad y la cultura', in N. Alsayyad and M. Castells (eds) Â¿*Europa musulmana o Euro-islam?*, Madrid: Alianza (English version: (2003) *Muslim Europe or Euro-islam*, Lanham, MD: University Press of America).

Alsayyad, N. and Castells, M. (eds) (2003) Â¿*Europa musulmana o Euro-islam?*, Madrid: Alianza (English version: (2003) *Muslim Europe or Euro-islam*, Lanham, Maryland (USA): University Press of America).

Anales de la Cátedra Francisco Suárez (2003) *Ciudadanía e Inmigración*, Special issue, No. 37.

Aubarell, G. and Zapata-Barrero, R. (eds) (2003) *Inmigración y procesos de cambio: Europa y Mediterráneo en un contexto global*, Barcelona: Icaria.

Balta, P. (1996) *El islam*, Madrid: Salvat-Le Monde.

Bastante, J. (2004a) 'Hacienda cambiará el formato de IRPF para incluir a musulmanes, judíos y evangélicos', *ABC*, 18 August.

Bastante, J. (2004b) 'Los musulmanes consideran que el plan de Alonso es propio de un Estado policíaco. Piden que se financie la formación de imanes para evitar su radicalización', *ABC*, 7 May: 15.

Bernal, A. M. (2002) 'Prólogo', in E. Martín Corrales, *La Imagen del magrebí en España una perspectiva histórica, siglos XVI-XX*, Barcelona: Bellaterra.

Borràs, A. and Mernissi, S. (eds) (1997) *El islam jurídico y Europa*, Barcelona: Icaria.

Carbayo Abengózar, M. (1998) 'La Hispanidad: un acercamiento deconstructivo', *Revista de estudios literarios*, No. 10.

Carens, J. (2000) *Culture, citizenship, and community*, New York: Oxford University Press.

Coca, J. M. (1995) 'Musulmanes de España. Crónica de una Federación', *Revista Verde Islam*, No. 2. Online. Available: http://www.verdeislam.com (accessed 14 September 2004).

De Lucas, J. (2002a) 'Algunas propuestas para comenzar a hablar en serio de política de inmigración', in J. de Lucas and F. Torres (eds) *Inmigrantes: Â¿cómo los tenemos?*, Madrid: Talasa Ediciones.

——— (2002b) 'Introducción: El vínculo social, entre ciudadanía y cosmopolitismo', in J. de Lucas (ed.) *El vínculo social: Ciudadanía y cosmopolitismo*, Valencia: Tirant lo Blanch.

Ferro, M. (1994) *Histoire des colonisations: des conquêtes aux indépendances*, Paris: Points.

FIMAM (Foro de Investigadores sobre el Mundo Árabe y Musulmán) (2002) 'Â¿Sospechosos habituales? La estigmatización de la figura de los musulmanes en España', SOS Racismo, *Informe anual 2002 sobre el racismo en el Estado Español*: 244–252.

Fundació Jaume Bofill (2004) 'El fet religiós: introducció a càrrec de J. Moreras', in *La immigració a debat: diversitat i ordenament jurídic*, Barcelona: Fundació Jaume Bofill.

García Morente, M. (1938) *Idea de Hispanidad*, Buenos Aires: Espasa Calpe.

González Antón, L. (1997) *España y las Españas*, Madrid: Alianza.

Granda, E. and Bárbulo, T. (2004) 'El gobierno carece de un registro de imanes y de mezquitas para controlar a los islamistas', *El País*, 5 May: 21.

López García, B. (1996) 'La evolución del origen de los inmigrantes marroquíes en España', in B. López García (ed.) *Atlas de la inmigración madrebí en España*, Madrid: Universidad Autónoma de Madrid.

——— (2003) 'El islam y la integración de la inmigración en España', Webislam, No. 212, 23 May: http://www.webislam.com (accessed 14 September 2004).

Luna Romero, M. (2003) 'La situación legal del islam en España', ponencia 43 del Primer Congreso Mundial de musulmanes de habla hispana, Sevilla, 3–5 April. Online. Available:

http://www.webislam.com/congresohispano (accessed 14 September 2004).

Martín Corrales, E. (2001) 'De las galeotas corsarias a las pateras del estrecho: la influencia del pasado en la imagen de los musulmanes y magrebíes en España', *Script nova: Revista electrónica de geografía y Ciencias Sociales*, 94.

―――― (2002a) *La Imagen del magrebí en España una perspectiva histórica, siglos XVI–XX*, Barcelona: Bellaterra.

―――― (2002b) 'La xenofobia histórica haca el vecino marroquí: la imagen de los norteafricanos a lo largo de los siglos', *El País*, 28 July: 6–7.

Martín-Muñoz, G. (1996) 'Prólogo', in P. Balta, *El islam*, Madrid: Salvat-Le Monde: 9–16.

―――― (ed.) (2003) *Marroquíes en España. Estudio sobre su integracóón*, Madrid: Fundación Repsol YPF.

Mateo Dieste, J. Ll. (2002) 'L'immigration et les paradoxes de la mémoire coloniale en Espagne', *Migrations Société*, 83–95.

Modood, T. (2000) 'Anti-essentialism, multiculturalism, and the "recognition" of religious groups', in W. Kymlicka and W. Norman (eds) *Citizenship in diverse societies*, New York: Oxford University Press.

Moreras, J. (1994) 'Reflexions entorn als Acords de Cooperació amb els musulmans a Espanya', in F. Carbonell (ed.) *Sobre interculturalitat*, Documents de Treball, Girona: Fundació Ser-Gi.

―――― (1999) *Musulmanes en Barcelona: espacios y dinámicas comunitarias*, Barcelona: Cidob edicions.

―――― (2003) 'Limits and contradictions in the legal recognition of Muslims in Spain', in W. Shadid and P. S. Von Koningsveld (eds) *Religious Freedom and the Neutrality of the State: The Position of Islam in the European Union*, Leiden: Peeters.

Motilla, A. (2003) 'El islam en España: marco legal', in M. A. Roque, *El islam plural*, Barcelona: Icaria.

Nagel, T. (1991) *Equality and partiality*, Oxford: Oxford University Press.

Navarro, J. M. (1997) *El islam en las aulas*, Barcelona: Icaria.

Osuna, A. (2002) 'Webislam se presenta en el "Foro sobre los medios de comunicación y la globalización" ', *Webislam*, No. 174, 27 May: http://www.webislam.com (accessed 14 September 2004).

Parekh, B. (2000) *Rethinking multiculturalism*, London: Macmillan.

Pérez-Díaz, V., Álvarez-Miranda, B. and Chuliá, E. (2004) *La inmigración musulmana a Europa: turcs a Alemanya, algerians a França i marroquins a Espanya*, Barcelona: Fundació 'La Caixa' (Colecció Estudis Socials, No. 15).

Ramos, I. (2004a) 'Â¿Sermón o Soflama?', *La Vanguardia (Revista)*, 9 May: 4.

―――― (2004b) 'En busca de un Islam imposible', *La Vanguardia*, 18 April: 33.

―――― (2004c) 'Una ley demasiado perfecta', *La Vanguardia*, 18 April: 34.

Roque, M. A. (2003) *El islam plural*, Barcelona: Icaria.

Sen, C. (2004) 'El Gobierno busca fórmulas para financiar la comunidad musulmana', *La Vanguardia*, 8 May: 17.

Simmel, G. (2003) *Le conflit*, Paris: Circé.

SOS Racismo (2002–2004) *Informe anaula sobre el racismo en el estado Español*, Barcelona: Icaria.

Spinner-Halev, J. (2000) *Surviving diversity: religion and democratic citizenship*, Baltimore, MD: Johns Hopkins University Press.

Todorov, T. (1991) *Les morales de l'histoire*, Paris: Grasset (le Collège de Philosophie).

Valenzuela, J. (2002) 'Perfidia Moruna. La democracia no ha curado a España de su morofobia secular', *El País* (suplemento Babelia), 25 May: 21.

—— (2003) 'Morofòbia i casticisme en els mitjans de comunicació', *Informe Anual 2003 de SOS Racisme*, Barcelona: Icaria: 220–225.

Vernet, J. (1993) *El islam en España*, Madrid: Editorial Maphre.

Vertovec, S. and Peach, C. (eds) (1997) *Islam in Europe: the politics of religion and community*, London: Macmillan.

Vila Selma, J. (1966) 'Hispanidad', *Enciclopedia de la Cultura Española*, Volume 3, Madrid: Editora Nacional: 551.

Webislam (2004) 'El ministro el Interior se reúne con la Comisión Islámica de España', Webislam, No. 255, 13 May:
http://www.webislam.com (accessed 14 September 2004).

Wieviorka, M. (2001) *La différence*, Paris: Éditions Balland.

Zapata-Barrero, R. (2002) *El turno de los inmigrantes: esferas de justicia y políticas de acomodación*, Imserso, Ministerio de Trabajo y Seguridad.

—— (2003a) 'Spain', in Y. Niessen and Y. Schibel (eds) *EU and US approaches to the management of immigration: comparative perspectives*, Brussels: Migration Policy Group: 459–489.

—— (2003b) 'La ciudadanía en contextos de multiculturalidad', *Ciudadanía e inmigración*, *Revista Anales: Cátedra Francisco Suárez*, Special issue, No. 37: 173–199.

—— (2003c) 'Spanish challenges and European dilemma: socialising the debate on the integration of immigrants', *Perspectives on European Politics and Society*, 4(2): 243–264.

—— (2003d) 'The "discovery" of immigration in Spain: the politicization of immigration in the case of El Ejido', *Journal of International migration and integration*, 4(4): 523–539.

—— (2004a) *Inmigración, innovación política y cultura de acomodación en España*, Barcelona: Cidob/Bellaterra.

—— (2004b) *Multiculturalidad e inmigración*, Madrid: Ed. Síntesis.

9 Secularism and the accommodation of Muslims in Europe*

Tariq Modood and Riva Kastoryano

Introduction

Secularism has long been regarded as a settled, non-controversial feature of Western societies. While a century or more of intra-Christian wars more or less gave way to the principle agreed in the Treaty of Westphalia of 1648, *Cujus regio, ejus religio* ('The religion of the prince is the religion of the people'), namely that the religion of the ruler was to be the religion of the state/country,[1] this principle was subsequently chipped away at. Not only did toleration come to be seen as equally important but the Enlightenment of the eighteenth century in various ways challenged the Christian faith, the authority of the Church, and the promotion of a religion by the state. With the militant example of the French Revolution, the secularist anti-Westphalian principle of the separation of Church and state, of religion and politics, has progressively become hegemonic. By the middle of the twentieth century it was universally taken for granted in Western societies – one of the few principles that was shared by liberalism, socialism and most versions of nationalism – and thought to be one of the defining features of modernity. Moreover, the Westphalian prioritizing of territorial allegiance over doctrinal truth and allegiance to a community of co-believers has been triumphant in the politics of Western societies. It has not been entirely without its challengers but the challengers have been forms of secular internationalism such as socialism or cosmopolitanism, rather than religious communities or movements.

Yet in the founding countries of secularism, the principle and its interpretation in specific contexts have gradually been challenged on the grounds of religion in the last twenty, and especially in the last ten, years. This challenge, especially in Western Europe, has been associated with the demand of some newly settled Muslim peoples to seek institutional expression for their Muslim identity. As this book has shown, Muslims today are citizens or long-term residents in many Western countries and are demanding institutional representation and recognition within these national societies. As Muslims are outside the long relationship between state and Church that made Western national histories, they do not always see the historical compromises of the relationships applied to their demands. Relatedly, Muslims do not sometimes appreciate the stresses and compromises of that history and why their demands are sometimes met with exasperation even by some of their political allies. Nevertheless, Muslim claims for religious recognition in one form or another are, as the previous chapters have demonstrated, central to multicultural debates. The truly democratic response to this unexpected development requires that the principles and the institutional and juridical arrangements of secularism must be revisited.

Varieties of secular states

At the heart of secularism is a distinction between the public realm of citizens and policies and the private realm of belief and worship. While all European Union countries are clearly secular in many ways, interpretations and the institutional arrangements diverge according to the dominant national religious culture and the differing projects of nation-state building and thus make secularism a 'particular' experience. This also applies to different forms of the Enlightenment rationalism. In Germany the Enlightenment philosophy (*Aufklärung*) was not really against religion as in France, just as rationality was not against Protestant piety. The concern for equality it embodied consisted mainly of destroying the barriers between the clergy, the nobility, the middle class and the peasantry (Müller, 1995). After the formation of the German state, the *Kulturkampf* was, as in France, characterized by an effort to guarantee social cohesion by minimizing the role of the Catholic Church while limiting Protestant influence on politics as well. Yet in Germany, the religious freedoms granted to Catholics and Lutherans assumed a corporative nature, 'granting equal rights only to communities formed as corporations', recognized by the public law (François, 1993: 239). This can be seen in the West German (FDR) social democratic model, in which (while the most formidable social partners in governance were industrialists and trade unions), the churches too had a corporatist place, with the state collecting funds for them (voluntary taxes) and paying for denominational teaching in schools out of general taxes. The churches have also been important political actors at various times. For example, some Protestant churches were active in the protest movements that led to the tearing down of the Berlin Wall in 1989.

British Enlightenment philosophers like David Hume were sceptical about the supernaturalistic claims of religion, which they felt should be subject to the claims of empirical science, but were not hostile to religion as such, which they thought had useful social functions such as a practical vehicle for the acquisition of morality. Moreover, the monarchical church in Britain, the Church of England, had much less social or political power than the Catholic Church in some countries. Hence there was no reason for a radical attack on the role of the Established Church in Britain. In other countries, whether within the Catholic sphere, such as Ireland and Poland, or outside it as in the case of Denmark and Greece, the national church was a source of resistance against an occupying power and so played a political role that was welcomed by many nationals and which too meant that radical secularism lacked support in those countries and few castigated the Church as anti-enlightenment, as 'infamy'. Hence, there are a number of churches within the EU states that have or recently had, formally or informally, a national political role. Of course that does not mean that they are not secular states. It means that countries such as England, Denmark and Greece believe that secularism is compatible with having state or 'established' churches. These and other states, such as the Netherlands and Germany, extensively support denominational schools, or denominational worship and lessons in schools, out of public funds. This is not because these societies are more religious than France or other members of the EU. In England, there is an established church, about a quarter of all school pupils are taught in state-funded religious schools and yet England is one of the most secular societies in Europe, measured in terms of worship, personal religious affiliation and theistic belief (De Graaf and Need, 2000). The case of England suggests a distinction between state and societies which can be used further to illustrate that secularism can take different, even contradictory, forms in contemporary, liberal democratic societies.

On the other side of the Atlantic, the US Constitution emphasizes the 'protection of religious diversity as a value' (Schuck, 2003). The United States has as its First Amendment to the Constitution that there shall be no established church; there is wide support for this and in the last few decades there has been a tendency amongst academics and jurists to interpret the Church–state separation in continually more radical ways (Sandel, 1994; Hamburger, 2002). Yet, as is well known, not only is the United States a deeply religious society, with much higher levels of church attendance than in Western Europe (Greely, 1995), but there is a strong Protestant, evangelical fundamentalism that is rare in Europe. This fundamentalism does not necessarily dispute the 'no establishment clause' in the Constitution but is one of the primary mobilizing forces in US politics and it is widely claimed that it decided the presidential election of 2004. The churches in question – mainly white, mainly in the South and Midwest – campaign openly for candidates and parties, indeed raise large sums of money for politicians and introduce religion-based issues into politics, such as positions on abortion, HIV/AIDS, homosexuality, stem-cell research, prayer at school and so on. It has been said that no openly avowed atheist has ever been a candidate for the White House and that it would be impossible for such a candidate to be elected. It is not at all unusual for politicians – in fact, for President George W. Bush, it is most usual – to talk publicly about their faith, to appeal to religion and to hold prayer meetings in government buildings. On the other hand, in establishment Britain, bishops sit in the upper chamber of the legislature by right and only the senior archbishop can crown a new head of state, the monarch, but politicians rarely talk about their religion. It was noticeable, for example, that when Prime Minister Blair went to a summit meeting with President Bush to discuss aspects of the Iraq War in 2003, the US media widely reported that the two leaders had prayed together. Yet Prime Minister Blair, one of the most openly professed and active Christians ever to hold that office, refused to answer questions on this issue from the British media on his return, saying it was a private matter. The British state may have an established church but the beliefs of the Queen's First Minister are his own concern.

France draws the distinction between State and religion differently again. Like the United States, there is no state church, but unlike the United States, the state actively promotes the privatization of religion. While in the United States organized religion in civil society is powerful and seeks to exert influence on the political process, French civil society does not carry signs or expressions of religion. Although the transition to the Republic and to secularism swept away religion from the public space, paradoxically it maintained a religious vocabulary to express the sacred character of the Republic. This is partly a reflection of historical debates about whether a public order is possible without the support that religion gives to the promotion of moral virtues such as truth-telling and fellow-feeling for others. It has, for example, led moralists like Rousseau to argue that a public order must take over one of the traditional functions of religion, the production of social virtues and responsible conduct, and so must go beyond legislation and law enforcement and seek to produce virtuous citizens. As a matter of fact the Republic, called 'the oldest daughter of the Church', has for some a holy character. Claude Nicolet has pointed to the religious metaphors used in the establishment of moral rules and of how the Republic has been described as an Enlightenment Church (Nicolet, 1995). Even Renan, in his famous lecture on the nation, spoke of 'the Jacobin Church' and defined it as a secular religion. When the republicans (secularists) defeated the anti-republicans (defenders of religion in public life) the representatives of the Church became civil servants, exercising certain functions allowed by the state, sometimes on behalf of the state. The state confers institutional legal status on the Catholic clergy, the Protestants of the National Federation of the Protestant Churches of France, and to the Jews governed by the Consistory created under Napoleon. Yet all references to religion disappeared from the public arena: its symbols, for example, were removed from the walls of public welfare hospitals. Public vocabulary also was secularized by using the adjective 'civil' in expressing the fundamental bonds in society: 'civil order', 'civil state', 'civil right', 'civil marriage', 'civil burial'. Thus, 'civil' replaced the holy (Nicolet, 1995). While the Constitution of 1795 introduced such a secularization of marriage, health and education, the full legal separation of Church and state dates from 1905, after the Dreyfus affair revealed extensive anti-Semitism amongst officials and soldiers of the state. Belief in God was now only a private matter. Even then it was not until the Constitution of 1946 that secularism became law, and that was reiterated in the Constitution of 1958, with Article 2 declaring: 'France is an indivisible, secular (*laïque*), democratic, and social Republic. It insures equality to all of its citizens before the law without distinction of origin, race and religion. It respects all beliefs.'

In this Article France is not necessarily different from the United States. What is different between these two countries is the organization of religious diversity: the place of religion in civil society and its relationship to the state, the interpretation – not its juridical definition – of the principle of separation of Church and state. In France, a republican state does not just separate itself from civil society but it leads civil society by creating a political culture that is opposed to clericalism, or perhaps even to 'Catholic culture' (*esprit*). For the French Republic, *laïcité* is considered an active movement from a community ruled by the Church to a society ruled by law, and thus integral to modernity. Emancipation, the political goal consequent upon the Enlightenment, is seen as extracting the individual from religious constraints and integrating him into the political community as an individual citizen. The secular state is not so much a product but the agent of this movement. The disappearance of the sacred, which for Weber characterized modernity, means a new structure of power replaces the religious community by a political community that is allegedly the only one necessary for modernity and that has political legitimacy because it is universal.

Therefore, what distinguishes France from the United States is not a fundamental juridical or constitutional principle, but rather the role of the state in civil society. While in the United States organized religion in civil society is powerful and seeks to exert influence on the political process, the French state promotes secularism in civil society through representative religious institutions and programmes of education. We might want to express this relationship as in Table 9.1, which also includes the German recognition of churches as corporations, which we elaborate later in the chapter.

Varieties of public/private mixes

We have seen, then, that the state/religion divide varies even amongst countries that subscribe to a version of secularism, to the claim that there must be some kind of a state/religion divide. In order to illustrate further that the public/private boundary – of which the question of an established religion is only part – is a complex one, and in which different secular societies can take different positions, consider some of the dimensions of religion on which a

Table 9.1 Religion *vis-à-vis* state and civil society in three countries

	State	*Religion in civil society*
England/Britain	Weak establishment	Weak
United States	No establishment	Strong and politically mobilized
France	Actively secular	Weak
Germany	Quasi-establishment by public law	Moderate

Table 9.2 Some dimensions of religion re private/public

1   Belief and worship
2   Family, community and voluntary organizations
3   Provision of (public) health, welfare and housing services and community services, etc.
4   (State) education
5   (Public) broad casting
6   Civil society debates and pressure groups
7   Political parties, e.g. Poale Zion, Black Sections, Women's Sections
8   Public moral leadership

public/private boundary decision has to be made. Table 9.2 lists some of these dimensions.

What are the appropriate limits of the state in relation to the dimensions in Table 9.2? Everyone will agree that there should be religious freedom and that this should include freedom of belief and worship in private associations. Family too falls on the private side of the line but the state regulates the limits of what is a lawful family – for example, polygamy is not permitted in many countries – not to mention the deployment of official definitions of family in the distribution of welfare entitlements. Turning to the third item on the list, religions typically put a premium on mutuality and on care of the sick, the homeless, the elderly and so on. They set up organizations to pursue these aims, but so do states. Should there be a competitive or a co-operative relationship between these religious and state organizations, or do they have to ignore each other? Can public money – raised out of taxes on religious as well as non-religious citizens – not be used to support the organizations favoured by some religious taxpayers? What of schools? Do parents not have the right to expect that schools will make an effort – while pursuing broader educational and civic aims – not to create a conflict between the work of the school and the upbringing of the children at home but, rather, show respect for their religious background? Can parents, as associations of religious citizens, not set up their own schools and should those schools not be supported out of the taxes of the same parents? Is the school where the private, the family, meets the public, the state; or is it, in some Platonic manner, where the state takes over the children from the family and pursues its own purposes? Even if there is to be no established church (item 8 on the list), the state may still wish to work with organized religion as a social partner, as is the case in Germany, or to have some forum in which it consults with organized religion, some kind of national council of religions, as in Belgium. Or, even if it does not do that because it is regarded as compromising the principle of secularism, political parties, being agents in civil society rather than organs of the state, may wish to do this and institute special representation for religious groups as many do for groups defined by age, gender, region, language, ethnicity and so on. It is clear then that the 'public' is a multi-faceted concept and in relation to secularism may be defined differently in relation to different dimensions of religion and in different countries.

We can all be secularists then, all approve of secularism in some respect, and yet have quite different ideas, influenced by historical legacies and varying prag-matic compromises, of where to draw the line between public and private. It would be quite mistaken to suppose that all religious spokespersons, or at least all political Muslims, are on one side of the line, and all others are on the other side. There are many different ways of drawing the various lines at issue. In the past, the drawing of them has reflected particular contexts shaped by differential customs, urgency of need and sensitivity to the sensibilities of the relevant reli-gious groups (Modood, 1994; 1997). Exactly the same considerations are relevant in relation to the accommodation of Muslims in Europe today – not a battle of slogans and ideological oversimplifications.

The 'universality' of secularism lies in the principle of equality according to which there is no domination of one religion – the majority, therefore the national – over other religions in a *de facto* minority situation. Hence the assumption of state neutrality in respect of religion: the state does not have a view about any of the religions in society but ensures the freedom to individuals to practise (or not) their religion. Yet today, the private/public distinction, the ideas of state neutrality and public equality between religious nation-states are sources of contradictions in relation to Muslims. More precisely, the multicultural interpretation of equality between religions, paralleling arguments of equality between the genders and between racial, ethnic and cultural groups, seems to lead in the direction of active policies of inclusion of Muslims (and others) rather than a principled indifference to organized religion. Hence, the claims of reli-gious equality are not decisively in alignment with some readings of secularist principles. We must therefore explore some meanings of multiculturalism and their implications for the public/private distinction (Modood, 1998a; 1998b).

Multiculturalism and the strict division between public and private spheres

There is a body of theoretical opinion that argues that the public/private distinc-tion is essential to multiculturalism. John Rex, for example, distinguishes between plural societies such as apartheid South Africa and the multicultural ideal. He contends that the fundamental distinction between them is that the latter restricts cultural diversity to a private sphere so all enjoy equality of oppor-tunity and uniform treatment in the public domain (Rex, 1986: chapter 7). Immigrants and minorities do not have to respect the normative power of a dominant culture, but there must be a normative universality in relation to law, politics, economics and welfare policy.

An important assumption contained in this way of seeing the public/private distinction is found in a discussion by Habermas. Although he maintains that a recipient society cannot require immigrants to assimilate – immigrants cannot be obliged to conform to the dominant way of life – he also contends that a democratic constitutional regime must seek to

> preserve the identity of the political community, which nothing, including immigration, can be permitted to encroach upon, since that identity is founded on the constitutional principles anchored in the political culture and not on the basic ethical orientations of the cultural form of life predominant in that country.
>
> (Habermas, 1994: 139)

But is this distinction between the political and cultural identities of a society valid? Politics and law depend to some degree on shared ethical assumptions and inevitably reflect the norms and values of the society they are part of. In this sense, no regime stands outside culture, ethnicity or nationality, and changes in these will need to be reflected in the political arrangements of the regime. Indeed, Habermas seems to concede this when he states that 'as other forms of life become established [that is, following immigration] the horizon within which citizens henceforth interpret their common constitutional principles may also expand' (*ibid.*: 139–140). But this concession begs the question of the coherence of his initial distinction. If the political identity of the regime is determined by reference to the 'constitutional principles anchored in the political culture', how can the articulation, interpretation and, therefore, operation of these constitutional principles not be subject to the 'basic ethical orientations' of new (religious) citizens, given these orientations provide the fundamental interpretative horizons for these principles? As the fundamental interpretative horizons of the citizenry 'expand' through the immigration of peoples with religions new to that society, so too the political identity of the regime is inevitably altered. Moreover, the interdependence between the political and the cultural, the public and the private, is not confined to the level of ethical generalities. On a practical level, as Rex recognizes, religious communities may look to the state to support their culture (for example, through support for religious schools and other educational institutions) and the state may, reciprocally, look to religious communities to inculcate virtues such as truth-telling, respect for property, service to others and so on, without which a civic morality would have nothing to build on.

Furthermore, if the public and private spheres mutually shape each other in these ways, then however 'abstract' and 'rational' the principles of a public order may be, they will reflect the 'folk cultures' out of which that particular public order has grown. If this is the case, then there can be no question of the public sphere being morally, ethnically or, indeed, religiously neutral. Rather, it will inevitably appeal to points of privately shared values and a sense of belonging found within the (religious and non-religious) communities that make up society, as well as to the superstructure of conventions, laws and principles which regulate it. And this can be so not only in the absence of any official state recognition of (a) religion but even in the absence of widespread adherence to historical state religions. Norris and Inglehart make this point well and are worth quoting at length:

> The distinctive worldviews that were originally linked with religious traditions have shaped the cultures of each nation in an enduring fashion; today these distinctive values are transmitted to the citizens even if they never set foot in a church, temple, or mosque. Thus, although only about 5% of the Swedish public attends church weekly, the Swedish public as a whole manifests a distinctive Protestant value system that they hold in common with the citizens of other historically Protestant societies such as Norway, Denmark, Iceland, Finland, Germany, and the Netherlands. Today, these values are not transmitted primarily by the church, but by the educational system and the mass media, with the result that although the value systems of historically Protestant countries differ markedly and consistently from those of historically Catholic countries – the value systems of Dutch Catholics are much more similar to those of Dutch Protestants than to those of French, Italian, or Spanish Catholics. Even in highly secular societies, the historical legacy of given religions continues to shape worldviews and to define cultural zones. As a distinguished Estonian colleague put it, in explaining the difference between the worldviews of Estonians and Russians, 'We are all atheists; but I am a Lutheran atheist, and they are Orthodox atheists.'
>
> (Norris and Inglehart, 2004)[2]

This will have the important implication that those citizens whose moral, ethnic or religious communal identities are most adequately reflected in the political identity of the regime, those citizens whose private identity fits most comfortably with this political identity, will feel least the force of a rigidly enforced public/private distinction. They may only become aware of its coercive influence when they have to share the public domain with persons from other communities, persons who may also wish the identity of the political community to reflect something of their own community too.

There is, therefore, a real possibility that the elaboration of a strict public/private distinction may simply act to buttress the privileged position of the historically 'integrated' folk cultures at the expense of the historically subordinated or newly migrated folk. This will not be equality between religions. In some contexts, therefore, a strict interpretation and application of the public/private distinction, far from underpinning multiculturalism, will work to prevent its emergence.

Public/private interdependence and the politics of recognition

If we recognize that the public sphere is not morally neutral, that public order is not culturally, religiously or ethnically blind, we can begin to understand why oppressed, marginalized or immigrant groups may want that public order (in which they may for the first time have rights of participation) to 'recognize' them, to be 'user-friendly' to the new folks. The logic of demanding that public institutions acknowledge their ways of doing things becomes readily intelligible, as does the whole phenomenon of minorities seeking increased visibility, of contesting the boundaries of the public, of not simply asking to be left alone and to be civilly tolerated.

What is important to recognize here is that the content of what is claimed today in the name of equality is more than that which would have been claimed in the 1960s. Iris Young expresses the new political climate when she describes the emergence of an ideal of equality based not just on allowing excluded groups to assimilate and live by the norms of dominant groups, but also on the view that 'a positive self-definition of group difference is in fact more liberatory' (Young, 1990: 157). She cites the examples of the Black Power movement, the Gay Pride assertion that sexual identity is a matter of culture and politics, and a feminism that emphasizes the positivity and specificity of female experience and values. Although these movements have not had the same impact in Europe as in parts of North America, they are nevertheless present here.

The shift in the content of these claims is from an understanding of equality in terms of individualism and cultural assimilation to a politics of recognition, to equality as encompassing public ethnicity. That is to say, equality as not having to hide or apologize for one's origins, family or community, but requiring others to show respect for them and adapt public attitudes and arrangements so that the heritage they represent is encouraged rather than ignored or expected to wither away.

There seem, then, to be two distinct conceptions of equal citizenship, with each based on a different view of what is 'public' and 'private'. Broadly speaking, the first equates with the content of the claims for equality proffered in the 1960s, the second accords more fully with the content of the claims presented by contemporary proponents of a politics of recognition. These two conceptions of equality may be stated as follows:

1   The right to assimilate to the majority/dominant culture in the public sphere; and toleration of 'difference' in the private sphere.
2   The right to have one's 'difference' (minority ethnicity, etc.) recognized and supported in the public and the private spheres.

These two conceptions are not mutually exclusive. Indeed multiculturalism requires support for both conceptions, for the assumption behind the first conception is that participation in the public or national culture is necessary for the effective exercise of citizenship (the only obstacles to which are the exclusionary processes preventing gradual assimilation). The second conception, too, assumes groups excluded from the public or national culture have their citizenship diminished as a result but proposes to remedy this by offering the right to assimilate while, at the same time, agreeing to widen and adapt the public or national culture (including the public and media symbols of national member-ship) to incorporate the relevant minority ethnicities.

It may be thought the second conception of equality involves something of a contradiction: it accepts that participation in national or shared culture(s) is necessary for effective equality but encourages individuals to cultivate minority identities and practices. There is indeed a genuine tension here, and perhaps it can only be resolved in practice, through finding and cultivating points of common ground between dominant and subordinate cultures, as well as new syntheses and hybridities. For an effective multicultural interaction, the impor-tant thing is this tension should not be heightened by the burdens of change – or the costs of not changing – all falling on one party to the encounter.

This leaves open the question who is to count as a relevant minority, who is allowed to make claims and is granted recognition? While different factors are relevant, 'difference' is not straightforwardly given but arises out of the interaction between a group and the socio-political context, which creates salience and establishes the limits of visibility or legitimacy. This explains why in some coun-tries religion has come to the fore and in particular that Islam has become a core element for minority community construction and a source of group mobilization (Kastoryano, 2002). The claim for equality and justice for Muslims thus often stems from the exclusion of religious associations from the process of resource distribution, while at the same time allowing religion to exist in and mobilize in civil society. At other times, as we saw in the chapter on Britain, it is the political marginalization or demotion of religious identity in favour of allegedly more acceptable identities, such as those of race and gender, that creates the grievances of misrecognition. The issue is not the cultural assimilation of individual immi-grants but the recognition of group identities, in this case a religious community. Certainly, the idea of equality as respect for difference has created a socio-political climate in which non-assimilation at a socio-cultural level is in many countries not regarded as a problem, and even in France the ideology and the term 'assimilation' with regard to culture have been replaced by integration. Moreover, institutionalization of a difference, whatever this difference might be, has emerged as a legitimate way of responding to new cultural and religious communities. The question of recognition of differences is therefore the same as how to assimilate/integrate difference institutionally. This leaves open the possi-bility that the state responds to the new presence of Islam through a form of structural assimilation or, paralleling integration at the level of civil society, in a more flexible way. We, the authors are divided on what form this structural assim-ilation may take. For Modood, institutional integration can take a pluralistic form, a variable geometry, in which Islam is integrated in ways that reflect existing national arrangements as well as the character of local Muslim needs and capacities. This reflects the experience of England, in which the Church of England, the Catholic Church, Protestant churches such as the Methodists, as well as Judaism, all enjoy some kind of state recognition and resources in relation to Parliament, schooling, the armed forces, hospitals, prisons and so on, but the relationship in each case is a product of its own history and population distribution. Thus, for Modood, if British Islam remains as decentralized and unhierarchical as it has started, then this should be taken into account in the political and structural accommodation that is offered to it in Britain. For Kastoryano, on the other hand, whatever the degree of cultural pluralism that becomes the norm in civil society, the state must promote equality and symmetry at the level of national representative institutions. As the existing arrangements in France require each recognized faith community to have a representative structure with 'chiefs' representation,, so French Islam has conformed to this pattern. It may be that this runs counter to Sunni Islam, with its traditions of autonomous mosques and sects, but it is the duty of French Muslim organizations to assimilate by producing representative structures that allow the state to extend recognition to Islam without compromising its symmetrical and equitable structures (see also Kastoryano, 2004). This would mean that Islam would be assimilated on an equal footing to all representative religious institutions in France. The result would be a genuinely French Islam and its freedom from foreign influences, especially the politics of countries of origin.

Pluralistic institutional integration/assimilation

Multicultural equality, then, when applied to religious groups means that secularism *simpliciter* can be an obstacle to pluralistic integration and equality. This does not, however, mean that there is an unresolvable conflict between secularism and multicultural equality, because, as we have seen, secularism pure and simple is not what exists in the world. The country-by-country situation is more complex, and indeed, far less inhospitable to the accommodation of Muslims than the ideology of secularsim – or, for that matter, the ideology of anti-secularism – might suggest (Modood, 1998a: table 1, p. 90). All actual practices of secularism consist of institutional compromises and these can, should be and are being extended to accommodate Muslims. The institutional reconfiguration varies according to the place of religion, therefore of Islam, in each country developed earlier. Today the appropriate response to the new Muslim challenges is pluralistic institutional integration/assimilation, rather than an appeal to a radical public/private separation in the name of secularism. The approach that is being argued for here, then, consists of:

1   A reconceptualization of secularism from the concepts of neutrality and the strict public/private divide to a moderate and evolutionary secularism based on institutional adjustments.
2   A reconceptualization of equality from sameness to an incorporation of a respect for difference.
3   A pragmatic, case-by-case, negotiated approach to dealing with controversy and conflict, not an ideological, drawing a 'line in the sand' mentality.

This institutional integration/assimilation approach is based on including Islam in the institutional framework of the state, using the historical accommodation between state and Church as a basis for negotiations in order to achieve consensual resolutions consistent with equality and justice. As these accommodations have varied from country to country, it means there is no exemplary solution, for contemporary solutions too will depend on the national context and will not have a once-and-for-all time basis. It is clearly a dialogical perspective and assumes the possibility of mutual education and learning. Like all negotiation and reform, there are normative as well as practical limits. Aspects of the former have been usefully characterized by Bhikhu Parekh as 'society's operative public values' (Parekh, 2000: 267). These values, such as equality between the sexes, are embedded in the political constitution, in specific laws and in the norms governing the civic relations in a society. Norms, laws and constitutional principles concerning the appropriate place of religion in public life generally and in specific policy areas (such as schools or rehabilitation of criminals) consist of such public values and are reasoned about, justified or criticized by reference to specific values about religion/politics as well as more general norms and values in a society, such as fairness, or balance or consensus and so on. We, therefore, recognize that the approach recommended here involves solutions that are highly contextual and practical but they are far from arbitrary or without reference to values. While the latter are not static because they are constantly being reinterpreted, realigned, extended and reformed, nevertheless they provide a basis for dialogue and agreement.

The institutional integration/assimilation that we are advocating is possible and is taking place to some extent, despite the presence sometimes of a vigorous version of secularism in the national political culture, especially amongst intellectuals.[3] For example, while in France there has been a revival of the old duality between religion and state in public discussions and some policies, at the same time the climate of controversy has accelerated the establishment of a representative institution of Islam on equal footing with other religions. Since the first headscarf affair in the late 1980s the concept of *laïcité* has gone through different interpretations with Islam serving as a mirror to its ambiguity and contradictions, and highlighting than in France religion is the main and long-term 'difference' that enjoys institutional recognition, for the separation of Church and state confers institutional legal status on the Catholic clergy, the Protestants of the National Federation of the Protestant Churches of France, and to the Jews governed by the Consistory. That 'recognition' is seen as an expression of respect for freedom of religion and the neutrality of the secular state. Since 1990, following the passionate debates concerning the place of religion in French society aroused by the headscarf affair, successive Interior Ministers, who are at the same time Ministers of Religion from both the Left and the Right, have worked to create representative Islamic institutions. In 1991, Pierre Joxe created a Council of Thought on Islam in France, the CORIF, in order to explore different means of adapting the requirements of Islam to the norms of society (or vice versa). The next Minister, Pasqua, of the Rally for the Republic (RPR), created a Representative Council of Muslims, with the idea that 'the issue of Islam must be treated as a French issue'. He declared in *Le Monde* of 11 January 1995: 'I have always wanted Islam to progress from the status of a tolerated religion in France to that of a religion accepted by all, and one that forms part of the French spiritual landscape'. His successor, Jean-Pierre Chevènement (Socialist Party), also declared that the recognition of Islam was 'not a question of left or right but a national question which affects the Republican state' and set up a commission called a 'Consultation' that also gave its name to a journal. In the first issue of that journal he declared his goal was to 'help Muslims to form themselves into a religious minority in France'. Most recently, in April 2003, Interior Minister Nicolas Sarkozy succeeded in creating a French Council of the Muslim Faith (Conseil Français du Culte Musulman), which subsequently elected its first national representative (see chapter 4).

The institutional approach is obviously an important way to achieve equality and representation for religious groups. Bringing Muslims into historic and existing institutional arrangements means a continuity with the old French scheme described by Danièle Lochak of a 'pragmatic handling of differences'. This consists of gradually introducing the minimal dose of institutionalization needed for a concrete resolution of the practical problems created by the existence of 'minority groups' who want to end up with 'official recognition', which would then produce the 'institutionalization of differences' (Lochak, 1989).

What is interesting about France is that while republican ideology is meant to be blind to 'difference', above all to religious difference, in its institutional architecture France not only recognizes difference at the level of organized religion but recognizes no other form of group difference to anything like the same degree. As Lochak states, 'the state's ignoring of the prohibition of differences is confined to religion' and that while France rejects the notion of 'minority' in all other contexts, the term 'religious minority' appears in legal texts (Lochak, 1989: 111–184).[4] This suggests to us that religion is – *pace* republican ideology – one of the fundamental cleavages in French society and its social, cultural and institutional representation.[5] The current effort to recognize Islam institutionally, then, is based in principle on the idea of equality of treatment of all religions in France, including the Catholic clergy.

Having seen that this is happening in a state that made *laïcité* its particularity, France, it is only to be expected this it is happening in other European states. Some of this has been reported in the previous chapters. This includes the development of a religious equality agenda in Britain, including the incorporation of some Muslim schools on the same basis as of schools of religions with a much longer presence. It also includes the recommendations of the Royal Commission on the Reform of the House of Lords (2000) that in addition to the Anglican bishops who sit in that House by right as part of the Anglican 'establishment', this right should be extended to cover those of other Christian and non-Christian faiths. The same point can be made in relation to the fact that as early as 1974 the Belgian state decided to include Islam within its Council of Religions as a full member, or to the way that Muslims in the Netherlands have long had state-funded religious schools and television channels as a progressive step in that country's traditional way of institutionally dealing with organized religion, namely 'pillarization'. This principle that recognized that Protestants and Catholics had a right to state resources and some publicly funded autonomous institutions officially ended in 1960. It is, however, still considered as a 'relevant framework for the development of a model that grants certain collective rights to religious groups' (Sunier and von Luijeren, 2002) in such matters as state funding of Islamic schools. So, the accommodation of Muslims is being achieved through a combination of pillarization and Dutch minority policies. In Germany, the question of the public recognition of Islam was raised as early as the 1980s, based on a definition of 'community' offered by the *Auslanderberauftragte*, the Commission on Foreigners, as 'a grouping of people who feel that they are linked to one or several deities and which eventually give rise to a faith'. This religious conception of community dates back to the nineteenth century when the religious freedom granted to both Catholics and Lutherans took on the corporate character of 'granting equal rights to communities constituted into organized bodies' (François, 1993). Recognition by public authorities of a 'Muslim community' was, therefore, suggested as a means of integrating Turkish immigrants into German society. The argument was firmly based on the official place of religion in German public space and the role of churches in taking care of foreigners in the manner of a 'religious society' (*Religionsgesellschaft*). It was appealed to by the Confederation of Islamic Cultural Centres in 1979 when it presented a request for recognition within the corporate body of public law (*Körperschaft des öffentlichen Rechts*) by the Islamic Federation of Berlin, hoping for recognition as *Religionsgemeinschaft* in the *Land* of Berlin in 1980, a status it finally won in 2000.[6] This precedent is being appealed to in other *Länder* (de Galembert and Tietze, 2002). Of course that is not to say that steps such as these were without controversy or that there is a simple, linear development. On the contrary, there can be on-going controversies and reversals, as earlier chapters have shown, and as has been particularly so since 9/11 and the so-called 'war on terrorism'.

We have not here attempted to discuss in a comprehensive way the kinds of legal and policy measures that are necessary to accommodate Muslims as equal citizens in European polities. These would include anti-discrimination measures in areas such as employment, positive action to achieve a full and just political representation of Muslims in various areas of public life, the inclusion of Muslim history as European history and so on. We have just been considering the inclusion of Islam as an organized religion and of Muslim identity as a public identity. Our argument has been that such inclusion is necessary to integrate Muslims and to pursue religious equality. While this inclusion runs against certain interpretations of secularism, it is not inconsistent with what secularism means in practice in Europe. We should let the latter and the spirit of compromise that it represents be our guide and not an ideological secularism that is unfortunately generating European domestic versions of 'the clash of civilizations' thesis and the conflicts that entails for European societies. That some people are today developing secularism as an ideology to oppose Islam and its public recognition is a challenge both to pluralism and equality, and thus to some of the bases of contemporary democracy.

Notes

* We are grateful to Talal Asad, Geoff Levey, Gregor McLennan and Anna Triandafyllidou for their comments on an earlier draft.
1 A special clause in the treaty allowed the two religions of the Empire – Catholicism and Protestantism – to live together.
2 Separate from this but also relevant is how the presence of assertive Muslim identities may be stimulating a revival of Christian cultural identities without a revival of Christian religious practices (for example, see Voas and Bruce (2004) on evidence in relation to the British 2001 Census).
3 We are not suggesting that it is merely a question of state ideology and state action. Sometimes difficulties arise from Muslim organizations, especially the competition between them, and sometimes from the intervention of the country of origin, such as Turkey in relation to Germany or Morocco in relation to France.
4 Even that very 'republican' Minister of Interior of the late 1990s, Chevènement, declared that he would like to see Islam 'develop in France as a minority religion like the Jews and Protestants' (*Consultation*, No. 1).
5 This is potentially a dynamic process: Muslims appeal to the institutional recognition given over many decades and longer to Christians and Jews, while the latter may at times be stimulated to strengthen a weakening institutional position by supporting Muslim demands or even by asking for extra powers in the context of the revisiting of state–religion arrangements prompted by the claims-making of Muslims.
6 See *Deutsches Verwlatungsblatt*, 1 July 2000: *Die Bremer Klausel des Art. 141 GG gilt in ganz Berlin*, S.1001–S.1006. Recognition, however, has raised questions about the place of Islam in state education instruction, just as with the Christian faiths. Since the 1990s, attempts have been made in three *Länder* to integrate Islam into the public schools. In Berlin, since religious instruction by and large is associated with the churches, instruction of the Koran has been placed under the supervision of the Turkish state through the intermediary of the *Diyanet*, its official organ. The presence of Islamic instructors has since 1984 been included in the bilateral agreements that initially governed the provision of Turkish-language classes. In Hamburg, a Social Democratic (SPD) *Land*, language teachers, even of Turkish nationality, enjoy the status of civil servants, and have established instruction in Islam within the *Religionspedagogik* programme that applies to all religions. In Northern Westphalia, teachers of theology, scientists and Christian pedagogues are responsible for implementing a curriculum of Islam.

References

De Galembert, C. and Tietze, N. (2002) 'Institutionalisierung des Islam in Deutschland. Pluralisierung der Weltanschauungen', *Mittelweg*, 36(11/1): 43–62.
De Graaf, N. D. and Need, A. (2000) 'Losing faith: is Britain alone', in R. Jowell, J. Curtice, A. Park and K. Thomson. (eds) *British Social Attitudes: Focusing on Diversity*, The 17th Report, London: Sage.
François, E. (1993) *Protestants et catholiques en Allemagne. Identités et pluralisme, Augsbourg 1648–1806*, Paris: Albin Michel.
Greely, A. (1995) 'The persistence of religion', *Cross Currents*, 45(Spring): 24–41.
Habermas, J. (1994) 'Struggles for recognition in the democratic constitutional state', in A. Gutmann (ed.) *Multiculturalism: Examining The Politics of Recognition*, Princeton, NJ: Princeton University Press.
Hamburger, P. (2002) *Separation of Church and State*, Cambridge, MA, and London: Harvard University Press.

Kastoryano, R. (2002) *Negotiating Identities: States and Immigrants in France and Germany*, Princeton, NJ: Princeton University Press.

––––– (2004) 'Religion and incorporation: Islam in France and Germany', *International Migration Review*, Fall: 1234–1256.

Lochak, D. (1989) 'Les minorités dans le droit public français: du refus des différences à la gestion des différences', *Conditions des minorités depuis 1789*, CRISPA-GDM, Paris: L'Harmattan.

Modood, T. (1994) 'Establishment, multiculturalism and British citizenship', *Political Quarterly*, 65(1): 53–73

––––– (ed.) (1997) *Church, State and Religious Minorities*, London: Policy Studies.

––––– (1998a) 'Multiculturalism, secularism and the state', *Critical Review of International, Social and Political Philosophy*, 1(3): 79–97 (Reproduced in Bellamy, R. and Hollis, M. (eds) (1999) *Pluralism and Liberal Neutrality*, London: Frank Cass).

––––– (1998b) 'British multiculturalism: some rival positions and thoughts on the way forward', Seminar paper to the Commission on the Future of Multi-ethnic Britain, London.

Müller, H. (1995) 'De l'*Aufklärung* à Weimar. Mouvement des idées et mutations politiques', in A.-M. LeGloannec (ed.) *L'État de l'Allemagne*, Paris: La Découverte: 33–37.

Nicolet, C. (1995) *L'Idée républicaine en France (1789–1924)*, Paris: Gallimard.

Norris, P. and Inglehart, R. (2004) *Sacred and Secular: Religion and Politics Worldwide*, Cambridge: Cambridge University Press.

Parekh, B. (2000) *Rethinking Multiculturalism: Cultural Diversity and Political Theory*, Basingstoke: Macmillan.

Rex, J. (1986) *Race and Ethnicity*, Milton Keynes: Open University Press.

Royal Commission on the Reform of the House of Lords (2000) *A House for the Future*, January, London: HMSO.

Sandel, M. (1994) 'Review of Rawls' political liberalism', *Harvard Law Review*, 107: 1765–1794.

Schuck, P. (2003) Diversity in America: Keeping government at a safe distance, Cambridge, MA: Harvard University Press.

Sunier, T. and von Luijeren, M. (2002) 'Islam in the Netherlands', in Y. Haddad (ed.) *Muslims in the West. From Sojourners to Citizens*, New York: Oxford University Press: 144–158.

Voas, D. and Bruce, S. (2004) 'The 2001 Census and Christian identification in Britain', *Journal of Contemporary Religion*, 19(1): 23–28.

Young, I. M. (1990) *Justice and the Politics of Difference*, Princeton, NJ: Princeton University Press.

10 Europe, liberalism and the 'Muslim question'

Bhikhu Parekh

In many influential circles in Europe, it is widely held that its over 15 million Muslims pose a serious cultural and political threat. Sometimes this view is explicitly stated; more often it is implied or simply assumed.[1] On other occasions it takes the form of an attack on multiculturalism for which Muslims are largely held responsible and which is a coded word for them.[2] It cuts across political and ideological divides and is shared alike, albeit in different degrees, by conservatives, fascists, liberals, socialists and communists. In this chapter I critically examine the basis of this view, paying particular attention to liberals and asking why the champions of minority rights, cultural diversity and civic as opposed to ethnic nationalism are drawn towards it.

The nature of European anxiety[3]

It is widely argued that although Muslim immigrants have now been in Europe for over four decades, they have, unlike their past and present counterparts, failed to integrate.[4] They show no commitment to its democratic institutions and mock its liberal freedoms. They do not feel at home in European societies and prefer to live among themselves, forming a relatively self-contained community maintaining only the minimum necessary ties with the wider society. They keep making unreasonable demands and feel deeply alienated and resentful when these are not met. They see themselves as part of the universal *Ummah*, have little loyalty to their country of settlement, and are more concerned about their fellow religionists in other parts of the world than their fellow citizens. They lag behind other groups of immigrants and the indigenous population educationally because, among other things, they have not fully taken to Western education and overburden their children with heavy doses of irrelevant Islamic education. They lag behind others economically partly because of their poor educational attainments and partly because they are not integrated into the economic and moral culture that underpins the Western economy. Predictably they remain an alienated underclass, in society but not of it, full of resentment and ill-directed anger and a potential source of unrest and violence. While conservatives hold them responsible for their predicament, liberals and others appreciate that the discrimination, hostility and disadvantages from which Muslims suffer are partly to blame. Even they, however, think that much of the responsibility lies with the Muslims themselves for failing to integrate, adjust and make European societies their cultural and political home.

Muslims have not integrated, it is argued, because they do not want to and cannot integrate. They cannot integrate because their ways of life and thought are fundamentally incompatible with those of Europe. They are collectivist, intolerant, authoritarian, illiberal and theocratic. This is why no Muslim society has so far thrown up a vibrant liberal democratic society, and almost every one of them strenuously resists internal and external attempts to introduce one.[5] Islam today is like what Christianity was during the Middle Ages, and badly needs a Reformation of the European or suitably Islamized kind. There are no signs of that happening now or in the near future. In fact many Muslims are positively opposed to it because they strongly disapprove of what they think it has done to Europe and the West in general. A Reformation in their view is a step towards secularization, and either undermines religion or emasculates it by confining it to the personal realm. Rather than see European history as pointing in the right direction, they draw the opposite conclusion and opt for 'fundamentalism' or holding on tenaciously to Islam in its original form. Some Muslims do see the need for radical reform, but are either daunted by the intellectual and theological task involved or, more often, frightened by the hostile reactions of the rest.

Another important reason why European Muslims are believed not to wish to integrate has to do with their alleged proselytizing mission. Integration involves accepting and adjusting to the basically secular culture of European society. Muslims do not think much of the 'heathen' and 'degenerate' West. They want to challenge and transform it, and think that their religion has equipped them for the task. It is in their view a perfect religion, the only one entitled to make such a claim. It is free from the errors and corruptions of and marks the fulfilment of the other two Abrahamic religions. And it is also incomparably superior to all others. Muslims therefore believe that they have a divine mission to proselytize and reshape the West in their image. They see no reason why they should fail. After all, they have chalked up remarkable successes in their short history, making theirs the second largest and fastest growing religion in the world today. Since they think they possess the Truth, face a morally and spiritually bankrupt West, and wield the strength derived from number, oil and conviction, they feel convinced that history is on their side. When they have a world to win, it makes no sense to integrate into a degenerate way of life.

Europeans who hold this view are convinced that since Muslims will not integrate for these and other reasons, they represent an unassimilable element. And since they harbour revolutionary aspirations, they are a hostile other, an enemy within. Europeans had hoped that the second and third generations of Muslims would integrate and become Europeans in all respects save their religion, but feel disappointed in them. They have turned out to be not just more religious but are so in a particularly unacceptable manner. The first generation of Muslim immigrants defined their identity in terms of their country of origin and saw their religion as one component of it. Their offspring are quite different. Their country of parental origin has no emotional or even cultural meaning for them, and its place has been taken by religion. Religion distinguishes them from their fellow citizens and is something they can call their own; it links them to Muslim immigrants from other countries and provides a basis of national unity; it connects them with the European and global *Ummah* and gives them a sense of power; it relates them to a splendid history and is the basis of their pride and self-respect. Their Islam thus is quite different from that of their parents.[6] It is not a taken-for-granted fact of life but a self-conscious public statement, not a quietly held personal faith but a matter of identity which they must jealously guard and loudly and repeatedly proclaim lest anyone else or even they themselves should ever be in doubt about it. It is not one component of their identity but its sole basis. It is intended not only to remind them of who they are but also to announce to others what they stand for. And since it performs political functions, it has a collective and political character. While their parents would have said that they were Muslims, their offspring say that they have a Muslim or Islamic *identity*. The difference is deep and striking.[7]

Since the proponents of the view I am considering feel disappointed and even betrayed by the Muslim youth in whom they had invested their hopes, they are deeply worried about how to integrate them. Liberals among them increasingly gravitate towards a dual strategy. Since young Muslims suffer from discrimination and disadvantage, a concerted programme is needed to tackle these by ensuring them equal opportunity, raising their educational achievement, improving their economic prospects, and giving them a stake in society. At the same a determined effort should be made to ensure their cultural integration. The state should stop flirting with multicultural experiments, lay down clear and firm limits which no one may transgress, foster the spirit and virtues of citizenship, cultivate pride in the country, redouble integrationist efforts in schools, disallow spouses from countries of parental origins who bring with them cultures and social ties that obstruct full integration, and so on.[8] In the liberal view the two parts of this strategy are interdependent and equally important. Cultural integration without economic equality fuels anger and resentment and is self-defeating. Economic equality without cultural integration is divisive and remains precarious.

The European anxiety about the Muslim threat that I have articulated above arises out of the belief that Muslims cannot and do not wish to integrate and are in fact engaged in a quiet but sustained conspiracy to subvert Europe. Very little evidence is offered or is indeed available to support such a view. As we saw recently in London and earlier in Madrid, a small group of militant Muslims do talk in such a language and engage in murderous terrorist deeds but as the widespread Muslim revulsion and condemnation has shown the militant youth have little support in their community. More importantly this view derives its plausibility from the dubious assertion that Muslims have so far made little or no effort to integrate.

Muslims have a good record as a law-abiding community. If we ignored such isolated incidents as the Rushdie affair in Britain, the murder of Theo Van Gogh in Holland, and the occasional riots often precipitated by genuine grievances, there is no evidence that Muslims have failed to show loyalty to their country of settlement. Even when subjected to blatant discrimination, such as not being allowed to build mosques in parts of Italy or denied state funding for their schools on the same lines as Christian and Jewish schools in Britain, they have either suffered quietly or protested peacefully but rarely taken the law into their own hands. They have also taken considerable pride in their country of settlement. Both young and old Muslims appreciate the rights and freedoms they enjoy in Europe, many of which are not available in most Muslim countries, and value the support of their fellow citizens in their struggle for equality and justice. In a recent British survey, 67 per cent of the Muslims said that they felt very or fairly patriotic, 11 per cent that they were mildly patriotic, and only 15 per cent claimed not to feel patriotic at all.[9] These figures are broadly comparable to those of the indigenous population and are reproduced in other European countries.

As for the extraterritorial loyalty to *Ummah*, it is neither unique to them nor amounts to much in practice. Jews press the cause of Israel, Indians of India, and blacks of Africa. Loyalty to *Ummah* has rarely led to disloyalty to their country of settlement. Barely a dozen British Muslims fought with the Taliban and were roundly condemned by the bulk of their community. Although we do not have exact figures for France, Italy, the Netherlands, Spain and elsewhere, the number there was not large either. When two French journalists were taken hostage by the Islamic Army in Iraq to put pressure on the French government to lift the ban on headscarves, the French Muslims mobilized as never before, and insisted that the Islamic Army had no right to speak in their name and that their primary loyalty was to their compatriots.

Like millions of their countrymen, a large number of European Muslims, though by no means all of them, were bitterly opposed to the war on Iraq, but remained content to join peaceful protests against it. Had they been so minded, they could have been far more noisy, could have tried to sabotage the war effort in countries belonging to the 'coalition of the willing', formed a human shield in Iraq and so on. The fact that they did not do any of these things speaks volumes. In Britain when the Imam of Finsbury Park Mosque, who preached hatred of the West and urged support for the terrorists, was arrested and his mosque raided, there was some outrage but also quiet satisfaction that some action had been taken against Abu Hamza and his associates.

Muslims have also shown respect for democratic institutions. They have participated in local and national elections, stood as candidates in fairly large numbers, joined mainstream political parties, and accepted the decisions of the majority. When a Muslim parliament was set up in Britain to discuss issues of common interest and provide Muslims with a distinct political voice, it received little general support and became defunct, largely because of widespread Muslim hostility and factionalism. A small group of Muslim activists formed the Islamic Party of Britain in 1989, arguing that only the Muslims could represent Muslims and that they should avoid secular political parties. It received little Muslim support and secured only 3 per cent of the vote in the Muslim majority wards in the Bradford North by-election a year later.

It is sometimes argued that the Muslim support for democratic institutions and loyalty to the state are prudential in nature and a matter of political expediency. Lacking a moral basis, they remain precarious and may be withheld at any time. The argument makes a valid point but does not apply to a large majority of European Muslims. Reasons for supporting democratic institutions do matter, for the support for them does not inspire trust and guarantee future conduct if it does not spring from the individual's deeply held beliefs. As the extensive debate among the European Muslims shows, they have seriously explored the moral dimension of their relationship to their country of settlement and articulated a theological–moral theory of political obligation.

While a small minority dismisses democracy as a form of polytheism (*shirk billah*) that deifies people and sets up their sovereignty in rivalry to that of Allah, most Muslims take a different view. Democracy, they argue, does not deify people, and subjects their will to clearly stated constitutional constraints including basic human rights. It shows respect for human dignity, protects fundamental human interests, ensures responsible use of power, guarantees freedom of religion and institutionalizes shura, all of which are not only consistent with but often enjoined by the Qur'ān. Although an enlightened monarchy might be able to achieve these objectives, it is heavily dependent on the character of the monarch and inherently risky. The Prophet was one such individual, and it is naive to imagine that all societies can throw up men like him on a regular basis. For most European Muslims democracy therefore remains a better form of government than any other, and they have a moral obligation to uphold it. This does not mean that they approve of its current liberal form. For many of them it should be more hospitable to religion and less secular in its orientation, but most of them agree that its basic institutional structure is sound and worthy of their support.

Political participation is given a similar theological-moral basis. While a small minority such as the Hizb al-Tahrir dismisses it as haram because it involves working with secular political parties and accepting secular Western political institutions, most Muslims take a very different view. The fatwa by Taha Jabir al-Alwani, Chairman of the North American Fiqh Council, asks Muslims to participate in political life because it enables them to promote worthwhile causes, protects basic human rights, ensures responsible rule, and improves the quality of information about Islam and Muslim interests. For Al-Alwani, political participation is not just a 'right' that can be surrendered, nor a 'permission' that may be ignored, but a 'duty' that must be discharged.[10]

Loyalty to the state too is defended on Qur'ānic grounds. The Qur'ān places high value on the sanctity of contracts, and enjoins Muslims to show loyalty to the state and respect its laws in return for its physical protection and respect for basic freedoms. This argument was commonly made by British Muslims when a small number of them wanted to go to Afghanistan to fight with the Taliban and against British troops. It was further clarified in the *Fatwa on British Muslims* issued by Shaykh Abdullah al-Judai, a member of the European Council for Fatwa and Research. The fatwa insisted that one of the Muslim's 'highest

obligations' was to respect agreements and contracts, that they were contractu-
ally bound to their country of settlement, and that they 'cannot take up arms'
against it even in order to defend Muslims elsewhere.[11] This last point is
disputed by some Muslims, but their number is small and confined to a militant
Shiite group lacking popular support.

As far as the basic European values and practices are concerned, Muslims
have no difficulty with many of these. Human dignity, equal human worth,
equality of the races, civility, peaceful resolution of differences and reciprocity
are all part of the Islamic tradition. Although polygyny and female circumcision
are practised by some groups of Muslims, they are disapproved of by others and
are in decline. It is therefore hardly surprising that the laws banning them
provoked little Muslim protest. Two areas that have proved particularly
contentious and provoked much liberal disapproval relate to gender equality
and freedom of expression.

Equality of the sexes is being increasingly accepted by a majority of European
Muslims. Women vote in elections and stand for public office without facing
much male opposition. Muslim girls go on to complete their school education
and do better than boys. A fairly large number of them go on to higher education,
though it is smaller than for boys often because of parental discouragement.
However, that is changing for the better. Muslim girls are discouraged from
pursuing certain occupations but that too is changing. They enjoy less social
freedom and are sometimes forced into arranged marriages, but they are
rebelling against this with some success. The struggle for gender equality is
fought in many families. And although the rebelling young girls and women are
subjected to intimidation and violence, they are taking collective action with
the judicious help of the state. Young girls also invoke the authority of the
Qur'ān in their struggle, arguing that sexist practices are conventional in origin
and lack a religious basis. This requires them to study the Qur'an well enough to
interpret it. While prima facie such a diligent study of religion appears conservative, its intentions and outcome are often radical, as is evident in the growing
popularity of Islamic 'feminism'.

Issues relating to free speech have provoked the greatest Muslim anger and
an equally fierce reaction against them. Muslims do not question the value of
free speech but its scope and limits. After all they use it to criticize the West,
highlight their grievances, press their demands, to challenge some of their own
ugly practices, and so on, and are its greatest beneficiaries. They value it not
only on instrumental but also on moral grounds and find a theological and
historical support for it. The sticking point comes when free speech is in
conflict with their religious sensibilities.

The Rushdie affair, the first Europe-wide public expression of Muslim anger
and a turning point in the European perception of Muslims, involved death
threats against a creative writer for 'mocking' and 'lampooning' Islam and its
founder, and that in a language most Muslims found 'filthy' and 'scurrilous'.
Ayaan Hirsi Ali, a member of the Dutch Parliament, was threatened with death
and had to go into hiding because her documentary *Submission* had words of the

Qur'ān written on the back, stomach and legs of a partly dressed woman to highlight women's oppression in the name of Islam. While she is now happily back in Parliament and intends to write *Submission Part II*, Theo Van Gogh, who directed the film and declined protection, was shot and brutally decapitated with a kind of a butcher's knife. When challenged by a petrified bystander, Muhammed, his assassin, is reported to have said that his victim had 'asked for it' and that 'now you all know what you can expect'.[12] The Moroccan–Dutch painter Rachid Ben Ali received death threats because of the homosexual themes in his work and his satirical treatment of fundamentalist imams. Fearing reprisals, several critical scholars of the Qur'an write under pseudonyms. 'Christoph Luxenberg', a pseudonymous author, argues that some key words in it are derived from Aramaic, the language group of most Middle Eastern Jews and Christians, and mean quite different from their conventional readings. He fears that even this might be too much for some Muslims.[13]

While a small group of Muslim militants have reacted violently against the works of 'Luxenberg', Ben Ali, and others like them, must either ignore or dismiss them with varying degrees of disapproval. *The Satanic Verses* and to a lesser extent *Submission* are in a separate category because of the kinds of issues they raise. Even here there is no unanimity among Muslims. While a sizeable group consider violence justified in such cases, many disapprove of it. Even they, however, think, often wrongly, that these works stretch the limits of freedom of expression beyond acceptable limits. There is thus a deep difference of opinion between the liberal and Muslim views on this point. One should not get it out of perspective, however. It is not a disagreement over the value of freedom of expression but rather over a trade-off between it and offence to religious sensibilities. Neither is it a disagreement between Muslims and liberals, for the Muslim view is shared by many other religious groups and some liberals, and the liberal view enjoys some support among an albeit small number of Muslims. As long as Muslim protests stay within the limits of the law, their dissenting voice need not arouse undue anxiety. Indeed liberals should welcome it both out of respect for the principle of freedom of expression and as a useful corrective to the excesses of its absolutist champions.

Logic of integration

I have argued that despite the rhetoric and murderous deeds of a militant minority and the cultural confusion and ambiguity of some others, the large majority of European Muslims can, wish to and have made sincere efforts to integrate. If they have not always succeeded, at least part of the responsibility lies with the hostility, racism and discrimination of the wider society and the inevitable disadvantages of all immigrants. This raises the question as to why an influential body of European people think otherwise. Some are narrow nationalists or racists and resent Muslim presence. Some concentrate on the militant minority, and either ignore the rest or interpret their silence to imply that they share or at least feel some sympathy for its views. Many are rightly disturbed by the rise of Islamic fundamentalism in different parts of the world and project it on to all Muslims including European immigrants. Some others see this as an opportunity to unite Europeans, firm up liberal resolve, put Muslims on the defensive, and to pressure their moderate majority into dissociating themselves from the militants more openly and loudly than they generally tend to do. While these and other factors play their part, there are also others that are internal to the European conservative and liberal thought. Since they are often ignored or insufficiently analysed, I shall concentrate on three of them.

When Europeans complain that Muslims have not integrated and cannot integrate, they rely on a narrow and dubious view of integration. European states have long seen themselves and many continue to see themselves as nation-states based on a shared national culture, including a shared view of the world, vision of the good life, personal and collective values, customs, and social and moral practices. For many Europeans cultural unity is the indispensable basis of political unity and must be maintained at all cost. If immigrants including Muslims wish to become and be accepted as full and equal members of society, they should assimilate into the national culture. If they insist on retaining their cultural identity and remaining different, they should not blame others for refusing to accept them as equals. The fact that most earlier European immigrants willingly or unwillingly accepted this view and opted for full assimilation gives this view historical legitimacy and makes it a norm for their post-war successors.

For all kinds of reasons assimilation has proved an unrealistic goal. Post-war immigrants are ethnically, culturally and religiously quite different from their predecessors, and resist assimilation. They also face greater discrimination, which hampers their assimilation. The moral climate has changed, and there is now greater tolerance of diversity. The traditional moral consensus has declined, and it is not clear how the immigrants can be assimilated into the much disputed national culture. Conservatives and liberals draw different conclusions from this. The former believe that the national culture has enough life left in it and can be revitalized, and that immigrants can be assimilated into it if society showed greater determination and stopped being a prey to shallow and suicidal multiculturalism. Liberals share the view that cultural unity is the basis of political unity, but insist that it can and should be limited to the public realm. In their view this represents the best way to reconcile the legitimate demands of political unity with respect for immigrant cultures. The public realm, in which citizens meet as citizens and which unites them in a single community, should be an area of uniformity based on a shared national culture. Their diversity belongs to the private realm where they may organize their personal lives as they please. Since this model unites members of society without suppressing their differences, integrates them without assimilating them, it has come to be called integration. Integration represents the liberal alternative to conservative assimilation.

When probed deeper, the moral and political distance between integration and assimilation is not as great as the liberal rhetoric suggests. Integration shares the basic assimilationist premise that political unity requires and is impossible without cultural unity, and differs only in limiting the latter to the public realm. Since this premise is the basis of the European nation-state, integration, like assimilation, operates within its framework and constantly runs up against its constraints. The public/private distinction on which it rests is not culturally neutral and is subject to much dispute. What is more, the boundary between the private and public realms is necessarily porous and few institutions and areas of life neatly fit into either category. Some, such as schools, belong to both and are subject to their conflicting demands, which is why they have been the site of struggle in almost every European country.

Since political unity depends in the integrationist view on the cultural unity of the public realm, there is a constant worry that the latter would remain precarious if its values were too much at odds with those governing the private realm. There is therefore a relentless pressure to bring the private realm into harmony with the values of the public realm, so that public values are internalized and become part of every citizen's moral identity and self-understanding. This is how the Lang Commission on Nationality in France defined integration, and justified state intervention in immigrant ways of life and thought. In Germany it is not considered enough if immigrants observe the country's public values; they must make an 'inner affirmation' of them. Muslim parents who send their children to religious classes and warn them against the influence of some Western values are said to 'act against integration'. Integration not only goes all the way down but also keeps extending sideways. It is not enough if immigrants integrate economically and politically but prefer to marry among themselves or lead culturally self-contained lives. The integrationist cannot understand why immigrants should hold themselves back and refuse to wholeheartedly throw in their lot with the rest if they are really committed to their country of settlement and wish to become its full and equal members. Liberals either fail to notice the totalist logic of integration or disapprove of it but lack a principled check against it.[14]

The totalist logic of integration at least partly explains the liberal complaint that Muslims are failing to integrate. Muslims have integrated economically and politically, but since they hold themselves back in some of the other areas of life, they fall short of the liberal expectation. Again, Muslims complain that since the cultural values of the public realm are constantly used to reshape the private realm, the latter is precarious and constantly violated. While liberals think that this is the only way to give the values a sound moral and social basis, Muslims see it as breaking the liberal commitment to respect the integrity of the private realm and accuse them of hypocrisy or even dishonesty. When Muslims take defensive measures such as sending their children to religious classes and schools, liberals see it as threat to common culture. Unless the liberal view of integration is made more hospitable to diversity and has built in theoretical and moral checks against its totalist logic, it will continue to alienate Muslims and other immigrants and provoke the very troubles it is designed to avoid.

Religion

The second cause of European anxiety about Muslim immigrants has to do with its attitude to religion, and has its source in European liberalism. Liberals in general and European liberals in particular have long been troubled by religion. For some it rejects many of the central principles of liberalism such as humanism, individualism, critical rationality, commitment to scientific enquiry, freedom of thought and belief in progress, and represents a reactionary and obscurantist form of thought. Other liberals take a more discriminating view of religion. They welcome it as a necessary corrective to human hubris, and a valuable moral resource if it is of the right kind, or when it is suitably rationalized and reformed, or if it stays within its prescribed limits and does not seek to dominate political life.

Whatever their attitude to religion, almost all liberals are convinced that political life should be organized along secular lines. The State, they argue, is concerned with this world not the next. It deals with matters that all citizens share in common, and its affairs should be conducted in a secular language which they all understand and share. It is inherently coercive and must stay clear of religious and other areas in which coercion has no place. It should treat all its citizens equally and respect their freedom of conscience, which it cannot do if it is tied to a particular religion. After civil wars and bitter experiences that nearly tore apart their societies, Europeans began to feel the force of these and related arguments. They arrived at a historical settlement according to which religion was to be confined to the private realm and the public realm was to be structured along secular lines. For liberals this marked a great turning point in European history and inaugurated the era of modern liberal democracy, as discussed in Chapter 9.

In the liberal view Islam challenges this historical consensus and threatens to reopen long-settled controversies. It rejects not just the comprehensive secularization of society but also the more limited form of political secularization. According to liberals, Muslims religionize political life at several levels. They make demands based on religion, such as a particular form of animal slaughter, time off for prayer during working hours, and exemption from certain laws and practices. They want the state to protect religious beliefs and practices by such means as restricting the freedom of expression and enforcing parts of the sharia. They reason about political matters in religious terms, debating whether the Qur'ān allows loyalty to the state, support for democratic institutions, political participation, equal rights for women or participation in a particular war. In so doing Muslims introduce a theological form of political reasoning in which others cannot participate but by whose outcome they are deeply affected. This rules out any form of shared public discourse, the *sine qua non* of common citizenship. Muslim introduction of religion in political life in these and other ways deeply disorients liberals. They cannot see how a secular political system can cope with this sudden intrusion of religion, especially one that rejects any form of private/public distinction on which all modern states are based. Their anxiety is further compounded by the fear that the Muslim example might encourage other religious groups and lead over time to the disintegration of the liberal political order.

Although liberals are right to highlight and worry about the danger militant Islam can pose, their anxiety in the European context is exaggerated and largely arises from a misunderstanding of how European societies are actually constituted and conduct their affairs. No European society or political system is secular in the sense in which liberals use the term. Its Christian heritage has profoundly shaped and continues to shape its vocabulary, self-understanding, institutions, ideals and practices. The ideas of human dignity, equal human worth, unity of humankind, freedom of conscience, etc., are all Christian in their origin, derive their moral energy from it, and reappear in liberalism in their secularized form. The views of human nature and history that inform much of the European political thought and practice, many of its current laws and practices, and even such trivial things as treating Sundays and Christmas as public holidays, are all further examples of the continuing influence of Christianity. The fact that their historical roots are often forgotten and that religion survives as culture does not mean that they do not have a religious basis and even religious overtones. Muslims and for that matter devout Christians do not introduce an alien element in an otherwise secular society. Rather they speak loudly in the same language that the rest of society speaks in a quiet whisper.

Legal and political arrangements of European societies have so far recognized and respected the beliefs and practices of Christianity and to some extent Judaism. They now need to take a similar account of Islam. In some cases this is straightforward; in others it requires adjustments and modifications in the prevailing practices. Since the British state funds Christian and Jewish schools, Muslims demand public funding for theirs. They ask for holidays on their religious festivals, halal meat, accommodation of their dress codes, etc., many of which do not involve special rights but are rather different ways of exercising the rights they enjoy equally with others. One might have perfectly good reasons to reject some Muslim demands, but the argument that their religious basis contravenes the constitutive principles of an otherwise secular society cannot be one of them.

The theological style of reasoning about political matter that worries liberals is not unique to Muslims. Anti-abortionists, pacifists, some groups of environmentalists, champions of global justice and opponents of Sunday trading reason from within the Christian, Judaic or some other religious tradition. And even some liberals only reproduce the basic Christian beliefs in a secular language, as becomes clear when they are pressed to articulate and defend them. Contrary to what liberals imagine, our public life does not and cannot rest on a uniform view of public reason.[15] It is inherently plural and made up of several different forms of reasoning, such as the secular, the religious, a mixture of the two, and the countless varieties of each of them. The standard liberal theory finds it difficult to explain how we can communicate across different moral and political languages. In fact we manage rather well.

Since many of these languages are precipitates of our history and form part of our common heritage, we grow up acquiring considerable familiarity and even a measure of sympathy with some of them, and do not even notice our society's mixed discourse. Unbeknown to us, we ourselves sometimes speak in several moral languages. And when we do not speak a language, we often understand it well enough to respond to its speakers. From time to time there are no doubt passages of incomprehension and breakdowns in communication, and then we seek to improve our knowledge of other languages, find a common language, turn to translators and interpreters, leave the matter unresolved, reach a tentative compromise, or do one of several other familiar things. What is troublesome about the Muslim political reasoning is not its religious character but its unfamiliarity. And the answer to that lies in greater interaction, sympathetic dialogue, multicultural education and Muslim spokespeople acquiring reasonable competence in other languages, especially the secular.

Secularism is a complex concept and some liberals take a simplistic and unrealistic view of it. Since religion matters to the vast majority of Europeans and shapes their behaviour, and since an attack on it can easily provoke public disorder, no European political system excludes it from political life or remains indifferent to it. At the same time no European state can allow religion to colonize political life and threaten its citizens' liberties. The history of every modern European state is a story of how best to balance these requirements. All European states are secular in the sense that they do not impose a religion on their citizens or make citizenship rights dependent on subscription to that religion, are not guided by religious considerations in making laws and policies, and do not derive their legitimacy from religious sources. They also, however, allow religion its proper place in political life, including religiously based political parties and a religiously grounded political rhetoric. They also have institutional mechanisms for maintaining regular contacts with major religious organizations, and many provide them with public funds to undertake secular activities. Britain funds Anglican, Catholic and Jewish schools, and its government informally but regularly consults religious bodies in matters relating to them. In Germany, the Jewish community, the Catholic dioceses and the regional Protestant churches enjoy the status of publicly recognized corporations. The state collects taxes from members of the churches on their behalf and hands over the money to the churches after deducting the agreed administrative charge. Nearly 80 per cent of publicly funded nursery schools are run by churches on behalf of the state, and so are a number of hospitals and other welfare institutions. The Netherlands has its 'pillars' which include its major religious communities. And while the most secular France refuses to take any notice of group differences, it recognizes those based on religion and regularly consults the representatives of the officially recognized national organizations of Catholics, Protestants and Jews.

Muslims pose no major problem. All that most of them ask for and what European states need to do is to find ways of accommodating them within the existing structure. As previous chapters have shown, this is broadly what is happening in practice, in some cases proactively, in others after considerable resistance. France has set up a Council of Muslim Faith, a national representative body, with the right to speak on behalf of French Muslims and enjoying a consultative status. In the Netherlands Muslims are part of 'pillarization' and have state-funded religious schools and television channels. In Belgium Islam has been a full member of the Council of Religions since 1974.[16] Spain, which had been subject to Muslim influence for centuries, tried for years to define its identity in opposition to Islam. In November 1992, it reached an accord with the Islamic Commission of Spain similar to that reached with other religious communities. The accord dealt with Muslim demands, such as the provision of halal meat, burial places, right to religious holidays, recognition of religious rights in hospitals, prisons and armed forces, tax relief, authority to perform civil marriages, and religious education in public schools. Although parts of the accord remain unimplemented because of lack of political will and funds, it represents a public acceptance of Muslims as an equal religious community with the rest.

While some liberal theorists worry deeply about the Muslim threat to secularism, European societies have in these and other ways accommodated them without compromising their secular character. Muslims are given regular access to power and are heard, their religious interests are taken into account, their demands discussed and conceded, shelved or rejected. At the same the secular historical settlement between religion and the state remains firmly in place, and most Muslims have neither asked for nor should be allowed any changes in it. Indeed since the existing arrangement treats them with respect and gives them full and equal religious freedom, it rightly claims and generally receives their whole-hearted moral support. It also makes it easier for them to challenge the militant minority's fulminations against the 'godless' land of 'crusaders'. Liberal society has far greater intellectual and moral resources and is far more subtle than its theorists imagine.

Rationalism

The third factor that generates European anxiety about Muslims has its roots in European rationalism. Although the latter's influence is noticeable in conservative, liberal, socialist, communist, nationalist, Fascist and other bodies of thought, it has found particular favour in certain forms of liberalism. To be sure, not all liberals are rationalists, but many classical and modern liberals are, and their influence on European thought and practice has been significant. I shall therefore concentrate on them.

For the rationalist liberal, reason is the highest human faculty. Human beings have dignity and intrinsic worth, and animals and trees do not, because they possess the capacity for reason. Freedom consists of self-determination, and for a rational being that involves acting on reason. The only proper way to deal with rational beings is to give them reasons and convince them why they ought to conduct themselves in a particular manner.

Compulsion is incompatible with human dignity, and is justified only when used in defence of reason against those acting irrationally. Ideally it has no place in a society that is based on rational principles and whose members habitually act rationally. In such a society, its members are asked to do what they would want to do anyway, obey only themselves and remain fully free. Since some human beings do from time to time act irrationally, compulsion sometimes becomes necessary. The goal of a liberal society is to minimize its need.

For the rationalist liberal, reason is impersonal and homogeneous in nature, capable of transcending time, place and individual circumstances and temperament and identical in all human beings. As such it is capable of convincing all with an open mind, and is inherently universal. Moral principles and values should be rationally arrived at and defended and not be based on human or divine authority, as otherwise they cannot convince rational beings and meet the demands of human freedom and rationality. Since reason is inherently universal, the moral principles and values it arrives at are universal in their validity and bind all human beings.

While some areas of human life raise moral questions and are governed by universal moral values, others deal with matters that are morally indifferent and are governed by customs and conventions. These include such things as forms of greeting, modes of dress, rituals and practices surrounding birth, marriage and death, and on which side of the road to drive. Unlike moral values, customs vary from society to society and are necessarily local in their nature and authority. Like all human actions and practices, customs too are subject to the authority of universal moral values and should be criticized and changed when they offend against the latter.

For the rationalist liberal, morality and customs involve different forms of reasoning.[17] Moral values can and should be rationally established, and convincing reasons should be given for them. Requiring human beings to respect and live by values whose point they cannot see is to violate their rational nature and dignity. Such compulsion as a society might exercise on individuals offending against its moral values is justified only if the values are defended by reasons that no rational person can deny. So far as customs are concerned, this form of defence is not possible. Once it is shown that they do not violate universal moral values and are not harmful, no further reason needs to be given for them than that 'this is how we do things here in this country'. This is not only a good but the only possible reason in matters that are morally indifferent and local in their origins and validity. Customs, conventions, etc., ensure the stable and smooth functioning of society, and what matters most is that they should be observed by all.

In the liberal rationalist view, liberalism represents many of the important universal moral values in a way that no other body of thought does. The liberal society embodies these values in its institutions and practices and seeks to live by them as best it can. Convincing reasons can be given why it is the most rational way to organize human society and why it deserves the fullest moral support of its members. Since liberal values are assumed to be universally valid, many liberals believe that they have a moral duty to spread them. This sense of universal mission, which has been an integral part of liberal thought almost from its very beginning, inspired or at least legitimized the European empires and remains a potent force even today.

Rationalist liberalism has its obvious strengths but also its limitations. As its critics have pointed out, it takes a transcendental view of human reason, homogenizes it, detaches it from other human faculties, and ignores its historicity, social embeddedness and the limitations imposed by the language in which it is necessarily articulated. I suggest that these and related limitations spring from, among other things, its inability to appreciate the importance of culture.[18]

Human beings seek to make sense of themselves and the world, and ask fundamental questions about the meaning and significance of human life, activities, relationships, their place in the universe, and so on. Their answers and the form of understanding they arrive at shape the way they structure their individual and collective lives. Culture refers to a historically created system of self-understanding or meaning and significance in terms of which a group of human beings make sense of and conduct their lives. Thanks to the human capacity to ask different questions and give the same ones different answers, their different geographical circumstances and historical experiences, and their powers of imagining different visions of the good life, different societies develop different systems of meaning and significance. They map out human faculties differently, develop different human capacities, emotions and traits of temperament, and cherish different ideals of human excellence. Since cultures are human creations and deal with common problems of human existence, their views and values overlap and no two cultures are totally distinct and mutually unintelligible. However, given the diversity of circumstances, plurality of human reason, etc., no two cultures are wholly alike either.

Moral life is necessarily embedded in and nurtured by the wider culture. Some cultures see morality as a separate realm; others weave it into customs and rituals. Some draw a sharp distinction between morality, truth and beauty; others subsume the latter two under it or vice versa and see morality as a form of truthful life or a way of creating a beautiful soul. Cultures also differ on what activities and human relations are moral in nature. For us our relation to food is morally indifferent; for many in Asia and Africa, it is profoundly moral because of the way the human body, the natural world and the human relation to it are understood.

In the light of all this, rationalist liberalism appears deeply problematic. Its distinction between morality and custom is specific to societies in which morality is abstracted from the rest of social life, and has no universal validity. Even in liberal societies there are practices that cannot be subsumed under either, or have elements of both. Take the French practice of *laïcité* as it is applied to schools. It is neither a custom that has somehow grown up nor a universal or even a local moral value. It is intimately tied up with the French views on the nature of the state, citizenship, national integration, public education and the role of the school. When pressed, the French do not simply say that this is their custom and should be enforced because this is 'how we do things here', but give an elaborate set of good theoretical, practical and historical reasons why they think it is a right political practice for them and should be retained as an integral part of their political culture. These reasons are not moral or universal in nature and have a local context and content. Since *laïcité* is neither a custom nor a moral value but a cultural practice that requires a distinct form of reasoning, it has not surprisingly caused the French and other liberals considerable difficulty. Those who see it as a moral and universal value need to give convincing moral reasons, which they cannot. Those who see it as a custom cannot explain why it should be sacrosanct and not allow exceptions. Both groups misidentify the nature of *laïcité* and look for kinds of reasons that are inappropriate for a cultural practice.

As for moral values, some of them are universal as the rationalist liberal rightly insists, but others are culturally specific. Deep humility and selflessness in the profound sense of dissolution of the jealously guarded boundary of the self and rejection of all forms of self-assertion are values in Buddhist societies but not in the modern West. Such other moral values as asceticism, minimum demands on the natural world, reverence for parents and cosmic piety are again deeply cherished in some societies but not others. The latter either do not see their point or feel their moral pull but are not convinced enough to want to adopt them. The values rest on good reasons, but these are not universal. And although they are local or limited to particular societies, they are moral in nature and not at all like customs and conventions.

So far as liberal moral values are concerned, the rationalist liberal exaggerates the case for them. While fairly compelling reasons can be given for some values, such as respect for human life, human dignity and equality of human worth, so that universal validity can be claimed for them, this is not so in relation to such other liberal candidates as personal autonomy, critical rationalism, individualism and private property, particularly the way liberals define them. We can certainly give good reasons for them, but these are not so compelling or convincing as to make those disagreeing irrational or intellectually obtuse.

All moral values need to be defined and interpreted, including those for which we can give compelling reasons as well as those for which we cannot. Respect for human life is a great universal moral value, but views vary between and within societies on when human life begins and ends, what respect for it entails, and how much moral weight to give it relative to animal life, scientific advance and national defence. What is true of such a basic moral value is even more true of others. Some of these disagreements can be resolved, but not all, and hence genuine and irresoluble differences are bound to remain.

Since values often conflict, they need to be prioritized, traded off, and their relative moral weights determined both in general and in relevant contexts. We discussed earlier the question of the limits of freedom of expression. Many liberals argue that it includes the freedom to offend religious sensibilities and even to mock and denigrate religious communities. Others, including some liberals, cannot see why it should be privileged and would limit it in appropriate ways. There are good arguments on both sides, and compelling ones for neither. The conflicts between civil liberties and national security, private property and collective well-being, liberty and equality, etc., often have good, sometimes even equally good, arguments on both sides. And we take stands based on which ones persuade us more or on other considerations than their intellectual force.

Like any other society, the liberal society is based on a broadly shared culture and the consequent consensus on the meanings of human activities and relationships, the nature and place of morality, the role of compulsion in social life, and so on. Some of its values are rationally compelling and rightly claim universal validity, while others are unique to it. There is also a broad consensus on how to define, prioritize and trade off universal values. The consensus is embodied in its major institutions and practices, and is maintained by suitably socializing its members. In some respects the consensus is deep and extensive, in others it is relatively shallow and narrowly based. Disagreements, some fairly profound, therefore arise from time to time, and are shelved, settled by compromise or lead to acute conflicts.

Disagreements become sharp when immigrants arrive, especially those from quite different cultural and religious backgrounds such as the Muslims. They do not share the wider culture and the prevailing moral consensus, yet are asked to respect the society's values and customs. This presents its spokespeople, especially the liberals, with a challenge. Liberals do not want to use compulsion as it violates their commitment to rationality and respect for persons. They need to give immigrants good and convincing reasons, and these in their view are of two kinds. So far as local customs are concerned, the liberals argue that this is how we do things here. And so far as the moral values are concerned, the liberals aim to give reasons that are compelling or at least powerful enough to secure the assent of immigrants. I shall take each in turn.

Local customs vary greatly in their nature and complexity. Immigrants could be asked to drive on the left- or right-hand side of the road because this is a local practice, and that settles the matter. There is a local custom in almost every European society that prayers should be conducted silently and not disturb local peace. Muslims use loudspeakers to call the faithful to prayer, not a religious requirement but a traditional practice. Should it be disallowed because this is not how we do things here? Or should it be changed to accommodate new arrivals? Different European societies took one or the other view until the courts ruled in favour of the latter, and even then some of them tried to circumvent or sabotage the court's decision by administrative and other means. Sometimes local customs conflict with immigrants' values as in the case of ritual slaughter, a religious requirement for Jews and Muslims. To say that 'this is not how we do things here' does not settle the issue, at least for the liberal who would not automatically wish to privilege a local custom over a religious–moral value, especially when good reasons can be given for it.

The problem for the rationalist liberals become particularly acute so far as moral values are concerned. The liberals need to give reasons capable of convincing immigrants. In some cases they can, in others they cannot. They cannot show, for example, that personal autonomy, individual choice and liberty, etc., should enjoy the privileged status that they do in the liberal society. Furthermore, some of the acute conflicts of recent years have centred not so much on the importance of liberal values as on their relative importance. When freedom of expression conflicts with deeply held religious beliefs, it is not easy to show that the former automatically trumps the latter as the liberals generally maintain. There are good reasons on both sides; and the liberals cannot show that theirs is the only rationally defensible view.

All this puts the rationalist liberals in a moral quandary. They need to give convincing reasons why immigrants should respect liberal values including the liberal interpretations and ways of resolving their conflicts, but they cannot. And they do not want to say that 'this is how we do things here', because such an argument has in their view no relevance in moral matters. Their difficulty is compounded by the fact that they have and know that they have good reasons for holding these values, because otherwise they would not themselves feel justified in subscribing to them. These reasons, however, are not impersonal, transcendental and transcultural; they are internal to the liberals' culture and bound up with their society's self-understanding, history, traditions and experiences. While these reasons convince the liberals and other members of society, they do not convince immigrants.

Since the rationalist liberals rightly think that their values rest on reasons they find convincing, they cannot understand why others fail to see the obvious. They accuse immigrants of being 'unreasonable', 'bigots', 'irrational', 'lacking an open mind', 'fundamentalist', 'obtuse', and see no possibility of a rational dialogue with them. For their part immigrants resent being so described, cannot see why the liberals fail to see what to them seems obvious, and return the abuse. While some groups of immigrants might give in out of self-doubt, prudential considerations, or the duty to fit in with the demands of liberal society, others do not, particularly those who are as certain of their values and as determined to live by them as the liberals and deeply worry about their likely erosion under liberal impact. This is the case with European Muslims.

The stage is now set for mutual hostility and suspicion. Each fears the other not just politically but morally and culturally, and sincerely believes that it cannot survive without defeating the other. The fear is particularly acute among liberals and leads to a veritable panic. Unlike the religious Muslims who feel sure that God is on their side, liberals have no such certainty and must protect their values and way of life themselves. Having long thought that history was on their side, they now find that it is acting capriciously and signalling the return of the 'Dark Ages' that they had successfully seen off several centuries ago. And while they think that their actions are restrained by moral scruples, those of their enemies are not, and there is no saying what degree of violence they might unleash. Like most such panics, the liberal panic is partly fuelled by a lingering self-doubt. Despite much agonized reflection in recent years, the more self-critical liberals realize that, although they can make a good case for liberal values, it is not transculturally convincing. Compelling others to live by them therefore gives them an uneasy conscience. Since Muslims precipitate the liberal crisis of confidence and identity they become a moral irritant, a persistent reminder that the liberals have failed to live up to their promise, and become an object of fear and resentment.

Rationalist liberals get into this situation because they set themselves an impossible task. They want Muslims and other immigrants not only to accommodate themselves to their way of life but also to give it their whole-hearted moral allegiance. And they think that they can do that only if they give them transculturally convincing reasons. Since the liberals cannot find such reasons beyond a certain point, they panic and worry deeply about how they are to defend their cherished way of life against its large number of determined critics who now are their fellow citizens. As I intimated earlier, the liberal panic is exaggerated and can be alleviated by redefining the liberal theory of moral and political rationality along the following lines.

The liberal way of life is historically contingent and embedded in a particular culture or form of social self-understanding. It is not underwritten by history, mandated by human nature, or grounded in a universal theory of humankind. Good internal and external reasons, however, can be given in support of it, such as those based on the society's history, experiences, moral traditions, cultural and religious heritage, circumstances and level of development, as well as known facts about human beings, lessons of human history and experiences of other societies. These reasons do not, and there is no reason why they should, convince all human beings and command their allegiance. It is enough if they are good reasons, are publicly debated and carry conviction with all or most members of society. The liberal society represents one good way to organize human life, and that is a strong enough moral basis to stand up for it and use such compulsion as is unavoidable and prudent. It is not the best, the most rational, or the only universally valid form of good society, and it need neither claim nor endeavour to show itself to be one in order to demand and deserve the allegiance of its members.

When immigrants join a liberal society, they naturally bring with them different ways of understanding and organizing human life. Their views and values and those of the receiving society converge on some points and diverge on others. Their commonalities should be explored and consolidated, and their differences debated and resolved. This calls for a dialogue, which is possible only if the liberal society recognizes itself as a distinct cultural community encountering other such communities represented by the immigrants. If it believed itself to be an embodiment of universal values and rationality, as it often tends to do, it would place itself on a higher pedestal, seeing itself as qualitatively superior to the immigrant communities and representing a universal civilization as against their local cultures, morality as different from their customs. No dialogue is possible under these conditions, only moral hectoring and high-minded sermonizing.

In its dialogue with immigrants, the liberal society needs to show why it deserves their moral allegiance. Its reasons are not transcultural but a mixture of internal and external reasons, and are designed to show not why the liberal society is the best but rather why its members think that this is for them the best way to organize their lives. Since these are good reasons, they should persuade most immigrants. Their power to do is enhanced by the fact that their aim is *limited* in the sense of defending *this* society rather than prescribe a universal model, and *modest* in the sense of making a good case for it without claiming that no rational person can fail to be convinced by it. And if some immigrants still remain unpersuaded, they would at least be able to see why others are persuaded and why they should go along with them.

Since culture is explicitly recognized and brought into the political discourse as a source of claims, an additional form of reasoning is available to both the liberals and the immigrants. The latter could legitimately argue that when they are able to offer good reasons for their cultural beliefs and practices, these should be respected and suitably accommodated. For their part the liberals could legitimately argue that immigrants should respect the prevailing cultural beliefs and practices when they can give good reasons for them. Such an appeal to mutual cultural respect has several advantages. It reassures immigrants that their culture is valued by the wider society and that they need not panic and turn inwards or become intransigent. It reassures the wider society that it remains in charge of its cultural affairs, that immigrants can be trusted not to undermine it by irresponsible demands, and that the relations between the two are based on a rational dialogue conducted in a spirit of mutual commitment to a common life. An appeal to mutual cultural respect also often avoids and sometimes even resolves otherwise intractable disagreements and controversies. Since the cultural argument works both ways, it is perfectly valid for the two parties to say that one of them cannot be expected to respect the deeply held cultural beliefs and practices of the other unless the latter too does the same. It is often forgotten in the heat generated by *l'affair du foulard* that over 95 percent of Muslim girls in French schools avoided the *hijab* largely out of respect for the French culture and its reasons for placing a high value on *laïcité*, not because it went against the French custom or some universal value.[19]

Difficult situations do arise when both parties feel equally strongly about their cultural norms. A few French Muslim girls insisted on wearing the *hijab*, and so did Fereshta Ludin, a teacher in Germany, to considerable public outrage. This is a clash between two important cultural norms, or between a human right and a cultural norm, and sometimes even between two human rights.[20] There are good arguments on both sides. The French *laïcité* and the German principle of religious neutrality should be modified to allow deeply held and defensible Muslim beliefs and practices. But equally these traditions are valuable historical achievements, and exceptions to them alienate the majority which is not in the immigrant's interest and set a precedent whose unexpected long-term conse-quences can be most unfortunate. In such situations it is wrong to claim that only one course of action is truly national. Equally balanced reasons on both sides require and create a space for a political solution, which is neither against reason nor mandated by it. What form it should take depends on the context.

When a society acknowledges culture as a valid reason, it incurs an obligation to respect minority cultures, but it also acquires a right to impose certain obligations on them such as making responsible demands, persuading others by rational arguments and respecting the society's deeply cherished cultural values and practices. While admitting culture as a source of claims has its obvious dangers, it also has great advantages. Our concern should be not to disallow it altogether, assuming that such an option is even open to a liberal society, but rather to decide when to allow it, in what form and what weight to assign it. This requires a well-considered theory of moral and political rationality that avoids the narrow and untenable extremes of rationalism and culturalism and grasps the proper relation between reason and culture.

Conclusion

Throughout this chapter I have spoken of 'Muslims'.[21] Although there are good reasons for this, they can paradoxically become bad reasons if their underlying complexity is ignored. Many European Muslim immigrants do identify themselves as and with other Muslims, make demands as Muslims, derive their inspiration from Islam, and so on. Outsiders too perceive and respond to them as Muslims including those for whom this is not their primary form of self-identification. For some their Muslim identity is self-chosen; for some others, externally imposed; for most it is a complex mixture of both.[22]

Like all human beings however, Muslim immigrants in Europe have several identities derived from their gender, occupation, citizenship, country of parental origin, religion, etc. While they define themselves in terms of any one or more of these depending on the context, they define themselves for political purposes as British, French, Dutch, Italian or German Muslims, stressing both their religion and citizenship. These terms mean one of three things. Take the term 'British Muslims'. It could mean *Muslims in Britain*, that is those Muslims who just happen to live in Britain or are its citizens but too alienated to have any commitment or attachment to it. Britain means virtually nothing to them, and the Islamic *Ummah* to which they are tied by their religious identity is all that matters. Second, the term could mean *Muslims of Britain*, that is those Muslims who see Britain as their home and feel loyalty and attachment to it. 'British' refers to their political, and 'Muslims' to their religious allegiance, and the two are kept more or less distinct. Finally, the term could refer, for want of a better word, to *Britishized Muslims*, that is those Muslims who not only feel loyal to Britain and see it as their home but are shaped by the British way of life and thought, values, attitudes, etc. The term 'British' refers to their cultural orientation, which influences their reading of the Qur'ān and Muslim history, and gives rise to a distinct British form of Islam. [23]

Of these three categories of European Muslims, the first forms the smallest minority. As I argued earlier, most Muslims feel a strong sense of loyalty and commitment to their respective countries of settlement. Since many of them have grown up in these countries, are educated in their schools, have learned their languages, etc., they are also inescapably shaped by their culture, often in a manner they do not even themselves recognize. Islam is important to them, but so is the culture of their new home, and the dialectic of the two governs their thoughts and lives. The last two groups, who form the overwhelming majority of European Muslims, rightly do not describe themselves as Muslims *sans phrase*.

A small minority of European Muslims feel uncomfortable with this dual identity, as does the global alliance of Islamists. They want to strip the Muslims of all other identities save the religious, and remove such constraints and influences as these exercise on it. Having homogenized all Muslims, they want to mould them in their image of 'true' Islam. They want to ensure that Muslims are nothing but Muslims, have no other sources of moral guidance than Islam, and no other loyalties, attachments and competing claims. When we refer to individuals and groups as Muslims *sans phrase*, we wittingly or unwittingly strip away or marginalize their other identities and walk into the Islamist trap. Our goal should be the opposite. We should reaffirm neglected identities, bring them into a creative interplay with the religious identity, and encourage individuals freely to define and relate them. So long as European Muslims remain Muslims in Europe, they will continue to arouse fear and anxiety. They need to become Muslims of Europe and hopefully over time even Europeanized Muslims. This requires them to acknowledge and discharge the responsibilities and obligations of citizenship, eschew mindless violence and reassure society of their moral commitment to it. For its part the liberal society should accept Muslims as its equal and legitimate members, cease demonizing and alienating them, and discharge its responsibilities and obligations towards them. My main concern in this chapter has been to show that this reciprocal process has been under way for years and should, despite the recent terrorist atrocities, continue to proceed smoothly if both sides avoid moral panic and respect the moral covenant regulating their relations.

Notes

1 Articles and editorials in major national local newspapers and magazines as well as parliamentary debates in European countries provide countless examples of this. This view is also reflected in serious works of political and social theory which draw many of their examples, of 'unreasonable' individuals and groups, limits of rational dialogue and threats to Western values from Muslim beliefs and practices.

2 In Britain multiculturalism has been welcomed by liberals and even conservatives since the 1970s. During the Thatcherite period, it was viewed with disfavour by conservatives but liberals remained its strong champions, and even the conservative government did little to arrest its progress. Although the Rushdie affair dampened liberals' enthusiasm for it, they continued to support it. In recent years, especially after the events of 9/11, more and more of them are turning against it, arguing that it ghettoizes communities, gives them a licence to continue dubious practices, and militates against common values and national cohesion. Most of the examples they give refer to Muslims (see Chapter 3). A similar trend is evident in the Netherlands where multiculturalism was much valued for years and where it is now blamed for

Muslim 'separatism'. France, Germany, Belgium and Spain were never very keen on multiculturalism and now think that they were right to do so.

3 For a variety of reasons Muslims in the United States do not arouse this kind of cultural anxiety. Historical memories of Islam there are different. The geographical distance from Muslim countries is greater. The percentage of Muslims is smaller, and since they are drawn from many different countries, they do not form organized communities. Moreover, about a third of American Muslims are African–Americans and not based on an immigration stream. The United States sees itself as a country of immigrants held together by the Constitution rather than as a nation-state based on a shared culture, and is less nervous of cultural and other differences. Its political structure both permits a greater range of ethnic diversity and prescribes clear limits to it, and channels immigrant demands in certain directions.

4 It is striking that Muslim immigrants arouse anxiety in a way that other religious groups do not. This has to do with their number, the kinds of demands they make, their forms and degrees of self-assertion, and of course the contemporary international situation. Historically speaking the anxiety provoked by Muslims bears a resemblance to that associated in earlier times in some countries with Jews and Catholics.

5 Contrary to popular misconception, Islam has undergone more drastic changes than almost any other religion. Turkey under Ata Turk underwent extensive secularization including even changes in dress, script, etc., that has no European parallel. Libya under Gadaffi broke the hold of the Ulema, imposed an official revolutionary interpretation of Islam, and even encouraged Muslims to date their calendar from the Prophet's death rather than the hegira. Nasser proclaimed a socialist interpretation of Islam and nationalized Al-Azhar University in 1961. Almost all these and other changes occurred during periods of crisis, were largely institutional and engineered by determined governments, and did not organically grow out of a sustained process of cultural criticism and change. This may partly explain why they remained precarious.

6 The Islam of the first generation of immigrants is heavily folkish, oral, tied up with local culture and traditional. That of their children and grandchildren is textual, learned in mosques and schools, 'purified' of culture, lacks historical continuity, is shaped by intellectuals rather than mullahs, and often free-floating.

7 The currently dominant language of identity is a peculiar product of the contemporary forms of modernity. It has much to do with the decline in traditional social structure and the emphasis on clear boundaries and neat self-definition. For a fuller discussion see my *Identity, Culture and Dialogue*, London: Palgrave–Macmillan, 2006.

8 In the Netherlands, Immigration Minister Rita Verdonk announced that immigrants from now on would be compelled to pass an examination in the Dutch language and culture and attend 350 hours of classes before becoming permanent residents. See *Time*, 28 February 2005, p. 37. In Belgium, Filip Dewinter, the leader of the far right Vlaams Belang Party, which won nearly a quarter of the total national vote in the regional elections in June 2004, wants to prevent Muslim immigrants from marrying in their home countries and bringing their spouses into Belgium. See *Time*, 28 February 2005, p. 38. In Britain the Labour government and many of its liberal supporters endorse this idea.

9 See ICM Survey for the BBC, Radio 4, 24 December 2002. Rather surprisingly the proportion of those claiming to be patriotic was higher among men than women (71 per cent as opposed to 59 per cent). Predictably it was higher among those at the top of the occupational hierarchy than those at the lower end (73 per cent as opposed to 60 per cent) and in the older generation than the younger (90 per cent as opposed to 60 per cent).

10 Cited in Mohammed Siddique Seddan, Dilwar Hussain and Nadeem Mallik (eds), *British Muslims Between Assimilation and Segregation*, Leicester: The Islamic Foundation, 2004, p. 182.

11 Ibid., p. 111. The Muslim Manifesto published by Kalim Siddiqui's London-based Muslim Institute in 1990 took a different view. While agreeing that Muslims have a duty of loyalty to the state in which they have settled, it argued that the loyalty was overridden if in conflict with the Ummah. The Institute is openly committed to Ayatollah Khomeini, and reflects a minority view.

12 See Paul Cliteur, 'Cast your discomfort aside, in matters of life and death, debate is the only thing that counts', The Times Education Supplement, 18 February 2005.

13 Ibid.

14 Kymlicka appreciates this and talks of 'thin' integration. His thin integration is too thin to satisfy many, and he does not explain what principles limit the expansionism inherent in integration. See Will Kymlicka and Magda Opalski (eds), Can Liberal Pluralism be Exported?, Oxford: Oxford University Press, 2001, p. 48. Michael Banton rightly calls integration a 'treacherous concept'. See his 'National integration in France and Britain', Journal of Ethnic and Migration Studies, 27(1), 2001.

15 Rawls is one of the ablest advocates of this view. For a critique of it, see my Rethinking Multiculturalism, London: Palgrave–Macmillan, 2000, pp. 87f. and 308ff.

16 These organizations reflect the tensions between liberal and traditionalist Muslims and between those coming from different countries, and often do not last long. The French Council of the Muslim Faith (CFCM) degenerated into squabbling factions, and one of its two French-born women board members resigned in protest at the conservatism of the older generation immigrant leaders. The Belgian Muslim General Assembly (MGA) has met a similar fate. See Time, 28 February 2005, p. 39.

17 For a clear statement of this view, see Brian Barry, Culture and Equality, Cambridge: Polity Press, 2000, pp. 284ff.

18 Although Brian Barry talks a great deal about culture, he does not offer a systematic analysis of it. He often equates it with customs and thinks that it rests on the authority of tradition. He does not appreciate that culture could involve reasons that are internal to it.

19 The French case is complicated by the fact that since Christian pupils are allowed to wear the crucifix, Muslims girls complained of discrimination, as discussed in Chapter 4. France could ban the crucifix as well, but dare not do so for fear of provoking public disorder and falling foul of human rights. It therefore argued that, unlike the crucifix, the hijab was ostentatious and had a proselytizing dimension, and subverted the principle of laïcité in a way that the crucifix did not. Although this argument is not as specious as its critics suggest, it cannot bear the weight France puts on it.

20 In Germany the teacher is a Beamter, a public servant representing the neutral and impartial state and expected to be above political, religious and other decisions. This is why s/he is required not to go on strike, to wear neutral dress, and so on. When Fereshta Ludin decided to wear a headscarf in the school she was told not to. She took the matter to the Federal Constitutional Court on the ground that she had a human right to practise her religion. Although the Court shared the general unease about her action, it ruled in her favour. There have been other such cases where exemptions from established practices were granted to accommodate the right to religion. Several commentators complained that human rights were being used to change their culture and that Germans were losing control over it.

While some commentators did not wish to change any established custom, others wanted to draw a line at practices they regarded as central to their way of life. The latter cases involve striking a delicate balance between respecting human rights and upholding valuable cultural traditions. It is not obvious that human rights should automatically trump the latter. Courts may feel legally constrained to take that view, and then their decisions alienate a large majority and lose popular legitimacy, as happened in Germany. Such matters may therefore be best settled politically. Johannes Kandel, a keen advocate of Christian–Muslim dialogue, expressed this view well when he asked Muslim organizations if they were right to use human rights to 'push through their interpretation of Islam by means of the German Courts' and introduce practices deeply offensive to the majority of Germans. See his article in *Islam und Gessellschaft*, Nr 2, Berlin: Friedrich-Ebert Stiftung, no date. See also Chapter 6 of this book.

Every liberal society contains a structural tension. It is committed both to human rights and to particular cultural traditions. When interpreted in a certain manner or pressed beyond a certain point, human rights might undermine the latter. Conversely, if the cultural traditions were to set the limits of human rights, they would emasculate them. Much good sense is required on the part of both the majority and minority to maintain their balance.

21 Muslim self-consciousness in Europe began to emerge, and Muslims began to define themselves as Muslims, in the mid 1970s in response to several national and international factors. The children of first-generation immigrants were reaching their adolescence, and parents were worried about how to bring them up, ensure cultural continuity, and counter the assimilationist thrust of the wider society. They naturally turned to religion. Not surprisingly the number of mosques, religious classes, etc., rose dramatically, and a new religiously self-conscious youth emerged.

Several international events also played an important part, and gave the emerging religious self-consciousness a new content and form. The Iranian Revolution of 1979 created the possibility of an Islamic society and gave Muslims a sense of political power and cultural self-confidence. The oil crisis and the Western dependence on oil gave them a sense of economic power. The Arab–Israeli conflict, the Israeli invasion of Lebanon, the Muslim struggle against injustices and oppression in different parts of the world, etc., gave Muslims a common cause and sharpened the awareness of the *Ummah*.

22 It is striking that Islam in Europe became an important area of research from the 1980s onwards. The European Science Foundation sponsored a collaborative Europe-wide project in the mid-1980s. Sweden convened a conference appropriately called 'The New Islamic Presence in Europe' in 1986. It is against this background that the Rushdie affair in Britain and the headscarf affair in France burst on the scene in the same year. Both involved young people, sometimes acting in opposition to their parents. Europe had now discovered and begun to fear its Muslims.

23 In the United States a distinct Americanized brand of Islam is beginning to emerge based on a clear separation between religious and secular matters, the individual's right to interpret the Qur'ān, giving the lay governing boards of mosques final authority over the imam, etc. Some commentators even call it Presbyterian or Baptist Islam. See Yvonne Yazback Haddad and Jane I. Smith (eds), *Muslim Minorities in the West: Visible and Invisible*, Walnut Creek, CA: Alternative Press, 2002, pp. 128ff. See also John Esposito and Francois Burgat (eds), *Modernising Islam*, London: Hurst, 2003.

Index

Afghanistan war 47, 51, 183–4
African immigrants from as Other 12, 13
African War (1860) 146
Agadshari, Hashem 105
Ali, Ayaan Hirsi 70, 185
Alleanza Nazionale 119, 129, 130–1
Allensbach Institute 112n
Alsace and Lorraine 63
al-Alwani, Taha Jabir 183
Amir-Moazami, S. 107, 113n
'amnesty' programmes 10, 119, 120
Amsterdam Treaty (AT) 11, 43
Anti-discrimination Directive (EU) 13
anti-discrimination measures 176
anti-essentialism 40
anti-racist movement in Britain 37, 38–9, 52
anti-Semitism 108–9, 110–11, 165
Anti-Terrorism Crime and Security Act (Britain) 53n
Antorini, Christine 88
arranged marriages 32, 184
Asia: Asian Muslims in Britain 37–53; immigrants from as Other 12, 13
assimilation: institutional assimilation 64, 172, 173–6, 191; integration as alternative to 186–7; see also integration
Ata Turk 201n
Avebury, Lord 44

Baden-Württemberg 97, 101
Balkan immigrants from as Other 13
banlieues and transnational Islam 65–8
Baptist Islam 203n
Barry, Brian 202n
Bauman, Zygmunt 96, 101
Bavaria 97
Bayrou, François 57–8, 59, 61
BBC: religious inclusion 45

Beckstein, Günther 111–12
Belgium 23–35; Council of Religions 175, 191; cultural diversity issues 31–4; headscarf debate 28, 29–31; immigration policies 8, 27, 201n; integration 2, 23; integration models 27–9; and multiculturalism discourse 25–6, 31–4; policy and ethnic diversity 24–5, 27–9, 31, 34; post-colonial migration 7
Ben Ali, Rachid 185
Ben Yehuda, N. 94
Berlusconi, Silvio 119, 129, 130, 133, 135
Bin Laden, Osama 32–3, 47, 149
black identity movement in Britain 41–2
black power 46
Blair, Tony 51, 164–5
blasphemy: and freedom of speech in Denmark 70, 87, 89; religious parity in Britain 44; see also Satanic Verses controversy
Böger, Klaus 96
Bossi, Umberto 130
Bossi Fini Law 121
Bourdieu, Pierre 66
Britain 1, 2, 37–54; anti-war unification 51, 183; 'British Muslims' 199–200; Census questions 37, 39, 45, 52; Church and state 164–5; faith schools 44, 49, 52, 164, 175, 189, 190; immigration policies 8, 201n; incitement to religious hatred offence 43, 44, 52; institutional assimilation 172–3, 182–3; integrationist discourse after 9/11 47, 48–9; multiculturalism debate 33, 51–3, 200–1n; Muslim activism 41–2, 46, 47–9, 53, 182–3; Muslim attitudes in 182–3; Muslim commentaries 49–51; Muslim population 37–8; positive

discrimination 44–6; post-colonial migration 7, 37–8; 'racial equality' approach 25, 38–9; religious claims 42–6; religious discrimination legislation 38–9, 43–4, 52; religious equality 175; secularism in 163, 164; support for terrorism in 47–9, 182
British National Party (BNP) 47, 53–4n
Brown, Yasmin Alibhai 33, 50
Brussels–Wallonia 27, 28
Bundesverband der jüdischen Studenten in Deutschland 108, 109
Buttiglione, Rocco 119, 120

Caliphate state 97, 105, 106
Camre, Mogens 82
Caritas 120, 121, 135
Catholic Church: Italy 126–8, 131, 134, 140n; Spain 153; *see also* Church and state
Catholic Young Community (Germany) 107–8, 109
Central and Eastern Europe (CEE) migration 9, 12
Chevènement, Jean-Pierre 175, 177n
Chirac, Jacques 59, 65
Christian Democrat Party (Italy) 130, 140n
Church and state in Europe 163–8, 190–1
citizenship: European citizenship 12; France 58, 68; Italy 121–2, 125–6, 134; multicultural citizenship 1–13, 31–3; Spain 154; Turkish migrants in Germany 94, 95–102
civic integration 71–4
civic nationalism 73; Denmark 76, 78–81, 83–4, 88–8
civic patriotism 73, 85–6
civic values in Italy 132, 135
civil culture 101, 102, 113n
claims-making 2, 26, 32; *see also* religious claims
'clash of civilizations' discourse 4, 176
Cohen, Stanley 94
COIFE (Collectif d'Associations Opposées à l'Interdiction du foulard à l'école) 34–5n
colonialism: and Maurophobia in Spain 145–8; and migration flows 7, 37–8
Commission on Islamophobia 52
Commission for Racial Equality (CRE) 48, 49, 52
'common good' discourse 37, 52, 88, 101–2, 104

Communist Party (PCF)(France) 58
community: civic integration 71–4; transnational Islam in French *banlieues* 66–7
compulsion and rationalist liberalism 192, 195
condensed symbols 106, 107
Confederation of Islamic Cultural Centres (Germany) 176
Conference of Algeciras (1906) 146
Conseil Français du Culte Musulman 64, 65, 175, 191, 202n
Conservative Party (Denmark) 70
constitutional patriotism 72, 84–5, 134
contracts and Quran 183–4
COREIS (Association of Italian Converts to Islam) 126, 131
Corriere della Sera 124–5, 129–33
Council of Religions (Belgium) 175, 191
Council of Thought on Islam (CORIF)(France) 174
crucifix and headscarf debate 202n
cultural integration 72, 181
cultural nationalism 77, 83–4, 186–7
cultural pluralism 40; and liberalism 189–90; and Western politics and political theory 71–4; *see also* multiculturalism
culture: immigrant threat to native culture 72, 112; influence of religion on 169–70, 189; Italian cultural tradition 125–6; politicization of culture in Denmark 71–89; and rationalist liberalism 193–4; *see also* political culture

Dahl, Hanne 90n
Danish Lutheran Church 77–8, 79–80, 84
Danish People's Party (DPP) 74, 76, 77, 79, 81, 82, 89n, 90n
Dantschke, Claudia 113n
Debré law 61
democracy: Muslim support for 182–3
Democrazia Cristiana *see* Christian Democrat Party
Denmark 8, 70–91; attitudes towards Muslims and political culture 74–6; blasphemy law 70, 87; common civic values 71, 78–9, 81–6, 88–9; Danish Lutheran Church 77–8, 79–80, 84; freedom of speech principle 70, 87, 89; headscarf debate 86; instrumental civic nationalism 78–81, 83–4; lack of integration of immigrants 2, 7–8, 74;

lack of provision for religious practice
75–6; liberal culture and religious
differences 86–8; liberal influence of
Lutheranism 79–80; privileging of own
religious culture 76–8; reunification
policies 74
Dewinter, Filip 201n
Dhondy, Farrukh 48–9
dialogical multiculturalism 73
DITIB (Turkish–Islamic Union of the
Office of Religion) 97
divorce: Islamic norms in Belgium 28–9
DuBois, W.E.B. 53

education: and integration in Italian
schools 122; Islamic teaching in
German schools 96, 104, 177n; see also
faith schools; headscarf debate
EMMA (German magazine) 105
Enlightenment and secularism 162, 163,
165, 166
equality 171; see also gender equality;
multicultural equality; racial equality
in Britain; religious equality
Erbakan, Mehmet Sabri 113n
Erbakan, Necmettin 97, 99
ethnic immigrant groups 7, 26
Eurobarometer 75
European Council for Fatwa and Research
184
European Court of Justice (ECJ) 11
European identity 10–11, 13
European Right 129
European Science Foundation 203n
European Social Forums 32
European Social Model 9–10
European Union (EU): anxiety over lack
of integration 179–88; categorization
of enlargement countries 12–13;
common immigration policy 11;
community of inclusion 10–11, 13;
East–West migration 12; European
citizenship rights 12; Italian
perception of 125; Muslim population
37, 53; and national identity 10–11,
13; secularism and Islamic religious
claims 32; varieties of secularism
163–6
'extracomunitari' 12

faith schools: Belgium 29; Britain 44, 49,
52, 164, 175, 189, 190; and public
funds 167, 190; in secular states 163,
164; Spain 150–1

family in secular state 167
Fatwa on British Muslims 184
fatwas see Satanic Verses controversy
Federal Association of Jewish Students in
Germany 108, 109
FEERI (Federación Española de Entidades
Religiosas Islámicas) 150
Feldmann, Peter von 114n
feminism 37, 40; Islamic feminism 184
Fergo, Tove 79
Ferry, Jules 61
Fini, Gianfranco 129, 130
First Amendment (US) 164
Flanders 27, 28
Foda, Farag Ali 105, 106
folk culture and religion 169–70
folkelighed 80
Fordism and migration flows 7
foreign workers see labour migration
Fortuyn, Pim 27, 33
Forum Against Islamophobia and Racism
(FAIR) 43, 52
Forza Italia Party 119, 129, 130
France 1, 57–69; banlieues and
transnational Islam 65–8; citizenship
and identity 58, 68; cultural
integration 72; headscarf debate 30,
57–60, 68, 148, 198; immigration
policies 8; integration 2, 57, 58, 72,
173, 187; multiculturalism and policy
25; post-colonial migration 7;
recognition of Islam 173, 174–5;
republicanism model 62;
secularism/laïcité 57–8, 59–60, 61–4,
165–6, 174, 190–1, 194, 198–9;
voluntary associations 58–9
Franco regime 146, 147, 154
freedom of speech/expression: in Denmark
70, 87, 89; Muslim attitudes towards
184–5; and rationalist liberalism 195,
196
French Council of the Muslim Faith 64,
65, 175, 191, 202n
Frevert, Louise 76
Friedrich-Ebert Stiftung 103, 114n
frisind (free-mindedness) 78, 80, 85
Fromm, Heinz 113n
fundamentalism see Islamism

Gadaffi, Muammar 201n
Gaserow, Vera 106, 108, 109
gender equality 184
Germany 7, 8, 94–114; background to
Muslims in 96–7; Church and state

163, 190; citizenship of Turkish migrants 94, 95–102; Constitution 102, 103; cultural integration 72; headscarf debate 102–7, 110, 113n, 198; Islamic teaching in schools 96, 104, 177n; lack of integration of immigrants 1, 2–3, 7, 95–7, 187; legal system and religious claims 102–7, 203n; minority rights of immigrants 95, 102–7; moral panic 94–5, 111–12; Muslim organizations and citizenship 97–102; Muslim Youth 97, 107–11; non-Muslim expert opinion on Islam 99; public funds for Muslim groups 95, 107–11; recognition of 'Muslim community' 176; republicanism model 62; secularism in 163, 166, 190

Giornale, il 124–5, 129–33

globalization and migration patterns 8–9

Gogh, Theo van 24, 32, 70, 87, 185

Goode, E. 94

Goodhart, David 54n

Great Britain *see* Britain

Greece 1, 10

Grey Wolves 97

Grundtvig, N.F.S. 80, 85

guest-workers 95

Habermas, Jürgen 84, 134, 168–9

Haider, Jörg 129

Hamza, Abu 182

headscarf (*hijab*) debate: Belgium 28, 29–31; Denmark 86; France 30, 57–60, 68, 148, 198; gender issues 31, 86; Germany 102–7, 110, 113n, 198

Hispanidad movement (Spain) 146–8, 154–5

Hizb al-Tahrir 183

Hornbech, B. 77, 80

Hume, David 163

identity: *see also* European identity; Muslim identity; national identity; religious practices and identity

identity movements 39

illegal immigrants: 'amnesty' programmes 10, 119, 120; positive economic effects 10

imams: regulation in Spain 151–2

immigration policies 8, 9, 11, 181

incitement to religious hatred offence in Britain 43, 44, 52

Inglehart, R. 170

institutional assimilation 64, 172, 173–6, 191

instrumental nationalism 72–3, 78–81, 83–4

integration 2, 5; anxiety over lack of integration 179–88; Belgian models 27–9; institutional assimilation 64, 172, 173–6, 191; integrationist discourse in Britain 47, 48–9; logic of 185–8; pluralistic integration 173–6; and rationalist liberalism 191–9; in Southern Europe 1, 2, 9; theoretical debate 26; *see also* headscarf debate; multiculturalism

intercultura 119, 122

Iraq war 51; Muslim attitudes 182

Islam, Yusuf 50

Islam: generational differences 180–1; historical changes 201n; proselytizing mission 180; resistance to reform 180; *see also* Islamism

Islamic Commission of Spain 150, 152, 191

Islamic Community Milli Görüş (Germany) 97, 98, 99–101, 109

Islamic Federation of Berlin 176

Islamic feminism 184

Islamic Party of Britain 182–3

Islamische Föderation 104

Islamism 48, 50–1, 60, 96; Islamist organizations in Germany 98–9; regulating imams in Spain 151–2

Islamophobia: anxiety over lack of integration 185–88; in Britain 43, 52; and Danish political culture 74–6, 82; in Germany 96, 105–12; in Italy 119; Lega Nord campaign in Italy 128–31; Maurophobia in Spain 143, 144, 145–8, 149; *see also* religious discrimination

Italy 117–40; amnesty for illegal migrants 10, 119, 120; Catholic Church and integration 121, 132, 135, 140n; citizenship rights 121–2, 134; immigrant population 117, 120–2; immigration policies 119–20, 120–1; and integration of immigrants 1, 2, 117–18, 119, 121, 131–3; migrant workers 10; mosque building and multiculturalism debate 118, 120, 123–31, 134; multiculturalism approach 128, 131–3, 134, 135; problematic national identity 117, 118–19, 132–3, 134–5

Iyidirly, Ahmet 95–6

Jensen, Frank 87
Jespersen, Karen 78
Jospin, Lionel 59
Joxe, Pierre 174
al-Judai, Shaykh Abdullah 184

Kandel, Johannes 103, 113n, 114n, 203n
Kaplan, Metin 105, 106
Kastoryano, R. 173
Katholische junge Gemeinde 107–8, 109
Khan, Dr Muqtedar 54n
Khomeini, Ayatollah 42, 105, 202n
King, Martin Luther, Jr 39
Knudsen, Fabienne 89
Koch, Hal 81, 88
Körting, Erhart 98–9
Krarup, Søren 76–7
Kulturnation 76, 78
Kymlicka, W. 7, 19n, 26, 202n

Laban, Abu 87
Laborde, Cécile 73, 85–6, 87–8
labour migration: amnesties for illegal
    workers 10, 119, 120; encouragement
    of migrant labour after WWII 7; ethnic
    specialization in Italy 121; European
    'zero immigration' policies 8, 9;
    globalization and changing labour
    market 8–9; recruitment of skilled and
    unskilled workers 9–10; *see also* Turkish
    migrants
Lacan, Jacques 34
laïcité in France 57–8, 59–60, 61–4, 165–6,
    174, 190–1, 194, 198–9
Lang Commission on Nationality (France)
    187
Latin America: immigrants from as Other
    12, 13
Lefringhausen, Klaus 114n
Lega Nord (Northern League) 118, 119,
    123, 124, 128–30, 131, 132, 134
Leitkultur 72, 76, 112
liberal democratic tradition 4; and church
    in Denmark 78–81, 85
liberal nationalism *see* instrumental
    nationalism
Liberal Party (Denmark) 70, 77, 79, 82
liberalism: challenge of multiculturalism
    4–5, 39–41, 72, 179–203; Danish
    culture and religious differences 86–8;
    and Danish Lutheran Church 79–80,
    84; and logic of integration 185–8;
    moral panic 196–7; rationalist
    liberalism 191–9; and religion 188–91

local customs 195–6
Lochak, Danièle 175
Lodi: mosque building 118, 120, 123–31,
    134
loyalty to state 183–4
Ludin, Fereshta 95, 104–7, 110, 198
Lutheranism in Denmark 76–8, 79–80, 84
Luxenberg, Christoph (pseudonym) 185

McCarthy era moral panic 94–5
Malcolm X 39
Malik, Kenan 48
marriage practices 32, 184
Martín Corrales, E. 145, 146
Martín-Muñoz, G. 148, 153
Martini, Cardinal 127–8
Maurophobia in Spain 143, 144, 145–8
media: constructs of Muslims in Spain
    149, 152–3; and multiculturalism
    debate in Italy 124–33; and Muslim
    extremism in Britain 49–50; Muslim
    voice in Britain 50; Muslim voice in
    Italy 126
Messaggero, Il 124–5, 129–33
migration: 'old' and 'new' migrations 7–10,
    117, 120; 'philosophies of integration'
    5; terrorism and securitization 1, 2–3,
    10
Milan: mosque building 118, 120, 123–31,
    134
militant Islamism 48, 50–1, 60
Miller, David 72–3, 78–9, 83, 84, 85
Milli Görüş 97, 98, 99–101, 109
minority rights: 'minority policy' in
    Netherlands 25, 33, 175–6; public
    recognition 171, 172; Turkish
    immigrants in Germany 95, 102–7; *see
    also* religious claims
models of incorporation: Belgium 28
'moderate' Muslims 48, 50–1
Modood, Tariq 32, 45–6, 85, 118, 134,
    172–3
monarchies 183
Moors *see* Maurophobia in Spain
moral panic: characteristics of 94; and
    media 124; Muslims in Germany
    94–5, 111–12; rationalist liberalism
    196–7
moral values and rationalist liberalism
    192–5, 196
morito bueno stereotype 146
Moroccan immigrants in Spain 143–58
mosques: discrimination in Spain 143,
    149; legal proceedings in Germany

103–4; new mosque building in Italy 118, 120, 123–31, 134
multicultural citizenship 1–13, 31–3; limitations of literature 4–7, 32
multicultural equality in Britain 39–40, 44–6
multiculturalism: Belgian models 27–9; cultural relativism charge 33, 78, 80; definition 26; in Europe 25–6, 31–3; impartiality argument 155–7; integrationist backlash in Britain 48–9; and lack of integration 179–88; lack of solidarity 78; and liberalism 179–203; Muslim support for 48, 52; policy and discourse in Europe 25–6, 32; and public/private spheres 168–70, 186–8
Muslim Association of Britain 51
Muslim Brotherhood 98, 109; *see also* Milli Görüş
Muslim Council of Britain 37, 46, 52
Muslim General Assembly (Belgium) 202n
Muslim identity 199–200
Muslim Institute (Britain) 202n
Muslim law (sharia): Belgium 28–9; Denmark 70–1
Muslim Manifesto 202n
Muslim power movements in Britain 46
Muslim schools: Spain 150–1; *see also* faith schools
Muslim Youth (Germany) 97, 107–11
Mussolini, Alessandra 130
Mutlu, Özcan 110

Nagel, T. 155–6
Nasser, Gamal Abdel 201n
National Assembly of Black People (Britain) 52
national identity: and European Union 10–11, 13; instrumental nationalism 72–3; and *laïcité* in France 61–2, 62–4; and multiculturalism 2, 186–7; problematic in Italy 117, 118–19, 125, 132–3, 134–5; *see also* religious practices and identity
national minorities 7
nationalist parties: Belgium 24, 27, 29; *see also* British Nationalist Party; Danish People's Party
naturalization *see* citizenship
Netherlands: immigration policy 1, 201n; 'minority policy' 25, 33, 175–6; multiculturalism and 'separatism' 201n; 'pillarization' 175–6, 190, 191
New Labour government (Britain) 48, 51

Nicolet, Claude 165
9/11 terror attacks 10; impact in Britain 47–9
Norris, P. 170
Northern League *see* Lega Nord
Norwood case 53n
Nurcu group 97

Oestreich, Heide 110
Osama Bin (Ben) Laden 32–3, 47, 149
Other/otherness: dynamics of 12–13, 111, 148; and EU inclusion 12–13; 'in-groups' and 'out-groups' in Italian mosque debate 128–31, 134–5
Ozouf, Mona 61

Padanian Republic movement 129, 131
Parekh, Bhikhu 26, 32, 88, 148, 174
Pasqua, Charles 174–5
patriotism to host countries 182
perspectivism 40
Phillips, Trevor 49
'philosophies of integration' 5
'pillarization' in Netherlands 175–6, 190, 191
pluralism: pluralistic integration 173–6; of secular societies 189–90; *see also* cultural pluralism
Polish immigrants and otherness 12
political culture: dominant culture and multiculturalism 168–9; and integration in Denmark 71–89; liberal views of Islam 188–9
political participation 183
Polo delle Libertà (centre–right coalition in Italy) 128, 129, 130–1, 133
polygamy 32
polytheism 183
populist parties 33
positive discrimination in Britain 44–6
post-industrial society and migration 8–9
Premià de Mar mosque 149
Presbyterian Islam 203n
press: Italy 124–33; *see also* media
private sphere *see* public/private sphere
prosopopoeia 106
public funds: Muslim groups in Germany 95, 107–11; and religious organizations 167, 190
public/private sphere: accommodating diversity in Belgium 23–4, 26, 27–8, 29, 30, 32; and multicultural citizenship literature 4; public recognition 26, 30, 39, 40–1, 58–9,

170–1; religion in private sphere 49, 73, 79, 186–8; religion in secular states 166–73

Q News 54n
Quran 183–4, 185

racial equality in Britain 25, 38–9
racialization in Britain 41–2
racism: Belgium 24; racial violence in French *banlieues* 66–7; in Southern Europe 9, 12; towards Muslim groups 13, 38–9; *see also* Islamophobia; religious discrimination
Rally for the Republic (RPR)(France) 174
Ramos, I. 152
Rasmussen, A.F. 70, 81–2
rationalist liberalism 191–9
reason 192–3
Reconquista 145, 150
Redder, G. 81
Reformation 79
regional identity in Italy 125
Reid, Richard ('shoe bomber') 47
relativism 33, 78, 80
religion: as basis for racism 13; Church and state in Europe 163–8, 190–1; Denmark's privileging of own religious culture 76–8; influence on culture 169–70, 189; liberal attitudes towards 188–91; and public/private sphere 49, 73, 79, 166–73, 186–8; *see also* Catholic Church; Islam; Islamism; Lutheranism; secularism
religious claims: Belgium 29, 31–4; Britain 42–6; Germany 95, 102–7, 203n; for mosques in Italy 118, 120, 123–31, 134; and multiculturalism 2, 32; and secular societies 162–3, 188–9
religious controversies: contextual and non-contextual approach 6–7; *see also* headscarf debate; *Satanic Verses* controversy
religious discrimination: anti-discrimination measures 176; legislation in Britain 38–9, 43–4, 52; in Spain 149; *see also* Islamophobia
religious equality: in Britain 42–6; pluralistic institutional assimilation 173–6, 191; public recognition 26, 30, 39, 40–1, 58–9, 170–1; in secular states 168, 170–3
religious practices 184; claiming rights in Germany 95, 102–7; generational

differences 180–1; and identity in Belgium 29–31; lack of provision in Denmark 75–6; as obstacle to integration in Denmark 86–7; Spain 148–9, 150–1, 191; *see also* headscarf debate
religious schools *see* faith schools
Renan, Ernest 63, 165
Representative Council of Muslims (France) 174–5
Repubblica, La 124–5, 129–33
republicanism: France as secular state 165–6; models of 62
Resnick, Philip 68
reunification policies in Denmark 74
Rex, John 168, 169
right wing *see* nationalist parties
Rorty, Richard 6
Rousseau, Jean-Jacques 91n, 165
Royal Commission on the Reform of the House of Lords 175
Royal Commissions on immigration policy (Belgium) 27–8
Runnymede Trust 52
Rushdie, Salman 38, 41–2; *see also Satanic Verses* controversy

Saadet Partisi (Turkey) 100
Salih, Chaban 110–11
Saracens 157–8n
Sardar, Ziauddin 50
Sarkozy, Nicolas 175
Satanic Verses controversy 29, 41–2, 47, 50, 184–5
Schavan, Annette 113n
Scheffer, Paul 33
schools *see* faith schools; headscarf debate
Schwarzer, Alice 105–6, 111–12
secularism 162–77; faith schools issue in Britain 49; integration in Italy 131–3; *laïcité* in France 57–8, 59–60, 61–4, 165–6, 174, 190–1, 194, 198–9; liberalism and Islam 188–91; and Muslim religious claims 2, 26, 32; pluralistic institutional integration approach 173–6, 191; and public/private spheres 166–73, 186–7; varieties of 163–8
September 11 attacks *see* 9/11 terror attacks
Severinsen, Hanne 90n
sexuality: attitudes in Denmark 86–7

sharia (Muslim law): Belgium 28–9;
  Denmark 70–1
'shoe bomber' 47
Siddiqui, Kalim 202n
social class and terrorist support in Britain
  47–8
Social Democrat Party (Denmark) 82
social exclusion: and Islam in French
  banlieues 66–7; 'Muslim schools' in
  Britain 49
Socialist People's Party (Denmark) 88
SOPEMI Report 122
SOS Racism (Spain) 147, 149
SOS Racisme (France) 30
Southern Europe: migration patterns 7, 8,
  9, 12; racism towards migrants 9, 12;
  see also Greece; Italy; Spain
Spain 143–58; citizenship preferences 154;
  composition of immigrant population
  147, 154; contact/conflict zones 144,
  148–9; dichotomy of Islam in 143–4;
  discourse on Muslim community
  152–5; 'ethnic filter' 154; *Hispanidad*
  movement 146–8, 154–5; historical
  legacy of Moors 143, 145–6, 153, 154;
  and impartiality argument 155–7;
  integration 1, 2, 153, 191; legal
  agreement for religious practice 144,
  149–52, 191; Maurophobia 143, 144,
  145–8; media constructs of Muslims
  149, 152–3; need for impartiality 144;
  recruitment of skilled and unskilled
  workers 10; resistance to mosque
  building 143
Spanish Civil War 146
Spiegel, Der 103–4, 105
Stasi Commission (France) 59–60, 65–6
Stevens, Cat (Yusuf Islam) 50
Submission (film) 70, 87, 185
Süleymanci group 97
Sunni Muslims: France 173; Germany
  96–7
Swann Report (Britain) 52
Sweden: multiculturalism 25

Tagesspiegel 106, 108, 109, 110
Taliban: support in Britain 47, 184
Taylor, Charles 76
terrorism: British connections 47–9, 182;
  Islam perceived as threat in Germany
  96; securitization of migration 1, 2–3,
  10; Spanish connections 151
Thatcher government (Britain) 200–1n
'thin integration' 202n

Tibi, Bassam 113n
totalist integration 187–8
Toynbee, Polly 49
trade unions in Italy 121
transnational Islam 65–8
Treaty of the European Communities
  (TEC) 11
Treaty of the European Union (TEU) 10,
  11
Treaty of Westphalia (1648) 162
Turkey: Islamic groups 96–7; migrants
  from *see* Turkish migrants
Turkish migrants: and citizenship rights in
  Germany 94, 95–102; as Other 12–13,
  96

UCIDE (Unión de Comunidades Islámicas
  de España) 150
Ulivo (centre–left coalition in Italy) 128,
  130, 132, 133, 135
Ummah 42, 46, 182; transnational Islam
  65–8
United Kingdom *see* Britain
United States (US): attitude towards
  Muslims 201n; Church and state 164,
  165–6; First Amendment 164; Islam in
  203n; multiculturalism literature 4–6;
  republicanism model 62
universalism: common civic values in
  Denmark 71, 78–9, 81–6, 88–9; and
  rationalist liberalism 192, 194; and
  secularism 168

Van Gogh, Theo 24, 32, 70, 87, 185
Verdonk, Rita 201n
Verfassungsschutz 97–9, 100–2, 109,
  111–12
Vieth-Enthus, Susanne 108–9
Vlaams Belang Party (Belgium) 201n
Vlaams Blok party (Belgium) 24, 27
voluntary sector: Catholic Church in Italy
  121, 132, 135, 140n; voluntary
  associations in France 58–9

Wallonia *see* Brussels–Wallonia
'war on terrorism' 51, 119, 182
Weber, Max 63, 166
Weil, Patrick 60
welfare democracy and common values
  78–9, 81
Werbner, Pnina 48
Westphalia, Treaty of (1648) 162
women: gender issues 86, 184; *see also*
  headscarf debate

xenophobia: Belgium 24; *see also*
Islamophobia; racism

Young, Hugo 48

Young, Iris M. 171
Yusuf, Hamza 54*n*

'zero immigration' policies 8, 9